MW00643840

A Treasury of
Buddhist Stories

About the Translator

The eminent American Orientalist Eugene Watson Burlingame was born in 1876 in Albany, New York. He obtained a BA and MA at Yale University, studied at Harvard, and obtained a Ph.D. from the University of Pennsylvania. He was a Fellow of the American Academy of Arts and Sciences and a professor at Yale. His other major publication, besides *Buddhist Legends*, was *Buddhist Parables* (1922). Burlingame died in 1932.

A Treasury of Buddhist Stories

from the Dhammapada Commentary

Translated from the Pali by
Eugene Watson Burlingame

Selected and revised by
Bhikkhu Khantipālo

Buddhist Publication Society

Buddhist Publication Society
P.O. Box 61
54, Sangharaja Mawatha
Kandy, Sri Lanka

Published in 1996
Reprinted 2012

Copyright © 1996 by the Buddhist Publication Society

National Library and Documentation Service Board-
Cataloguing-In-Publication Data

Tripitaka. Sutrapitaka. Dhammapada
  A Treasury of Buddhist Stories: From the Dhammapada
Commentary/ed. by Bhikkhu Khantipalo.- Kandy: Buddhist
Publication Society Inc., 2011.
  BP 220S.- 240p.; 22cm.

  ISBN 978-955-24-0147-3

  i. 294.382322 DDC 22   ii. Bhikkhu Khantipalo ed.

  1. Dhammapada
  2. Buddhism

ISBN 978-955-24-0147-3

Typeset at the BPS
Text set in URW Palladio Pali

Printed in Sri Lanka by
Samayawardana Printers,
Colombo 10.

Contents

Part IV: Noble Attainments

Part V: What Novices Can Do

Part VI: How Dhamma is Practised

Part VII: The Attainments of Monks

Part VIII: The Attainments of Nuns

Publisher's Note

This anthology has been compiled from Eugene Watson Burlingame's classic translation of the background stories from the Dhammapada Commentary, *Buddhist Legends*. Originally published in the Harvard Oriental Series, *Buddhist Legends* has been maintained in print since 1969 by the Pali Text Society. With the latter's permission, the Buddhist Publication Society had issued a selection of these stories in booklet form in the Wheel series, edited and arranged by Bhikkhu Khantipālo (now Laurence Mills). It is this same selection of stories that is now being issued in a single volume. The publisher gratefully acknowledges the kindness of the Pali Text Society for granting permission to publish this anthology. Readers who would like to obtain the complete three-volume collection of *Buddhist Legends* may contact the Pali Text Society, U.K., or inquire from bookshops specializing in Asian literature.

Introduction

This book comprises Buddhist stories which have been selected from the old commentary to the Dhammapada. This anthology of fifty-six stories represents only a small part of the very large original work, which in its complete translation fills three large volumes. The stories selected here are perhaps among the best, and they will be those most appealing to us at a time more than two thousand years after their origin.

The Dhammapada itself is the best known of all the collections of the Buddha's sayings, for it has been translated many times into English and into many other languages of the East and the West. It consists of 423 verses arranged into twenty-six chapters. A few of these verses were spoken as pairs and, more rarely, three or more of them were uttered by the Buddha together. Most are single stanzas which sum up the Dhamma that was necessary at that particular time.

No one knows how the Dhammapada was compiled. A great many of its verses are found elsewhere in the Pāli Canon, but a few are peculiar to this collection. Why these particular verses were formed into what we now call the Dhammapada is not clear, but we know that other Buddhist schools had Dhammapadas of their own which varied a good deal from the Pāli version.

If all the stories go back to the Buddha's days (which is unlikely, though the traditional view), then the collection could have been made for teaching purposes since many of the tales are both absorbing and instructive. But the random arrangement of the Dhammapada itself points to a time when the Buddha's words were orally transmitted and when a more logical rearrangement would have been difficult. Yet there is some order indeed, for the first verses point to the very heart of the Buddha's Teaching:

"Mental states are forerun by mind,
Mind is chief, mind-made are they..."

The last chapter of verses on the arahant, the person who is of supreme worth since without any defilements, gives one a clear picture of the final goal reached in this world by patient effort and

1

perseverance. But in between there is a mixture of verses and topics which are arranged more for ease of memorization than anything else.

It is likely that many of the Dhammapada stories do record events that happened in the Buddha's time, for they often quote from the Suttas or are based on them. In the latter case they always amplify the rather sparse accounts found in the Suttas. Sometimes the process of embroidery can be clearly seen, as when teachings or classifications not known during the Buddha's lifetime are attributed to him or to that period. Examples of this are the mention of the Three Piṭakas (the "baskets" into which the Buddha's words were arranged), which probably began to be compiled from the time of the First Council onwards; and mention of the two duties (*dhura*) for monks and nuns, that is, either scholarship (which meant oral repetition of the Buddha's words to pass them on to the next generation of students) or meditation—a dichotomy not clearly found in the Buddha's time. Many other examples could be given.

Some of the stories have no counterparts in the Suttas and we do not know where they came from. But as some of them are good stories, well told, conveying the taste of Dhamma, they have been included here. "The Weaver's Daughter" (No. 24) and the next tale of "A Certain Layman" are noteworthy examples.

The Dhammapada Commentary as we have it now was written down by the great Buddhaghosa and his pupils, nearly fifteen hundred years ago. They converted the collections of stories as found in old Sinhalese, together with the word-commentary explaining the verses, into Pāli, which even a thousand years after the Buddha was still a *lingua franca*. In that language it has remained, preserved on palm-leaf manuscripts, until modern times. The whole work has always been used as an enjoyable and easy text for novices learning the Pāli language.

After this brief sketch of the history of the Dhammapada stories it might be a good idea to give some hints on how to read them and how not to. They come from a culture far separated from us in time, though if we live in a Buddhist country the "distance" is not so great. However, modern Western-type education is based on very different assumptions from those which lie behind the world of the Dhammapada stories, a fact which may make some of them difficult to understand. Stories which I felt would not have much impact now, or which might easily lead to misunderstandings, have been left out of this selection. Even so, the ancient commentators did not hesitate to embroider them with the strange and marvellous, sometimes in the middle of an otherwise straightforward account. In this case I have included the tale thinking that its teaching will be remembered while the embroidery can be forgotten. The purpose of the stories, after all, is to illustrate the Dhamma and to provide memorable incidents which will serve as a pattern for one's own Dhamma practice. If this is forgotten (as seems to have been the case in later collections of Buddhist legends), then the marvellous takes over and the Dhamma teaching disappears. So when reading these stories it is the Dhamma which is important, not whether the incident concerned really happened. The old commentators were not concerned with history or whether precisely these words were spoken or those things done, but they preserved and passed on these stories as examples: either as warnings of what should not be done, or as encouragements for Dhamma practice. This emphasis needs to be remembered, otherwise a reader with a critical mind, thinking, "That's impossible," will miss the real point of the story.

It is recommended that these stories be read and re-read so that they stick in the mind. When they can be remembered easily, one has then a store of Dhamma to carry around which can be related to everyday life. For oneself and for other people to whom one may relate them, they can convey "the taste of Dhamma."

When these stories are related in Buddhist countries during sermons in temples or at Dhamma-study classes, they are not repeated word for word as found in the Dhammapada Commentary. Though their main features are unaltered, by being told orally they vary a great deal in the amount of detail included. Here they are presented as the text gives them, but some of the details may not be appropriate to repeat when retelling them. However, care should be taken that the story is not distorted, and even more care taken to see that the Dhammapada verse which is the Buddha's word is not incorrectly quoted.

These stories, as the reader will see, range from the comic to the tragic. Indeed, some of the longest, not included here, have all the material for extended drama and have been used as dramatic presentations of the Dhamma. But however amusing or disturbing,

3

the message is always that *kamma has its appropriate results*. Actually there is no real tragedy in the Western sense of this word because what is painful is also impermanent. Though one may be afflicted in this life, one's suffering cannot continue forever. Past life stories are quite common in the Dhammapada Commentary and are often related by the Buddha to account for some attainment of happiness or misery in the lives of the people with whom he came into contact.

What is reproduced in these pages is a partly revised version of E.W. Burlingame's translation, entitled *Buddhist Legends*. The revision of these stories was undertaken at the behest of Ven. Nyanaponika Mahāthera. I have left much of the translator's work as it is found in the complete translation: his English style is excellent and his renderings usually very accurate. However, in reading through that three-volume work, a few question marks were inserted into the margins where the meaning was not clear. These points I have cleared up after consulting the Pali Text Society's edition of the Dhammapada Commentary. Also, as the translation was made more than fifty years ago, some of the renderings of terms have now been more accurately translated. Generally I have followed the suggestions of the *Buddhist Dictionary* of Ven. Nyanatiloka Mahāthera, and those of Ven. Ñāṇamoli Thera in his various books.

I have used my own verse translation of the stanzas of the Dhammapada to replace the prose renderings in the original translation. It now only remains for me to give thanks to the late I.B. Horner, President of the Pali Text Society, for permission to base this book on the complete translation of the Dhammapada Commentary published by the Society. Hopefully, this selection will whet the appetite and lead more people to read the entire work.

BHIKKHU KHANTIPĀLO

4

Part I

Making Good Kamma

1. The Story of Magha

BY HEEDFULNESS DID MAGHA GO TO THE LORDSHIP OF THE GODS.... This instruction was given by the Teacher while in residence at a summer-house near Vesālī with reference to Sakka king of gods.[1]

Story of the Present: Mahāli's Question

A Licchavi prince named Mahāli, who lived at Vesālī, hearing the Teacher recite the Suttanta entitled Sakka's Questions,[2] thought to himself, "The Supremely Enlightened One has described the great glory of Sakka. Has the Teacher seen Sakka? Or has he not seen Sakka? Is the Teacher acquainted with Sakka? Or is he not acquainted with Sakka? I will ask him."

So the Licchavi prince Mahāli drew near to where the Exalted One was, and having drawn near, saluted the Exalted One and sat down on one side.[3] And having sat down on one side, the Licchavi prince Mahāli spoke thus to the Exalted One: "Reverend sir, has the Exalted One seen Sakka king of gods?"—"Yes, Mahāli, I have indeed seen Sakka king of gods."—"Reverend sir, it must certainly have been a counterfeit of Sakka; for, reverend sir, it is a difficult matter to see Sakka king of gods."—"Nevertheless, Mahāli, I know Sakka; I know what qualities made him Sakka; I know by the cultivation of what qualities Sakka attained to the state of Sakka.

"Mahāli, in a previous state of existence Sakka king of gods was a human being, a prince named Magha: therefore is he called Maghavā. Mahāli, in a previous state of existence Sakka king of gods was a human being who in a previous state of existence gave gifts (*pure dānaṃ adāsi*); therefore he is called Purindada. Mahāli, in a previous state of existence Sakka king of gods was a human being who gave alms assiduously (*sakkaccaṃ*); therefore is he called Sakka. Mahāli, in a previous state of existence Sakka king of gods

---

1. Sakka was the ruler of the gods in the Tāvatiṃsa heaven, the realm of the Thirty-three, one of the celestial realms in the sensual sphere.

2. See *Sakka's Questions* (BPS Wheel No. 10).

3. The portion of the story from this sentence through the verses is found at Saṃyutta Nikāya 11:3.

7

was a human being who gave a dwelling-place (*āvasathā*); therefore is he called Vāsava. Mahāli, in a previous state of existence Sakka king of gods was a human being who could think of as many as a thousand things (*sahassaṃ atthaṃ*) in an instant: therefore is he called Sahassakkha. Mahāli, Sakka king of gods has an asura maiden named Sujātā for his wife; therefore is he called Sujampati. Mahāli, Sakka king of gods bears sway as lord and master over the gods of the Thirty-three; therefore is he called King of Gods. Mahāli, Sakka king of gods in a previous state of existence as a human being took upon himself and fulfilled seven vows. Because he took upon himself and fulfilled these seven vows, Sakka attained to the state of Sakka.

"Now what were the seven? 'So long as I live, may I be the support of my mother and father. So long as I live, may I honour my elders. So long as I live, may I speak gentle words. So long as I live, may I never give way to back-biting. So long as I live, may I live the life of a householder with heart free from taint of avarice, generous in renunciation of what is mine, with open hand, delighting in liberality, attentive to petitions, delighting in the distribution of alms. So long as I live, may I speak the truth. So long as I live, may I be free from anger. Should anger spring up within me, may I quickly get rid of it.' Mahāli, Sakka king of gods in a previous state of existence took upon himself and fulfilled these seven vows. Because he took upon himself and fulfilled these seven vows, Sakka attained to the state of Sakka."

> If a man support his mother and father,
> If he honour his elders in the household,
> If he be gentle and friendly in conversation,
> If he avoid backbiting,
> If he steadfastly put away avarice,
> If he be truthful, if he conquer anger,
> Such a man the gods of the Thirty-three
> Call a good man.

When the Teacher said, "This, Mahāli, was what Sakka did in his previous existence as Prince Magha," Mahāli, desiring to hear the whole story of his conduct, asked the Teacher, "Reverend sir, how did Prince Magha conduct himself?"—"Well then," said the Teacher, "listen." So saying, he related the following story.

8

Story of the Past: How Magha Became Sakka

In times long past a prince named Magha lived in the village of Macala in the kingdom of Magadha. One day he went to the place where the business of the village was carried on, removed with his foot the dust from the place where he stood, and having made a comfortable place for himself, stood there. Thereupon another struck him with his arm, pushed him aside, and took his place. But instead of becoming angry at the man, he made another comfortable place for himself and stood there. Thereupon another struck him with his arm, pushed him away, and took his place. But neither did he allow himself to become angry at this man; he merely made another comfortable place for himself and stood there. In like manner one man after another came out of his house, struck him with his arm, and pushed him away from the place which he had cleared for himself.

The prince thought to himself, "All these men appear to be pleased. Since this work of mine conduces to the happiness of men, it must be a meritorious work." So on the following day he took a spade and cleared a space as big as a threshing-floor, whereupon all the men came and stood there. In cold weather he built a fire to warm them, so that the place became a favourite resort for all. Then he thought to himself, "It behooves me to take upon myself the task of making the road smooth and even." So early in the morning he started out to make the road smooth and even, cutting down and removing all the branches of trees that needed to be removed. Thus did he spend his time.

Another man saw him and said to him, "Master, what are you doing?" He replied, "Master, I am treading the path that leads to heaven."—"I also am your companion."—"Be my companion, master; heaven is a pleasant place for many." Seeing these two, a third man asked the same question, received the same answer, and joined them; then a fourth, then a fifth, until finally there were thirty-three. All these men worked together with spades and axes and made the road smooth and even for a distance of one or two leagues. The village headman saw them and thought to himself, "These men are all following the wrong occupation. If they would only fetch fish and flesh from the forest, or indulge in strong drink, or do something else of the sort, I should make something by it."

So he sent for them and asked them, "What is it you are doing?"—"Treading the path to heaven, master."—"That is no proper occupation for men living the lives of laymen. What you should do is to bring fish and flesh from the forest, indulge in strong drink, and have a general good time." But they refused to follow his suggestion, and the more he urged them, the more firmly they refused to do as he suggested.

Finally the village headman became angry. "I will destroy them," said he. So he went to the king and said to him, "Your majesty, I see a band of thieves going about committing depredations." The king replied, "Go and catch them and bring them before me." So the village headman arrested the thirty-three youths and took them before the king. Without instituting an inquiry into their conduct, the king gave the following order: "Cause them to be trampled to death by an elephant." Thereupon Magha admonished his companions as follows, "Friends, we have no refuge but love. Therefore let your hearts be tranquil. Cherish anger towards no one. Let your hearts be full of love for the king and the village headman and the elephant that tramples you under his feet." The thirty-three youths followed the admonition of their leader. Such was the power of their love that the elephant dared not approach them.

When the king heard of this, he said, "If the elephant sees so many men, he will not venture to trample them under his feet. Have the men covered with heavy matting, and then order the elephant to trample them." So the village headman had the men covered with heavy matting and drove the elephant forwards to trample them. But when the elephant was yet a long way off, he turned round and went back. When the king heard what had happened, he thought to himself, "There must be some reason for this." So he caused the thirty-three youths to be brought before him and asked them, "Friends, is there anything which you have failed to receive at my hands?"—"Your majesty, what do you mean?"—"I am informed that you are a band of thieves and that you rove about the forest committing depredations."—"Your majesty, who said that?"—"Friends, the village headman so informed me."

"Your majesty, it is not true that we are thieves. The fact is, we are clearing a path to heaven for ourselves, and we do this and that. The village headman tried to persuade us to adopt an evil

10

mode of life, and when we refused to follow his suggestions, he became angry at us and determined to destroy us. That is why he said this about us."—"Friends, this animal knows your good qualities; but I, who am a man, was unable to discern them. Pardon me." So saying, the king made the village headman their slave, together with his children and wife, gave them a riding-elephant, and presented that village to them to do with as they saw fit. Thought the thirty-three youths, "Even in this life the advantage to be derived from the performance of work of merit is clearly to be seen." And mounting the elephant by turns, they rode about the village.

As they went about the village, they took counsel together, saying, "It is our duty to perform yet more abundant works of merit. What shall we do?" Thereupon the following thought occurred to them, "Let us build at the crossing of the four highways a rest-house for the multitude, making it secure and strong." So they summoned a builder and ordered him to build a hall for them. And because desire for women had departed from them, they resolved to give women no share in the building of the hall.

Now there were four women living in Magha's house named Joy, Thoughtful, Goodness, and Wellborn. Goodness went secretly to the builder, gave him a bribe, and said to him, "Brother, give me the principal share in the building of this hall."—"Very well," replied the builder, agreeing to her proposal. Accordingly he first marked a tree out of which to make a pinnacle, felled it, and laid it aside to season.

Then he hewed it and planed it and bored it, and having fashioned it in the form of a pinnacle, carved the following inscription on it: "This is the Hall of Goodness." Having so done, he wrapped it in a cloth and laid it aside.

Now when he had completed the hall and the day came to erect the pinnacle, he said to the thirty-three youths, "Noble sirs, there is something we have forgotten."—"What is it, sir?"—"A pinnacle."—"Let us procure one."—"It is impossible to make one out of a freshly hewn tree. We should procure for a pinnacle a tree felled long ago and laid away to season."—"What had we best do under the circumstances?"—"If in anybody's house there is a completed pinnacle which has been laid away to season and which is for sale, that is the thing for you to search for." So they searched

11

everywhere, and finding what they wanted in the house of Goodness, offered her a thousand pieces of money for it. But they were unable to secure it for the price they offered. Said Goodness, "If you will give me a share in the building of the hall, I will give you the pinnacle." But they replied, "We have resolved to give women no share in the building of this hall." Thereupon the builder said to them, "Noble sirs, what are you doing? With the exception of the world of Brahmā, there is no place from which women are excluded. Take the pinnacle, for if you do, our work will speedily be finished."—"Very well," said they. So they took the pinnacle and completed the hall. And they divided the hall into three parts, reserving one chamber for kings, another for the poor, and another for the sick.

Then the thirty-three youths built thirty-three seats, and having so done, gave the following orders to the elephant, "If a visitor comes and sits down in a seat, take him and lodge him in the house of whoever built and owns that seat. It then becomes the duty of the owner of that seat to see that his guest's feet and back are rubbed, to provide him with food both hard and soft, and with lodging; to perform for him, in fact, all the duties of hospitality." Accordingly, whenever a visitor came, the elephant would take him and conduct him to the house of the owner of the seat in which he had sat, and the owner of the seat would on that day perform for him all the duties of hospitality.

Magha planted an ebony-tree near the hall and built a stone seat at the foot of the ebony-tree. All those who entered the hall looked at the pinnacle, read the inscription, and said, "This is the Hall of Goodness." The names of the thirty-three youths did not appear.

Joy thought to herself, "The youths who built this hall resolved to deprive us of a share in the building thereof. But Goodness by her own cleverness obtained a share. I also ought to do something. What can I do?" Thereupon the following thought occurred to her, "Those who come to the hall should be provided with water for drinking and water for bathing. I will have a place dug for a pool." Accordingly Joy caused a bathing-pool to be built.

Thoughtful thought to herself, "Goodness has given a pinnacle, and Joy has caused a bathing-pool to be built. What can I do?" Thereupon the following thought occurred to her, "After those who come to the hall have drunk water and bathed they should be decked with garlands when they are ready to depart. I will cause a flower garden to be laid out." So Thoughtful caused a beautiful flower garden to be laid out. So many and so various were the flowers that grew therein that it was impossible for anyone to say, "Such and such a flower-bearing or fruit-bearing tree does not grow in this garden."

Now Wellborn thought to herself, "I am the daughter of the brother of the mother of Magha and likewise the wife of Magha. The merit of the work he has wrought accrues to me only, and the merit of the work I have wrought accrues to him only." Accordingly she did nothing but spend her time adorning herself.

Thus did Magha minister to his mother and father, honour his elders in the household, speak the truth, avoid harsh words, avoid backbiting, put away avarice, and not become angry. Even thus did he fulfill the seven precepts, as it is said:

> If a man support his mother and father,
> If he honour his elders in the household,
> If he be gentle and friendly in conversation,
> If he avoid backbiting,
> If he steadfastly put away avarice,
> If he be truthful, if he conquer anger,
> Such a man the gods of the Thirty-three
> Call a good man.

Having attained so praiseworthy a state, Magha, upon reaching the end of the term of life allotted to him, was reborn in the world of the Thirty-three as Sakka king of gods. His companions were likewise reborn there. The builder was reborn as the god Vissakamma.[4]

Now at that time there were asuras dwelling in the world of the Thirty-three, and when they learnt that new gods had been reborn there, they prepared celestial drink for them.[5] But Sakka gave orders to his retinue that no one should drink it. The asuras, however, drank freely and became intoxicated. Thereupon Sakka thought to himself. "Why should I share my kingdom with these deities?" Then, giving a sign to his retinue, he caused them to pick

---

4. Celestial architect or engineer-in-chief of the heavenly world.

5. The asuras are the perennial enemies of the gods, frequently engaging them in battle.

up the asuras by the heels and fling them into the great ocean. So the asuras fell headlong into the ocean. By the power of their merit there sprang up at the foot of Mount Sineru the palace of the asuras and the tree that is called pied trumpet-flower.

When the conflict between the gods and the asuras was over and the asuras had been defeated, there came into existence the city of the Thirty-three. The distance from the eastern gate to the western gate was ten thousand leagues, and the distance from the southern gate to the northern gate was the same. Now this city was provided with a thousand gates and was adorned with gardens and pools, and in the midst thereof, as the fruit of the building of the hall, there arose a palace called the Palace of Victory. Its height was seven hundred leagues, and it was decked with banners three hundred leagues long. On staffs of gold were banners of jewels, and on staffs of jewels were banners of gold; on staffs of coral were banners of pearls, and on staffs of pearls were banners of coral; on staffs of the seven precious stones were banners of the seven precious stones. Such was the palace that arose as the fruit of the building of the hall; a thousand leagues was its height, and it was composed of the seven precious stones.

As the result of the planting of the ebony-tree, there arose the coral-tree, a hundred leagues in circumference. As the result of the building of the stone seat, there came into existence at the foot of the coral-tree the Yellowstone Throne, of a reddish yellow colour like that of the jasmine flower, sixty leagues in length, fifty leagues in breadth, and fifteen leagues thick. When Sakka sits down on this throne, half its mass sinks into the ground; when he rises, it is all above ground. The elephant was reborn as god Erāvaṇa. There are no animals in the world of the gods; so when he went into the garden to play, he would quit his form as a god and become the elephant Erāvaṇa, a hundred and fifty leagues in size. For the thirty-three youths, Erāvaṇa created thirty-three vessels, each two or three quarters of a league around.

In the centre of all, Erāvaṇa created for Sakka a vessel called Beautiful. It was thirty leagues in circumference, and above it was a canopy, twelve leagues in size, made entirely of precious stones. At regular intervals about the canopy there arose banners a league in length, made entirely of the seven precious stones. And from the lower edge of each banner depended a row of tinkling bells,

14

which, when they were shaken by the gentle wind, gave forth sweet music like the mingled strains of the music of the five kinds of instruments or the singing of the celestial choir. In the centre of the pavilion a jewelled couch a league in length was prepared for Sakka. There Sakka reclined in state. Erāvaṇa created thirty-three vessels for the thirty-three gods. Each vessel bore seven tusks, each fifty leagues long; each tusk bore seven lotus-tanks; each lotus-tank bore seven lotus-plants; each lotus-plant bore seven flowers; each flower, seven leaves; and on each leaf danced seven celestial nymphs. Thus on all sides round about for a space of fifty leagues there were dancing assemblies poised on elephants' tusks. Such was the glory in the enjoyment of which lived Sakka king of gods.

When Goodness died, she was also reborn there. And at the same time there came into existence Goodness, the meeting hall of the gods, nine hundred leagues in extent, the most charming of all places. Here, on the eighth day of the month, the Dhamma is preached. Even today, when men behold a charming place, they say, "It is like Goodness, the meeting hall of the gods." When Joy died, she also was reborn there. And at the same time there came into existence a lotus-tank called Joy, five hundred leagues in extent. When Thoughtful died, she also was reborn there. And at the same time there came into existence Thoughtful's creeper-grove, five hundred leagues in extent. There they conduct the gods whose prognostics have appeared,[6] till they are overcome by confusion. But when Wellborn died, she was reborn as a crane in a certain mountain cave.

Sakka surveyed his wives and considered within himself, "Goodness has been reborn here and likewise Joy and Thoughtful. Now where has Wellborn been reborn?" Perceiving that she had been reborn as a crane in a mountain-cave, he thought to himself, "Because she did no work of merit, the foolish girl has been reborn as an animal. It is my duty to have her perform some work of merit and bring her here." So saying, he laid aside his proper form, and assuming a disguise, he went to her and asked, "What are you doing here?"—"But, master, who are you?"—"I am your

---

6. There are five signs of the impending death of a god: their garlands wither, their clothes become soiled, they sweat profusely, their radiance fades, and they become uneasy.

husband, Magha."—"Where were you reborn, husband?"—"I was reborn in the heaven of the Thirty-three. Do you know where your companions were reborn?"—"No, husband, I do not."—"They also were reborn in the heaven of the Thirty-three as my wives. Should you like to see your companions?"—"How can I get there?" Said Sakka, "I will carry you." Placing her in the palm of his hand, he carried her to the realm of the gods and set her free on the bank of the lotus-tank named Joy. Then he said to the other three, "Should you like to see your companion Wellborn?"—"Sire, where is she?"—"On the bank of the lotus-tank named Joy." So the three went and looked at her. "Alas!" they cried out, "See what has been the result of the noble woman's spending her life in adorning herself! Look now at her beak! Look at her feet! Look at her legs! She presents a beautiful appearance indeed!" Thus did they ridicule her. Having so done, they departed.

Sakka went once more to her and said, "Did you see your companions?"—"Yes," replied Wellborn, "I saw them. They ridiculed me and then went their way. Take me back again." So Sakka took her back again, set her free in the water, and then asked her, "Did you see their celestial glory?"—"Yes, sire, I did."—"You also should employ such means as will enable you to obtain rebirth there."— "Sire, what shall I do?"—"If I admonish you, will you keep my admonition?"—"Yes, sire, I will keep your admonition." So Sakka taught her the Five Precepts. Having so done, he said to her, "Be zealous in keeping the precepts," and departed.

Thenceforth she sought after and ate only such fish as had died a natural death. After a few days had passed, Sakka determined to test her. So he went, and taking the form of a fish, lay down on the surface of the sand, pretending to be dead. When she saw the fish, thinking that it was dead, she took it in her beak. Just as she was about to swallow the fish, it wriggled its tail. The instant she discovered the fish was alive she released it in the water. Sakka waited a little while, and then lay down before her on his back once more. Again thinking it was a dead fish, she took it in her beak. But just as she was about to swallow the fish, it moved the tip of its tail. The instant she saw the fish move its tail she knew it was alive, and therefore let it go. When Sakka had thus tested her three times and had satisfied himself that she was keeping the precepts faithfully, he revealed his identity to her and said, "I came here for the purpose of testing you. You are keeping the precepts faithfully. If you continue thus faithfully to keep them, before long you will be reborn as one of my wives. Be heedful." Having spoken thus, he departed.

Thenceforth she used for food either fish that had died a natural death or none at all. After only a few days had passed, she shrivelled up and died, and solely as the fruit of her virtuous conduct was reborn at Benares as the daughter of a potter. When she was about fifteen or sixteen years old, Sakka considered within himself, "Where has she been reborn?" Perceiving that she had been reborn at Benares as the daughter of a potter, he said to himself, "I ought now to go to her."

So filling a cart with the seven kinds of precious stones disguised as cucumbers, he drove into the city of Benares. "Come, get cucumbers!" he cried, as he entered the street. But when people came to him with coins in their hands, he said, "I do not part with my cucumbers for a price."—"On what terms do you part with them, then?" the people asked him. "I give them to the woman that keeps the precepts," he replied. "Master, what do you mean by 'precepts'? Are they black or brown or of some other colour?"—"You don't even know what precepts are; much less will you keep them. I will give my cucumbers to the woman who keeps the precepts."

"Master, there is a potter's daughter who is always going about saying, 'I keep the precepts.' Give them to her." The potter's daughter said to him, "Very well, master, give them to me."—"Who are you?"—"I am a maiden that has never failed to keep the precepts."—"For you alone have I brought these," said Sakka. And driving his cart to her house, he presented to her, in the guise of cucumbers, celestial treasure which cannot be taken away by others. And making his identity known to her, he said, "Here is wealth sufficient for you to live on. Keep the Five Precepts unbroken." So saying, he departed.

At the end of her existence as a potter's daughter she was reborn in the world of the asuras as the daughter of Vepacitti, king of asuras, a bitter enemy of Sakka. Since she had kept the precepts in two successive existences, she was fair of form, her skin was of a golden hue, and she was endowed with beauty and comeliness the like of which had never been seen. Vepacitti, king of asuras,

17

said to all the asura princes who sought her in marriage, "You are not fit to marry my daughter." Having thus refused to give her in marriage to any of the asura princes, he said, "My daughter shall choose for herself such a husband as she sees fit." So saying, he assembled the host of asuras, and placing a garland of flowers in the hand of his daughter, said to her, "Choose for yourself a husband who suits you."

At that moment Sakka looked to see where she had been reborn. Perceiving what was taking place, he assumed the form of an aged asura and went and stood in the outer circle of the assembled company. The daughter of Vepacitti looked this way and that. Suddenly, because in a previous state of existence she had lived with Sakka, she was overwhelmed as by a mighty torrent by the power of the love for him which sprang up within her. And crying out, "He is my husband!" she threw the garland of flowers over his head. Said the asuras, "For a long time our king has been unable to find a husband suitable for his daughter. Now, however, he has found one. This fellow is old enough to be his daughter's grandfather." And they departed, hanging their heads with shame.

Sakka took her by the hand, cried out, "I am Sakka," and flew up into the air. The asuras exclaimed, "We have been fooled by Old Sakka," and started up in pursuit. Mātali the charioteer brought up the chariot called Chariot of Victory and stopped by the way. Thereupon Sakka assisted his bride to mount and set out for the city of the gods. Now when they reached the Forest of Silk-cotton Trees, the garuḍa fledglings, hearing the sound of the chariot and fearing they would be crushed to death, cried out.

When Sakka heard their cries, he asked Mātali, "What are they that are crying?"—"Garuḍa birds, sire."—"Why are they crying?"—"They hear the sound of the chariot and fear they will be crushed to death."—"Let not so numerous a host perish, crushed by the impact of the chariot, because of me alone. Cause the chariot to turn back." Thereupon Mātali gave the sign with the lash to the thousand Sindh horses and caused the chariot to turn back.

When the asuras saw that the chariot had turned back, they said, "Old Sakka started out in flight from the city of the asuras, but has just caused his chariot to turn back. Doubtless he has received reinforcements." And turning back, the asuras entered the city of the asuras by the same road by which they had come out and nevermore lifted up their heads. Sakka bore the asura maiden Wellborn to the city of the gods and installed her as the chief of twenty-five million celestial nymphs.

One day Wellborn asked Sakka for a boon, saying, "Great king, in this world of the gods I have neither mother nor father nor brother nor sister; therefore please take me with you wherever you go."—"Very well," replied Sakka, promising to do for her as she had asked. Thenceforth, when the tree that is called pied trumpet-flower blooms, the asuras cry out, "Now is the time when our heavenly coral-tree blooms," and straightway they sally forth to attack Sakka. Therefore Sakka posts a guard to defend the nāgas in the sea below, and likewise affords protection to the supaṇṇas and the kumbhaṇḍas and the yakkhas, and likewise to the Four Great Kings. And over all, for the purpose of averting disaster, he places before the gates of the city of the gods images of Indra bearing the thunderbolt in his hands. When the asuras, after defeating the nāgas and the other supernatural beings, approach the city of the gods and see the images of Indra, they cry out, "Sakka has made a sally," and flee away. (*End of Story of the Past.*)

"Thus, Mahāli, Prince Magha adopted the way of heedfulness. Because he was so heedful, he obtained such sovereignty so exalted and came to rule over the two worlds of the gods.[7] Heedfulness is praised by the Buddhas and by others likewise. For it is through heedfulness that all attain the higher attainments, both those that are worldly and those that transcend all worlds." So saying, he pronounced the following stanza:

30.   Heedfulness is always praised,
       Heedlessness is ever blamed;
       By heedfulness did Magha go
       To the lordship of the gods.

---

7. The Four Great Kings and the Thirty-three gods.

2. The Old Brahmin and His Sons

THE TUSKER DHANAPĀLAKA NAMED.... This instruction was given by the Teacher while he was in residence at Sāvatthī with reference to the sons of a certain brahmin who had reached the decrepitude of old age.

The story goes that there lived in Sāvatthī a certain brahmin who had four sons and whose wealth amounted to eight hundred thousand pieces of money. When his sons reached marriageable age, he arranged marriages for them and gave them four hundred thousand pieces of money. After the sons had married, the brahmin's wife died, whereupon the sons took counsel together, saying, "If this brahmin marries again, the family fortune will be divided among his wife's children and there will be nothing left of it. Come then! Let us succour our father and win his favour." Accordingly they waited upon him faithfully, providing him with the choicest food and the finest clothes, rubbing his hands and feet, and performing all of the other duties.

One day they went to wait upon him and found that he had fallen asleep, although it was broad daylight. As soon as he awoke, they rubbed his hands and his feet, and while thus engaged, spoke to him of the disadvantage of living in separate houses. Said they, "We will wait upon you after this manner so long as you live; give us the rest of your wealth also." In compliance with their request the brahmin gave each of them a hundred thousand more. He kept nothing for himself but his under and upper garments; all the rest of his wealth and possessions he divided into four portions and handed over to his sons.

For a few days his eldest son ministered to his needs. One day, however, as he was returning to the house of his eldest son after his bath, his daughter-in-law, who stood at the gate, saw him and said to him, "Did you give your eldest son a hundred or a thousand pieces of money more than you gave your other sons? You certainly gave each of your sons two hundred thousand pieces of money. Do you not know the way to the house of any of your other sons?" The brahmin answered angrily, "Perish, vile woman!" and went to the house of his second son. But in a few days he was driven from the house of his second son as he had been from the house of the first, and in like manner from the houses of his two youngest sons. Finally he found himself without a single house he could enter.

Thereupon he retired from the world and became a monk of the Paṇḍaranga Order,[1] begging his food from door to door. In the course of time he became worn out by old age, and his body withered away as a result of the poor food he ate and the wretched quarters in which he was obliged to sleep. One day, after he had returned from his begging rounds, he lay down on his back and fell asleep. When he awoke from sleep and sat up and surveyed himself and reflected that there was no one of his sons to whom he might go for refuge, he thought to himself, "They say that the monk Gotama has a countenance that does not frown, a face that is frank and open, that his manner of conversing is pleasant, and that he greets strangers in a kind and friendly way. Possibly if I go to the monk Gotama, I shall receive a friendly greeting." So adjusting his under and upper garments, taking his alms bowl, and grasping his staff, he went to the Exalted One, even as it is said:[2]

Now, a certain brahmin, a man who had formerly possessed wealth and social position, clad in rough garments, drew near to where the Exalted One was, and having drawn near, sat down respectfully on one side. And as he sat respectfully on one side, the Exalted One greeted him in a pleasant manner and said this to him, "How comes it, brahmin, that you are rough and clad in rough garments?"—"Sir Gotama, I have four sons living in this world, but instigated by their wives, they have driven me out of their houses."—"Well then, brahmin, learn these stanzas thoroughly, and when the people are gathered together in the hall and your sons are gathered together with them, recite them before the assembled company:

"They at whose birth my heart was glad,
They for whose being much I longed,
They, instigated by their wives,
Are as a dog that drives off swine.

---

1. A non-Buddhist sect.
2. Saṃyutta Nikāya 7:14.

21

Wicked and worthless they say to me,
'Dear father' or 'Dear Dad' again:
Demons are they in guise of sons
Forsaking me in my old age;

Just as a worn-out useless horse
Is no longer led to its food
So is the father of these fools;
Though old, he begs at others' doors.

Better in truth the staff for me
Than sons who are disobedient.
It serves to drive off savage bulls
And likewise keeps off savage dogs.

It goes before me in the dark
And in the deeps it steadies me,
And by the power of this staff
Having slipped, I stand up again."

The brahmin, taught by the Teacher, learned these stanzas by heart. On the day appointed for the brahmins to assemble, the sons of the brahmin pushed their way into the hall, dressed in their costliest garments, adorned with all their jewels, and sat down on a costly seat in the midst of the brahmins. Thereupon the brahmin said to himself, "Now is my opportunity." So he entered the hall, made his way into the midst of the assemblage, lifted up his hand, and said, "I desire to recite certain stanzas to you; please listen to me."—"Recite them, brahmin; we are listening." So the brahmin stood there and recited the stanzas which he had learned from the Teacher.

Now at that time this was the law of mankind: *If any devour the substance of mother and father, and support not mother and father, he shall be put to death.* Therefore the sons of that brahmin fell at their father's feet and begged him to spare their lives, saying, "Dear father, spare our lives!" Out of the softness of a father's heart the brahmin said, "Sirs, do not kill my sons; they will support me." The men said to his sons, "Sirs, if from this day you do not take proper care of your father, we will kill you." The sons, thoroughly frightened, seated their father in a chair, raised the chair with their own hands, and carried their father home. They anointed the body

22

of their father with oil, flying this way and that in their haste, bathed him, employing perfumes and aromatic powders, and having so done, summoned their wives and said to them, "From this day forth you are to take proper care of our father; if you neglect this duty, we shall punish you." And they set the choicest dishes before him.

As the result of the wholesome food which the brahmin was given to eat and the comfortable quarters in which he slept, strength came back to him after a few days and his senses were refreshed. As he surveyed his person, he thought to himself, "I have gained this success through the monk Gotama." So desiring to make him a present, he took a pair of cloths and went to the Exalted One, and after exchanging friendly greetings, took his seat respectfully on one side. Then he laid the pair of cloths at the feet of the Exalted One, and said to him, "Sir Gotama, we brahmins desire that a teacher shall receive the offering which is his due; may my lord Gotama, my teacher, accept the offering which is due to him as a teacher." Out of compassion for the brahmin, the Teacher accepted the present which he had brought, and taught Dhamma to him. At the conclusion of the sermon the brahmin was established in the Refuges. Thereupon the brahmin said to the Teacher, "Sir Gotama, my sons provide me regularly with four meals; two of these I give to you." The Teacher replied, "That is well, brahmin; but we shall go only to such houses as we please." So saying, he dismissed him.

The brahmin went home and said to his sons, "Dear sons, the monk Gotama is my friend, and I have given him two of the meals with which you regularly provide me. When he arrives, be not heedless of your duty."—"Very well," replied his sons, promising to do as he said. On the following day the Teacher set out on his alms round and stopped at the door of the house of the brahmin's eldest son. When the brahmin's eldest son saw the Teacher, he took his bowl, invited him into the house, seated him on a costly couch, and gave him the choicest foods. On the succeeding days the Teacher went to the houses of the other sons in order, and all of them provided hospitable entertainment for him in their houses.

One day when a holiday was at hand, the eldest son said to his father, "Dear father, in whose honour shall we make merry?" The brahmin replied, "The monk Gotama is my friend, and I know no

23

others."—"Well then, invite him for tomorrow with his five hundred monks." The brahmin did so. So on the following day the Teacher came to the house with his attendant monks. The house was smeared with fresh cow dung and decked in festive array. The brahmin provided seats within the house for the Order of Monks presided over by the Buddha, and served them with rich porridge sweetened with honey and with the choicest foods, both hard and soft. In the course of the meal the brahmin's four sons sat down before the Teacher and said to him, "Sir Gotama, we care tenderly for our father; we never neglect him. Just look at him!" The Teacher replied, "You have done well. Wise men of old likewise cared tenderly for their mother and father." So saying, he related in detail the Mātuposaka Nāgarāja Jātaka (Jāt. No. 455), in which the story is told of how the *sallakī*-tree and the *kuṭaja*-plant grew up and blossomed in the absence of the elephant. Having so done, he pronounced the following stanza:

324. The tusker Dhanapālaka named,
Pungent rut exuding, uncontrolled,
Bound, he does not eat a mouthful,
The tusker mourns the elephant-wood.

Word Commentary

Dhanapāla: At this time the king of Kāsi sent an elephant-trainer to a charming elephant-grove and caused an elephant to be taken captive; this is the name of the elephant. *Pungent but exuding*: acrid juice; for in the rutting season the root of the elephant's ear bursts. As a rule, when trainers try to subdue elephants at this time with hook or spear or lance, the elephants become fierce. But this elephant was excessively fierce; therefore it is said: *Pungent rut exuding, uncontrolled/Bound, he does not eat a mouthful.* When by command of the king this elephant was led, bound to the elephant-stable and made to stand in a place screened with a curtain of many colours, decked with festoons, and garlands, overhung with a variegated canopy, although the king himself offered him food of various choice flavours and fit for a king, he refused to eat. It is with reference to his entrance into the elephant-stable that the words are employed. *Bound, he does not eat a mouthful,/The tusker mourns*

24

the elephant-wood: No matter how delightful the place in which he lodged, nevertheless he remembered the elephant-wood. Now his (blind) mother, who remained in the forest, suffered greatly by reason of separation from her son. Her son thought to himself, "I am not fulfilling the obligation of a son to succour his mother. What do I care for this food?" Thus he remembered only the solemn obligation resting upon a son to succour his mother. Now inasmuch as it was possible for him to fulfill this obligation only by being in the elephant-grove, therefore it is said: *The tusker mourns the elephant-wood.*

As the Teacher related this Jātaka, detailing his own deed in a previous state of existence, his hearers shed floods of tears, and by reason of the softness of their hearts became fully attentive. Thus did the Exalted One, knowing full well what would be of advantage to them, proclaim the Truths and teach the Dhamma. At the conclusion of the lesson the brahmin, together with his sons and daughters-in-law, was established in the fruit of stream-entry.

3. A Certain Brahmin

BY GRADUAL PRACTICE FROM TIME TO TIME.... This instruction was given by the Teacher while he was in residence at Jetavana in Sāvatthī with reference to a certain brahmin.

The story goes that early one morning this brahmin went out of the city, stopped at the place where the monks put on their robes, and stood and watched them as they put on their robes.[1] Now this place was thickly overgrown with grass. As one of the monks put on his robe, the edge of the robe dragged through the grass and became wet with drops of dew. Thought the brahmin, "The grass should be cleared away from this place." So on the following day he took his mattock, went there, cleared the place and made it as clean and smooth as a threshing-floor. The day after, he went to that place again. As the monks put on their robes, he observed that the edge of the robe of one of the monks dropped to the ground and dragged in the dust. Thought the brahmin, "Sand should be sprinkled here." So he brought sand and sprinkled it on the ground.

Now one day before breakfast the heat was intense. On this occasion he noticed that as the monks put on their robes, sweat poured from their bodies. Thought the brahmin, "Here I ought to cause a shelter to be erected." Accordingly he caused a shelter to be erected. Again one day, early in the morning, it rained. On this occasion also, as the brahmin watched the monks, he noticed that their robes were wetted by the drops of rain. Thought the brahmin, "Here I ought to cause a hall to be erected." So there he caused a hall to be erected. When the hall was finished, he thought to himself, "Now I will hold a festival in honour of the completion of the hall." Accordingly he invited the Order of Monks presided over by the Buddha, seated the monks within and without the hall, and gave alms.

At the conclusion of the meal he took the Teacher's bowl to permit him to pronounce the words of thanksgiving. "Reverend

---

1. This means that they had the lower robe on already but carried the upper robe folded until they reached the city when it (and the outer robe of patches if it had been instituted at this time) was put on over both shoulders for entering an inhabited area.

sir," said he, "as I stood in this place when the monks were putting on their robes and watched them, I saw this and that, and I did this and that." And beginning at the beginning, he told the Teacher the whole story. The Teacher listened to his words and then said, "Brahmin, a wise man by doing good works, time after time, little by little, gradually removes the stains of his own evil deeds." So saying, he pronounced the following stanza:

239. By gradual practice from time to time,
Little by little let the sage
Blow off his own blemishes
Just as a smith with silver.

4. The Bondswoman Puṇṇā

FOR THOSE WHO ARE EVER VIGILANT.... THIS INSTRUCTION was given by the Teacher while he was in residence on Mount Vulture Peak with reference to Puṇṇā, a bondswoman of the treasurer of Rājagaha.

The story goes that one day they gave her much rice to pound. She pounded away until late at night, lighting a lamp to work by; finally she became very weary and, in order to rest, stepped outside and stood in the wind with her body moist with sweat. Now at that time the Venerable Dabba Mallaputta was the one who allotted lodgings to the monks. Having listened to the Dhamma, he then lighted his finger so that he might show the monks the way to their respective lodgings, and preceding them, he created, by power of meditation, a light for them.

The light enabled Puṇṇā to see the monks making their way along the mountain. She thought to herself, "As for me, I am oppressed by my own discomfort, and so, even at this time, am unable to sleep. Why is it that the reverend monks are unable to sleep?" Having considered the matter, she came to the following conclusion, "It must be that some monk who resides there is sick, or else is suffering from the bite of some reptile." So when it was dawn, she took some rice-flour, placed it in the palm of her hand, moistened it with water, and having thus mixed a chapatti, cooked it over a bed of charcoal. Then, saying to herself, "I will eat it on the road leading to the bathing-place on the river," she placed the chapatti in a fold of her dress, and taking a water-pot in her hand, set out for the bathing-place on the river.

The Teacher set out on the same path, intending likewise to enter that village for alms. When Puṇṇā saw the Teacher, she thought to herself, "On other days when I have seen the Teacher, I have had no alms to give him, or if I have had alms to give him, I have not seen him; today, however, not only do I meet the Teacher face to face, but I have alms to give him. If he would accept this chapatti without considering whether the food is of inferior or superior quality, I would give it to him." So setting her water-pot down on one side, she saluted the Teacher and said to him, "Reverend sir, accept this coarse food and bestow your blessing upon me."

28

The Teacher looked at the Elder Ānanda, whereupon the elder drew a bowl out from under a fold of his robe and presented it to the Teacher. The Teacher held out the bowl and received therein the offering of the chapatti. When Puṇṇā had placed the chapatti in the Teacher's bowl, she bowed down to him respectfully and said to him, "Reverend sir, may the Truth which you have beheld be of avail to me also." The Teacher replied, "So be it." And remaining standing as before, he pronounced the words of thanksgiving. Thereupon Puṇṇā thought to herself, "Although the Teacher bestowed on me a blessing as he took my chapatti, yet he will not eat it himself. He will doubtless keep it until he has gone a little way and will then give it to a crow or a dog. Then he will go to the house of some king or prince and make a meal of choice food."

Thought the Teacher to himself, "What was the thought in the mind of this woman?" Perceiving what was in her mind, the Teacher looked at the Elder Ānanda and intimated that he wished to sit down. The elder spread out a robe and offered the Teacher a seat. The Teacher sat down outside the city and ate his breakfast. The deities squeezed out nectar, food proper to gods and men alike throughout the circle of the worlds, even as one squeezes a honeycomb, and imparted it to the Teacher's food. Puṇṇā stood looking on. At the conclusion of the Teacher's breakfast the elder gave him water. When the Teacher had finished his breakfast, he addressed Puṇṇā and said, "Puṇṇā, why have you blamed my disciples?"—"I do not blame your disciples, reverend sir."—"Then what did you say when you saw my disciples?"

"Reverend sir, the explanation is very simple. I thought to myself: 'As for me, I am oppressed by my own discomfort, and so am unable to sleep. Why is it that the reverend monks are unable to sleep? It must be that some monk who resides there is sick, or else is suffering from the bite of some reptile.' " The Teacher listened to her words and then said to her, "Puṇṇā, in your own case it is because you are afflicted with discomfort that you are unable to sleep. But my disciples are assiduously watchful and therefore they do not sleep." So saying, he pronounced the following stanza:

226. For those who are ever vigilant
And train themselves by night and day,
Upon Nibbāna ever intent,
Their pollutions are eradicated

At the conclusion of the lesson Puṇṇā, even as she stood there, was established in the fruit of stream-entry; the assembled company also profited by the lesson.

The Teacher, having eaten the chapatti which Puṇṇā made of rice-flour and cooked over a bed of coals, returned to the monastery. Thereupon the monks began a discussion in the Hall of Truth:

"Brethren, how hard it must have been for the Supremely Enlightened One to eat the chapatti of rice-flour which Puṇṇā cooked over a bed of coals and gave him!" At that moment the Teacher drew near and asked them, "Monks, what are you discussing now as you sit here all gathered together?" When they told him, he said, "Monks, this is not the first time I have eaten red-rice powder which she gave me; the same thing happened to me in a previous state of existence also." And the Teacher related the Kuṇḍakasindhavapotaka Jātaka in detail (Jāt. No. 254).

5. Treasurer Catfoot

DO NOT DISREGARD MERIT, SAYING.... This instruction was given by the Teacher while he was in residence at Jetavana with reference to Treasurer Catfoot, Biḷālapādaka.

For once upon a time the residents of Sāvatthī banded themselves together and gave alms to the Order of Monks presided over by the Buddha. Now one day the Teacher, in rejoicing (with their merits), spoke as follows, "Lay disciples, here in this world one man himself gives, but does not urge others to give; in the various places where he is reborn, such a man receives the blessing of wealth but not the blessing of a following. A second man does not himself give, but urges others to give; in the various places where he is reborn, such a man receives the blessing of a following but not the blessing of wealth. A third man neither himself gives nor urges others to give; in the various places where he is reborn such a man receives neither the blessing of wealth nor the blessing of a following. Lastly, a man both himself gives and urges others to give; in the various places where he is reborn, such a man receives both the blessing of wealth and the blessing of a following."

Now a certain wise man who stood listening to the Teacher's discourse on the Dhamma thought to himself, "This is indeed a wonderful thing! I will straightaway perform works of merit leading to both of these blessings." Accordingly he arose and said to the Teacher, as the latter was departing, "Reverend sir, accept our offering of food tomorrow."—"But how many monks do you need?"—"All the monks you have, reverend sir." The Teacher graciously consented to come. Then the layman entered the village and went here and there, proclaiming, "Women and men, I have invited the Order of Monks presided over by the Buddha for tomorrow's meal. Give rice and whatever else is needed for making rice-porridge and other kinds of food, each providing for as many monks as his means permit. Let us do all the cooking in one place and give alms in common."

Now a certain treasurer, seeing that the layman had come to the door of his shop, became angry and thought to himself, "Here is a layman who, instead of inviting as many monks as he could himself accommodate, is going about urging the entire village to give alms." And he said to the layman, "Fetch the vessel you brought with you." The treasurer took grains of rice in three fingers, and presented them to the layman similarly with different kinds of pulses. Ever after that the treasurer bore the name Catfoot, Bilālapāda. Likewise in presenting ghee and jaggery to the layman, he placed a little pot in the layman's vessel and dribbled out his offering drop by drop into one corner, giving him only a very little.

The lay disciple placed together the offerings which the rest presented to him, but placed apart by themselves the offerings of the treasurer. When the treasurer saw the layman do this, he thought to himself, "Why does he place apart by themselves the offerings I have presented to him?" In order to satisfy his curiosity, he sent a serving-boy with orders to follow the layman, saying to the serving-boy, "Go find out what he does with my offerings." The layman took the offerings with him, and saying, "May the treasurer receive a rich reward," put two or three grains of rice into the porridge and cakes, distributing beans and drops of oil and jaggery-pellets in all the vessels. The serving-boy returned and told the treasurer what the layman had done. When the treasurer heard his report, he thought to himself, "If the layman blames me in the midst of the assembled company, I will strike him and kill him the moment he takes my name upon his lips."

On the following day, therefore, the treasurer hid a knife in a fold of his undergarment and went and stood waiting at the refectory. The layman escorted into the refectory the Order of Monks presided over by the Buddha, and then said to the Exalted One, "Reverend sir, at my suggestion the populace has presented these offerings to you. All those persons whom I urged to give have given rice and other provisions according to their respective ability. May all of them receive a rich reward." When the treasurer heard this, he thought to himself, "I came here with the intention of killing the layman in case he took my name upon his lips by way of blame; in case, for example, he said, 'So and so took a pinch of rice and gave it to me.' But instead of so doing, this layman has included all in his request for a blessing, both those who measured out their gifts in pint-pots and those who took pinches of food and gave, saying, 'May all receive a rich reward.' If I do not ask so good a man to pardon me, punishment from the king will fall upon my head!" And straightaway the treasurer prostrated himself before the layman's feet and said, "Pardon me, master."—"What do you mean?" asked the layman. Thereupon the treasurer told him the whole story.

The Teacher, seeing this act, asked the steward of the offerings, "What does this mean?" Thereupon the layman told him the whole story, beginning with the incidents of the previous day. Then the Teacher asked the treasurer, "Is his story correct, treasurer?"—"Yes, reverend sir." Then said the Teacher, "Disciple, one should never regard a good deed as a small matter and say, 'It is a mere trifle.' One should never regard lightly an offering given to a Buddha, or to the Order of Monks presided over by the Buddha, and say of it, 'It is a mere trifle.' For wise men who do works of merit, in the course of time, become filled with merit, even as a water-vessel which stands uncovered becomes filled with water." So saying, he showed the connection, and teaching the Dhamma, pronounced the following stanza:

122. Do not disregard merit, saying:
'That will not come to me'—
For by the falling of water drops
A water jar is filled:
The sage with merit fills himself,
Gathering it little by little.

6. The Brahmin with a Single Robe

MAKE HASTE TOWARDS THE GOOD.... This instruction was given by the Teacher while he was in residence at Jetavana with reference to the brahmin Little One-Robe, Cūḷa Ekasāṭaka.

For in the dispensation of the Buddha Vipassī there lived a brahmin named Mahā Ekasāṭaka, Big One-robe, and he it was who was reborn in the present dispensation in Sāvatthī as Cūḷa Ekasāṭaka, Little One-robe. For Cūḷa Ekasāṭaka possessed only a single under garment, and his wife possessed only a single under garment, and both of them together possessed only a single upper garment. The result was that whenever either the brahmin or his wife went out of doors, the other had to stay at home. One day an announcement was made that there would be a preaching at the monastery. Said the brahmin to his wife, "Wife, an announcement is made that there will be a preaching at the monastery. Will you go to hear the Dhamma by day or by night? For we do not have enough upper garments between us to go together." The brahmin's wife replied, "Husband, I will go in the daytime." So saying, she put on the upper garment and went.

The brahmin spent the day at home. At night he went to the monastery, seated himself in front of the Teacher, and listened to the Dhamma. As he listened to the Dhamma, the five sorts of joy arose within him, suffusing his body. He greatly desired to do honour to the Teacher, but the following thought restrained him, "If I give this garment to the Teacher, there will be no upper garment left for my wife or me." A thousand selfish thoughts arose within him; then a single believing thought arose within him. Then thought of self arose within him and overmastered the believing thought. Even so did the mighty thought of self seize, as it were, and bind and thrust out the believing thought. "I will give it! No, I will not give it!" said the brahmin to himself.

As he thus reflected, the first watch passed and the second watch arrived. Even then he was not able to bring himself to give the garment to the Teacher. Then the last watch came. Finally the brahmin thought to himself, "While I have been fighting with thoughts of faith and thoughts of self, two watches have elapsed.

34

If these powerful thoughts of self increase, they will not permit me to lift up my head from the four states of suffering.[1] I will therefore give my gift." Thus the brahmin finally overmastered a thousand thoughts of self and followed the lead of a thought of faith. Taking his garment, he laid it at the Teacher's feet and thrice cried out with a loud voice, "I have conquered! I have conquered!"

King Pasenadi of Kosala happened to be listening to the Dhamma. When he heard that cry, he said, "Ask him what he has conquered." The king's men asked the brahmin the question, and the brahmin explained the matter to them. When the king heard the explanation, he said, "It was a hard thing to do what the brahmin did. I will do him a kindness." So he caused a pair of garments to be presented to him. The brahmin presented these garments also to the Tathāgata. Then the king doubled his gift, presenting the brahmin first with two pairs of garments, then with four, then with eight, finally with sixteen. The brahmin presented all these garments also to the Tathāgata. Then the king directed thirty-two pairs of garments to be presented to the brahmin. But to avoid having it said, "The brahmin has not kept a single pair for himself, but has given away every pair he received," he said to the brahmin, "Keep one pair for yourself and give another pair to your wife." So saying he caused the brahmin to keep two pairs and let him give the remaining thirty pairs to the Tathāgata alone. Even had the brahmin given away what he possessed a hundred times, the king would have met his gifts with equal gifts.

(In a former state of existence Mahā Ekasāṭaka kept for himself two pairs of garments out of sixty-four he received; Cūḷa Ekasāṭaka kept two out of thirty-two.)

The king gave orders to his men, "It was indeed a hard thing to do what the brahmin did. Fetch my two blankets into the presence-chamber." They did so. The king presented him with the two blankets, valued at a thousand pieces of money. But the brahmin said to himself, "I am not worthy to cover my body with these blankets. These are suitable only for the religion of the Buddha." Accordingly he made a canopy of one of the blankets and hung it up in the Perfumed Chamber over the Teacher's bed;[2] likewise he made a canopy of the other blanket and hung it up in his own

---

1. Asuras, ghosts, animals, and hell-realm beings.

house over the spot where the monk who resorted to his house for alms took his meals. In the evening the king went to visit the Teacher. Recognizing the blanket, he asked him, "Reverend sir, who was it that honoured you with the gift of this blanket?"— "Ekasāṭaka." Thought the king to himself, "Even as I believe and rejoice in my belief, even so does this brahmin believe and rejoice in his belief." Accordingly he presented to him four elephants, four horses, four thousand pieces of money, four women, four female slaves, and four most excellent villages. Thus therefore did the king cause the brahmin to be given the "gift of fours."

The monks started a discussion in the Hall of Truth: "Oh, how wonderful was the deed of Cūla Ekasāṭaka! No sooner done than he received all manner of presents of four! As soon as he did a good deed, straightway the fruit thereof was given to him." The Teacher approached and asked the monks, "Monks, what are you sitting here now talking about?" When they told him, he said, "Monks, had Ekasāṭaka been able to bring himself to give me his gift in the first watch, he would have received the 'gift of sixteens'; had he been able to do so in the middle watch, he would have received the 'gift of eights'; because it was not until late in the last watch that he gave me his gift, he received only the 'gift of fours.' He who does good works should not put away the impulse to good that arises within him, but should act on the instant. A meritorious deed tardily done brings its reward, but tardy is the reward it brings. Therefore a man should perform a good work the instant the impulse to good arises within him." So saying, he showed the connection, and teaching the Dhamma, pronounced the following stanza:

> 116. Make haste towards the good
> And check one's mind from evil;
> If one is slow in making merit,
> One's mind delights in evil

---

2. The "Perfumed Chamber" (*gandhakuṭī*) is the name of the Buddha's personal cottage in Jetavana.

7. Pāṭhika the Naked Ascetic

THE FAULTS OF OTHERS.... This instruction was given by the Teacher while he was in residence at Sāvatthī with reference to Pāṭhika the naked ascetic.[1]

At Sāvatthī, we are told, the wife of a certain householder ministered to the needs of a naked ascetic named Pāṭhika, treating him as she would her own son. Of her nearest neighbours, those who went to hear the Teacher teach the Dhamma returned praising the virtues of the Buddhas in manifold ways, saying, "Oh, how wonderful is the preaching of the Buddhas!" When the woman heard her neighbours thus praise the Buddhas, she desired to go to the monastery and hear the Dhamma. So she put the matter to the naked ascetic, saying, "Noble sir, I desire to go and hear the Buddha." But as often as she made her request, the naked ascetic dissuaded her from going, saying, "Do not go!" The woman thought to herself, "Since this naked ascetic will not permit me to go to the monastery and hear the Dhamma, I will invite the Teacher to my own house and hear the Dhamma right here."

Accordingly, when it was evening, she summoned her own son and sent him to the Teacher, saying to him, "Go and invite the Teacher to accept my hospitality for tomorrow." The boy started out, but went first to the place of residence of the naked ascetic, saluted him, and sat down. "Where are you going?" asked the naked ascetic. "By my mother's direction I am going to invite the Teacher."—"Do not go to him."—"All very well, but I am afraid of my mother. I am going."—"Let the two of us eat the fine things prepared for him. Do not go."—"No, my mother will give me a scolding."—"Well then, go. But when you go and invite the Teacher, do not say to him, 'Our house is situated in such and such a place, in such and such a street, and you may reach it by taking such and such a road.' Instead, act as if you lived nearby, and when you leave, run off as if you intended to take a different road, and come back here."

The boy listened to the instructions of the naked ascetic and then went to the Teacher and delivered the invitation. When he

---

1. See Dīgha Nikāya No. 24.

had done everything according to the instructions of the naked ascetic, he returned to the latter. Said the naked ascetic, "What did you do?" Said the boy, "Everything you told me to do, noble sir."— "You have done very well. Now we shall both of us eat the good things prepared for him." On the following day, very early in the morning the naked ascetic went to that house, taking the boy with him, and the two sat down together in the back room.

The neighbours smeared that house with cow-dung, decked it with the five kinds of flowers, including the *lāja* flower, and prepared a seat of great price, that the Teacher might sit therein. (People who are not familiar with the Buddhas know nothing about the preparation of a seat for them. Nor do the Buddhas ever need a guide to direct them on their way. For on the day of Enlightenment, when they sit under the Bodhi-Tree, causing ten thousand worlds to quake, all paths become plain to them: "This path leads to hell, this path leads to the world of beasts, this path leads to the world of ghosts, this path leads to the world of humans, this path leads to the world of the gods, this path leads to the Deathless, to Great Nibbāna." There is never any need of telling them the way to villages, market-towns, or other places.)

Therefore the Teacher, very early in the morning, took bowl and robe and went straight to the house of the great female lay disciple. She came forth from the house, respectfully bowed down to the Teacher, escorted him into the house, poured the water of donation into his right hand, and gave him the choicest of food, both hard and soft. When the Teacher had finished his meal, the female lay disciple, desiring to have him pronounce words of thanksgiving, took his bowl, and the Teacher with his own sweet voice began the address of rejoicing. The lay disciple listened to the teaching of the Dhamma and applauded the Teacher, saying, "Well said! Well said!"

The naked ascetic, sitting there in the back room, heard the words of applause uttered by the lay disciple as she heard the Teacher teach the Dhamma. Unable to control himself, he remarked, "She is my disciple no longer!" and came out. And he said to the lay disciple, "Hag, you are lost for applauding this man thus." And he reviled both the female lay disciple and the Teacher in all manner of ways, and then ran off.

The lay disciple was so embarrassed by the naked ascetic's insulting words that her mind became completely distraught, and she was unable to concentrate her attention on the Teacher's discourse. The Teacher asked her, "Lay disciple, are you unable to fix your mind on my discourse?"—"Good and reverend sir," she replied, "my mind is completely distraught by the insulting words of this naked ascetic." Said the Teacher, "One should not consider the talk of such a contrary person; one should pay no attention to such as he; one should regard only what one has committed and omitted to do." So saying, he pronounced the following stanza:

50. Not the faults of others,
     Nor what they did and did not;
     But in oneself should be sought
     Things done and left undone.

8. Coppertooth the Thief-killer

THOUGH A THOUSAND SPEECHES ARE MADE OF MEANINGLESS LINES.... This instruction was given by the teacher while he was in residence at Veḷuvana with reference to Coppertooth, a public executioner.

We are told that five hundred thieves less one made a living by plundering villages and other acts of violence. Now a certain man with copper-coloured teeth and tawny skin, his body covered with scars, came to them and said, "Let me also live with you." They took him to the ringleader of the thieves, saying, "This man also wishes to live with us." The ringleader of the thieves looked at the man and thought to himself, "This man's nature is inordinately cruel. He is capable of cutting off the breast of his mother and eating it, or of drawing the blood from the throat of his father and drinking it." Therefore he refused his request, saying, "It will not do for this man to live with us."

Although he had thus been refused admission to the band of thieves, he went and won the favour of a certain pupil of the ringleader by his courteous attention to him. This pupil took the man with him, approached the ringleader of the thieves, and said to him, "Master, this man is a dutiful servant of ours; bestow your favour on him." Having made this request, he turned the man over to the ringleader of the thieves.

One day the citizens joined forces with the king's men, captured those thieves, took them to court, and arraigned them before the lords of justice. The justices ordered their heads to be chopped off with an axe. "Who will put these men to death?" said the citizens. After a thorough search they were unable to find a single man who was willing to put them to death. Finally they said to the ringleader of the thieves, "You put these men to death, and we will spare your life and give you a rich reward besides. You kill them." But because they had lived with him, he also was unwilling to put them to death. In like manner also all of the five hundred less one refused when asked. Last of all they asked that scarred, tawny, coppertooth. "Yes, indeed," said he, consenting. So he put to death all the thieves, and in return received his life and rich gifts besides.

40

In like manner also they brought in five hundred thieves from the country to the south of the city and arraigned them before the justices. When the justices ordered their heads to be chopped off, they asked each thief, beginning with the ringleader, to put his companions to death, but found not a single one willing to act as executioner. Then they said, "The other day a certain man put five hundred thieves to death. Where is he?"—"We saw him in such and such a place," was the reply. So they summoned him and said to him, "Put these men to death, and you will receive a rich reward."—"Yes, indeed," said he, consenting. So he put them all to death and received his reward.

The citizens consulted together and said, "This is a most excellent man. We will make him permanent executioner of thieves." So saying, they gave him the post. Later on they brought in five hundred thieves also from the west and still later five hundred also from the north, and he put them all to death. Thus he put to death two thousand thieves brought in from each of the four cardinal points. As time went on, and one or two men were brought in each day, he put them all to death. For a period of fifty-five years he acted as public executioner.

In old age he could no longer cut off a man's head with a single blow, but was obliged to deliver two or three blows, causing much unnecessary suffering to the victims. The citizens thought to themselves, "We can get another executioner of thieves. This man subjects his victims to much unnecessary torture. Of what use is he any longer?" Accordingly they removed him from his office. During his term of office as executioner of thieves, he had been accustomed to receive four perquisites: old clothes for him to wear, milk-porridge made with fresh ghee for him to drink, jasmine flowers wherewith to deck himself, and perfumes wherewith to anoint himself. But these four perquisites he received no longer. On the day he was deposed from office he gave orders that milk-porridge should be cooked for him. And taking with him old clothes and jasmine flowers and perfumes, he went to the river and bathed. Having so done, he put on the old clothes, decked himself with garlands, anointed his limbs, and went home and sat down. They set before him milk-porridge made with fresh ghee and water for rinsing the hands.

At that moment the Elder Sāriputta emerged from his meditation. He said to himself, "Where ought I to go today?" Surveying

41

his rounds for alms, he saw milk-porridge in the house of the former executioner. Considering within himself, "Will this man receive me kindly?" he became aware of the following: "This excellent man will receive me kindly and will thereby gain a rich reward." So the elder put on his robe, took his bowl, and showed himself at the door of the former executioner's house.

When the man saw the elder, his heart was filled with joy. He thought to himself, "For a long time I have acted as executioner of thieves, and many are the men I have put to death. Now milk-porridge has been prepared in my house, and the elder has come and stands at my threshold. Now I ought to present alms to his reverence." So he removed the porridge which had been set before him, approached the elder, and paid obeisance to him. And escorting him into his house, he provided him with a seat, poured the milk-porridge into his bowl, spread fresh ghee thereon, and standing beside him, began to fan him.

Now for a long time he had not received milk-porridge, and therefore desired greatly to drink thereof. The elder knowing his desire, said to him, "Lay disciple, drink your own porridge." The man placed the fan in the hand of another and drank the porridge. The elder said to the man who was fanning him, "Go fan the lay disciple instead." So while he was being fanned, the former executioner filled his belly with porridge, and then went and resumed fanning the elder. When the elder had finished his meal, he took his bowl.

When the elder began the words of thanksgiving to his host, the man was not able to fix his mind on the elder's discourse. The elder, observing this, said to him, "Lay disciple, why is it that you are not able to fix your mind on my discourse?"—"Reverend sir, for a long time I have done deeds of cruelty; I have put many men to death. It is because I keep recalling my own past deeds that I am unable to fix my mind on your reverence's discourse." The elder thought to himself, "I will play a trick on him." So he said to the man, "But did you do this of your own free will, or were you made to do it by others?"—"The king made me do it, reverend sir."—"If that is the case, lay disciple, what wrong did you do?" The bewildered disciple thought, "According to what the elder says, I have done no wrong." Said he to the elder, "Very well,

42

reverend sir, continue your discourse."

As the elder pronounced the words of thanksgiving, the man's mind became tranquil; and as he listened to the Dhamma, he developed the quality of patience, and progressed in the direction of the path of stream-entry. When the elder had completed the words of rejoicing, he departed. The lay disciple accompanied him a little way and then turned back. As the lay disciple was returning, an ogress came along in the form of a cow, struck him with her shoulder, and killed him. So he died and was reborn in the world of the Tusita gods.

The monks began a discussion in the Hall of Truth: "He who was an executioner of thieves, he who for fifty-five years committed acts of cruelty, today was relieved of his office, today gave alms to the elder, today met death. Where was he reborn?" The Teacher came in and asked them, "Monks, what are you sitting here now talking about?" When they told him, he said, "Monks, that man has been reborn in the world of the Tusita gods."—"What did you say, reverend sir? He who killed men for so long a time has been reborn in the world of the Tusita gods?"—"Yes, monks. A great and good spiritual counsellor did he receive. He heard Sāriputta teach the Dhamma, and profiting thereby, acquired knowledge. When he departed from this existence, he was reborn in the world of the Tusita gods." So saying, he pronounced the following stanza:

"He who was executioner of thieves in the city
Listened to words well spoken.
Having gained patience accordingly,
He went to heaven, and is in joy."

"Reverend sir, there is no great power in words of thanksgiving, and this man had done much wrong. How could he gain something special with so little?" The Teacher replied, "Monks, do not measure the Dhamma I have taught as being little or much. One saying possessed of meaning is of surpassing merit." So saying, he instructed them in the Dhamma by pronouncing the following stanza:

100. Though a thousand speeches
Are made of meaningless lines,
Better the single meaningful line
By hearing which one is at peace.

43

9. Husband-honourer

ONLY GATHERING FLOWERS INDEED .... This instruction was given by
the Teacher while he was in residence at Sāvatthī with reference to
a woman named Husband-honourer, Patipūjikā. The story begins
in the world of the Thirty-three gods.

The story goes that a god named Garland-wearer, Mālabhārī,
entered the pleasure-garden in the world of the Thirty-three, accompanied by a thousand celestial nymphs. Five hundred of these
nymphs climbed trees and threw down flowers; five hundred others gathered up the flowers that fell and decked the god with them.
One of these nymphs, even as she sat on the branch of a tree,
passed from that state of existence, her body vanishing like the
flame of a lamp, and received a new conception in Sāvatthī in a
certain family of station. Born with a recollection of her former
states of existence, and remembering that she had been the wife of
the god Garland-wearer, she made offerings of perfumes and
garlands when she grew up, making the earnest wish to be reborn
with her former husband.

When she was sixteen years of age, she married into another
family. And even then, whenever she gave the monks ticket-food
or fortnightly-food or food for the rainy season,[1] she would say,
"May this offering assist me to obtain rebirth with my former
husband." Said the monks, "This woman, ever busy and active,
yearns only for her husband." Therefore they called her Husband-
honourer, Patipūjikā. She cared regularly for the Hall of Assembly,
supplied water for drinking, and provided seats for the monks.
Whenever others desired to give ticket-food or fortnightly-food,
they would bring it and give it to her, saying, "Dear lady, please
present these to the Order of Monks." Going to and fro in this
manner, she obtained at one and the same time the "fifty-six
qualities of goodness." She became pregnant and at the end of ten
lunar months gave birth to a son; when her son was old enough to
walk, she gave birth to another son, and then to another, until she
had four sons.

---

1. These are special types of meal-offerings that lay people make to the monks.

One day she gave alms, rendered honour to the monks, listened to the Dhamma and undertook the precepts, and at the end
of that day died of some sudden sickness and was reborn with her
former husband. During all that time the other celestial nymphs
were decking the god with flowers. When the god Garland-wearer
saw her, he said, "We have not seen you since morning. Where
have you been?"—"I passed from this existence, husband."—"What
do you say?"—"Precisely so, husband."—"Where were you
reborn?"—"In a family of station at Sāvatthī."—"How long a time
did you remain there?"—"At the end of the tenth lunar month I
issued from the womb of my mother. When I was sixteen years
old, I married into another family. I bore four sons, gave alms,
and rendered honour to the monks, making an earnest wish to
return and be reborn with you, husband."—"How long is the life
of men?"—"Only a hundred years."—"So short as that?"—"Yes,
husband."—"If men are reborn with so short a time as that to live,
do they spend their time asleep and heedless, or do they give alms
and render honour?"—"What do you say, husband? Men are ever
heedless, as if reborn with an incalculable number of years to live,
as if in no way subject to old age and death."

The god Garland-wearer was greatly agitated. Said he, "If, as
you say, men are reborn with only a hundred years to live, and if
they lie heedless and asleep, when will they ever obtain release
from suffering?" (Now a hundred of our years are equivalent to a
night and a day in the world of the Thirty-three gods, thirty such
nights and days make up a month, twelve such months make up a
year, and the length of their lives is a thousand such celestial years;
or, in human reckoning, thirty-six million years. Thus it was that
for that god not a single day had passed; nay, not more than a
moment of time. Therefore he thought to himself, "If the life of
men is so short, it is highly improper for them to give themselves
up to a life of heedlessness.")

On the following day the monks, on entering the village, found
the Hall of Assembly uncared for, no seats provided, no water
supplied for drinking. "Where is Husband-honourer?" they asked.
"Reverend sirs, how could you expect to see her? After your reverences had eaten and departed, she died in the evening." Thereupon monks who had not yet attained the fruit of stream-entry,
remembering her kindly services to them, were unable to restrain

45

their tears, while monks who had attained arahantship were deeply moved by Dhamma.

After eating their breakfast, they went to the monastery and asked the Teacher, "Reverend sir, Husband-honourer, busy and active, performed all manner of work of merit and yearned only for her husband. Now she is dead. Where was she reborn?"— "Monks, she was reborn with her own husband."—"But, reverend sir, she is not with her husband."—"Monks, she yearned not for that husband. Her husband was the god Garland-wearer in the world of the Thirty-three. She passed from that state of existence while decking him with flowers. Now she has returned to where she was before and has been reborn with him."—"Reverend sir, is what you say true?"—"Yes, monks, what I say is true."—"Oh, how short, reverend sir, is the life of creatures in this world! Early in the morning she served us with food, and in the evening she sickened and died." The Teacher replied, "Yes, monks, the life of creatures in this world is indeed short. Therefore while creatures in this world yet yearn for the things of earth and have not yet satisfied their desires for sensual pleasures, death overpowers them and carries them off wailing and weeping." So saying, he pronounced the following stanza:

48.   Only gathering flowers, indeed,
      Insatiate in sensual desire,
      With a mind clinging—just such a man
      Must the Ender bring under his sway.

10. A Certain Monk

THE MIND IS VERY HARD TO CHECK.... This instruction was given by the Teacher while he was in residence at Sāvatthī with reference to a certain monk.

In the country of the king of the Kosalans, it appears, at the foot of a mountain, was a certain thickly settled village named Mātika. Now one day sixty monks, who had received from the Teacher a subject of meditation leading to arahantship, came to this village and entered it for alms. Now the headman of this village was a man named Mātika. When Mātika's mother saw the monks, she provided them with seats, served them with rice-porridge flavoured with all manner of choice flavours, and asked them, "Reverend sirs, where do you desire to go?"—"To some pleasant place, great lay disciple." Knowing that the monks were seeking a place of residence for the season of the rains, she prostrated herself at their feet and said to them, "If the noble monks will reside here during these three months, I will take upon myself the Three Refuges and the Five Precepts and will perform Uposatha-day practices." The monks consented, thinking to themselves, "With her assistance we shall be free from anxiety on account of food and shall be able to effect escape from the round of existence."

Mātika's mother superintended the erection of a monastery to serve as their place of residence, presented it to them, and the monks took up their residence there. On a certain day they met together and admonished each other as follows, "Brethren, it behoves us not to live the life of heedlessness, for before us stand the eight great hells with gates wide open, even as our own houses. Now we have come here thus, having received a subject of meditation from the living Buddha. And the favour of the Buddhas cannot be won by a deceitful person, even though he walk in their very footsteps. Only by doing the will of the Buddhas can their favour be won. Therefore be heedful. Two monks may neither stand nor sit in any one place. In the evening we shall meet together to wait upon the elder, and early in the morning we shall meet together when it is time to go the rounds for alms. At other times two of us must never be together. If, however, a monk is taken

47

sick, let him come to the monastery court and strike the block.[1] At the signal given by a stroke on the block, we will come together and provide a remedy for him." Having made this agreement, they entered upon residence.

One day, while the monks were in residence, that female disciple took ghee, molasses, and other kinds of medicine and in the evening, accompanied by a retinue of bondsmen and servants, went to the monastery. Seeing no monks, she asked some men, "Where have the noble monks gone?"—"My lady, they must be sitting in their own respective night quarters and day quarters."—"What must I do in order to see them?" Men who knew about the agreement made by the Order of Monks said; "If you strike the block, my lady, they will assemble." So she struck the block. When the monks heard the sound of the block, they thought to themselves, "Someone must be sick." And coming forth from their several quarters, they assembled in the monastery court. No two monks came by the same path.

When the female lay disciple saw them approach one at a time, each from his own quarters, she thought to herself, "My sons must have had a quarrel with each other." So, after paying obeisance to the Order of Monks, she asked them, "Have you had a quarrel, reverend sirs?"—"No, indeed, great lay disciple."—"If, reverend sirs, there is no quarrel among you, how is it that whereas in coming to our house you came all together, today you do not approach in that manner, but instead approach one at a time, each from his own quarters?"—"Great lay disciple, we were sitting each in his own cell engaged in the practice of meditation."—"What do you mean, reverend sirs, by this expression, 'practice of meditation'?"—"We rehearse the thirty-two constituent parts of the body[2] and thus obtain a clear conception of the decay and death inherent in the body, great lay disciple."—"But, reverend sirs, are you alone permitted to rehearse the thirty-two constituent parts of the body and thus obtain a clear conception of the decay and death inherent in the body; or are we also permitted to do this?"—"This practice is forbidden to none, great lay disciple."

---

1. A hollow or solid block of hardwood, still used in Asian monasteries.

2. Beginning: hair of the head, hair of the body, nails, teeth, skin. See *Mirror of the Dhamma* (BPS Wheel No. 54).

"Well then, teach me also the thirty-two constituent parts of the body and show me how to obtain a clear conception of the decay and death inherent in the body."—"Very well, lay disciple," said the monks, "learn them." So saying, they taught her all. She began at once to rehearse the thirty-two constituent parts of the body, striving thereby to obtain for herself a clear conception of the decay and death inherent in the body. So successful was she that even in advance of those monks she attained the three paths and the three fruits, and by the same paths won the four analytical knowledges and mundane super-knowledge.[3]

Arising from the bliss of the paths and the fruits, she looked with divine vision and considered within herself, "At what time did my sons attain this state?" Immediately she became aware of the following, "All these monks are still in the bondage of lust, hatred, and delusion. They have not yet, by the practice of deep meditation, induced insight." Then she pondered, "Do my sons possess the dispositions requisite for the attainment of arahant-ship or do they not?" She perceived, "They do." Then she pondered, "Do they possess suitable lodgings or do they not?" Immediately she perceived that they did. Then she pondered, "Have they proper companions or have they not?" Immediately she perceived that they had. Finally she pondered the question, "Do they receive proper food or do they not?" She perceived, "They do not receive proper food."

From that time on she provided them with various kinds of rice-porridge and with all manner of hard food and with soft food flavoured with various choice flavours. And seating the monks in her house, she offered water of donation[4] and presented the food to them, saying, "Reverend sirs, take and eat whatever you desire."

As the result of the wholesome food they received, their minds became tranquil; and as the result of tranquillity of mind, they developed insight and attained arahantship together with the analytical knowledges. Then the thought occurred to them, "The great female lay disciple has indeed been our support. Had we

---

3. That is, she attained the path and fruit of non-returning, accompanied by certain other advanced types of meditative knowledge and psychic powers.

4. She offered the water of donation as a symbol of offering merits to her relatives or other beings born in states of suffering.

not received wholesome food, we should never have attained the paths and the fruits. As soon as we have completed our residence and done the ceremony of Pavāraṇā[5] let us go and visit the Teacher." Accordingly they took leave of the great female lay disciple, saying, "Lay disciple, we desire to see the Teacher."— "Very well, noble sirs," said she. So she accompanied them on their journey a little way, and then, saying, "Look in on us again, reverend sirs," and many other pleasant words, she returned to her house.

When those monks arrived at Sāvatthī, they paid obeisance to the Teacher and sat down respectfully on one side. The Teacher said to them, "Monks, you have evidently fared well, had plenty to eat, and have not been troubled on account of food." The monks replied, "We have indeed fared well, reverend sir, had plenty to eat, and have by no means been troubled on account of food. For a certain female lay disciple, the mother of Mātika, knew the course of our thoughts, in so much that the moment we thought, 'Oh, that she would prepare such and such food for us!' she prepared the very food we thought of and gave it to us." Thus did they recite her praises.

A certain monk, who heard his fellow monks praise the virtues of their hostess, conceived a desire to go there. So obtaining a subject of meditation from the Teacher, he took leave of the Teacher, saying, "Reverend sir, I intend to go to that village." And departing from Jetavana, he arrived in due course at that village and entered the monastery. On the very day he entered the monastery he thought to himself, "I have heard it said that this female lay disciple knows every thought that passes through the mind of another. Now I have been wearied by my journey and shall not be able to sweep the monastery. Oh, that she would send a man to make ready the monastery for me!" The female lay disciple, sitting in her house, pondering within herself, became aware of this fact and sent a man, saying to him, "Go make ready the monastery and turn it over to him." The man went and swept the monastery and turned it over to him. Then the monk, desiring to have water to drink, thought to himself, "Oh, that she would send me some

---

5. A ceremony held at the end of the rains residence, when monks invite admonition from their fellow-monks.

sweetened water!" Straightaway the female lay disciple sent it. On the following day, early in the morning, he thought to himself, "Let her send me soft rice-porridge with some dainty bits!" The female lay disciple straightway did so. After he had finished drinking the porridge, he thought to himself, "Oh, that she would send me such and such solid food!" The female lay disciple straightaway sent this also to him.

Then he thought to himself, "This female lay disciple has sent me every single thing I have thought of. I should like to see her. Oh, that she would come to me in person, bringing with her soft food seasoned with various choice seasonings!" The female lay disciple thought to herself, "My son wishes to see me, desires me to go to him." So procuring soft food, she went to the monastery and gave it to him. When he had eaten his meal, he asked her, "Lay disciple, is your name Mātika's Mother?"—"Yes, dear son."— "You know the thoughts of another?"—"Why do you ask me, dear son?"—"You have done for me every single thing I have thought of; that is why I ask you."—"Many are the monks who know the thoughts of another, dear son."—"I am not asking anyone else. I am asking you, lay disciple." Even under these circumstances the female lay disciple avoided saying, "I know the thoughts of another," and said instead, "Those who do not know the thoughts of another do thus, my son."

Thereupon the monk thought to himself, "I am in a most embarrassing position. They that are still worldings like me entertain both noble and ignoble thoughts. Were I to entertain a single inappropriate thought, she would doubtless change her attitude towards me, as they seize a thief with the goods by his hair. Therefore I had best run away from here." So he said to the female lay disciple, "Lay disciple, I intend to go away."—"Where are you going, noble sir?"—"To the Teacher, lay disciple."—"Reside here for a while, reverend sir."—"I can no longer reside here, lay disciple. I must positively go away." With these words he departed and went to the Teacher.

The Teacher asked him, "Monk, are you no longer residing there?"—"No, reverend sir, I cannot reside there any longer."— "For what reason, monk?"—"Reverend sir, that female lay disciple knows every single thought that passes through my mind. It occurred to me, 'They that are still worldlings like me entertain

51

both noble and ignoble thoughts. Were I to entertain a single inappropriate thought, she would doubtless change her attitude towards me, as they seize a thief with the goods by his hair. That is why I have returned."—"Monk, that is the very place where you ought to reside."—"I cannot, reverend sir. I will not reside there any longer."—"Well then, monk, can you guard just one thing?"—"What do you mean, reverend sir?"—"Guard your thoughts alone, for thoughts are hard to guard. Restrain your thoughts alone. Do not concern yourself with anything else, for thoughts are unruly." So saying, he pronounced the following stanza:

35. The mind is very hard to check
    And swift it falls on what it wants;
    The training of the mind is good,
    A mind so tamed brings happiness.

When the Teacher had admonished that monk, he dismissed him, saying, "Go, monk, concern yourself with nothing else. Resume residence in that same place." And that monk, after being admonished by the Teacher, went to that same place and did not think thoughts concerned with exterior things.

The great female lay disciple looked with divine vision and seeing the elder, she determined by her own knowledge alone the following fact, "My son has now gained a Teacher who gives admonition and has returned once more." And at once she prepared wholesome food and gave it to him. Once having received wholesome food, in but a few days the elder attained arahantship.

As the elder passed his days in the enjoyment of the bliss of the paths and the fruits, he thought to himself, "The great female lay disciple has indeed been a support to me. By her assistance I have gained release from the round of existence." And he considered within himself, "Has she been a support to me in my present state of existence only or has she been a support to me in other states of existence also, as I have passed from one state of existence to another in the round of existences?" With this thought in mind he recalled a hundred states of existence less one. Now in a hundred states of existence less one that female lay disciple had been his wife, and her affections had been set on other men, and she had caused him to be deprived of life. When, therefore, the elder beheld the huge pile of demerit she had accumulated, he thought to himself, "Oh, what wicked deeds this female lay disciple has committed!"

The great female lay disciple also sat in her house, considering within herself the following thought, "Has my son reached the goal of the holy life?" Perceiving that he had attained arahantship, she continued her reflections as follows, "When my son attained arahantship, he thought to himself, 'This female lay disciple has indeed been a powerful support to me.' Then he considered within himself, 'Has she been a support to me in previous states of existence also or has she not?' With this thought in mind he recalled a hundred states of existence less one. Now in a hundred states of existence less one I conspired with other men and deprived him of life. When, therefore, he beheld the huge pile of demerit I thus accumulated, he thought to himself, 'Oh, what wicked deeds this female lay disciple has committed!' Is it not possible that, as I have passed from one state of existence to another in the round of existences, I have rendered assistance to him?"

Considering the matter further, she called up before her mind her hundredth state of existence and became aware of the following: "In my hundredth state of existence I was his wife. On a certain occasion, when I might have deprived him of life, I spared his life. I have indeed rendered great assistance to my son." And still remaining seated in her house she said, "Discern further and consider the matter." By the power of the divine ear the monk immediately heard what she said. Discerning further, he called up before his mind his hundredth state of existence and perceived that in that state of existence she had spared his life. Filled with joy, he thought to himself, "This female lay disciple has indeed rendered great assistance to me." Then and there, reciting the questions relating to the four paths and fruits, he attained the remainderless element of Nibbāna.[6]

---

6. This means, in ordinary terms, that he passed away.

Part II

Doing Evil

11. The Lay Disciple Atula

FROM DAYS OF OLD IT HAS BEEN, ATULA.... This instruction was given by the Teacher while he was in residence at Jetavana with reference to the lay disciple Atula.

Atula was a lay disciple who lived at Sāvatthī, and he had a retinue of five hundred other lay disciples. One day he took those lay disciples with him to the monastery to hear the Dhamma. Desiring to hear the Elder Revata teach the Dhamma, he saluted the Elder Revata and sat down respectfully on one side. Now this Elder Revata was a solitary recluse, delighting in solitude even as a lion delights in solitude, and thus he had nothing to say to Atula.

"This elder has nothing to say," thought Atula. Provoked, he arose from his seat, went to the Elder Sāriputta, and took his stand respectfully on one side. "For what reason have you come to me?" asked the Elder Sāriputta. "Reverend sir," replied Atula, "I took these lay disciples of mine to hear the Dhamma and approached the Elder Revata. But he had nothing to say to me; therefore I was provoked at him and have come here. Teach the Dhamma to me." – "Well then, lay disciple," said the Elder Sāriputta, "sit down." And forthwith the Elder Sāriputta expounded the Abhidhamma at great length.

Thought the lay disciple, "The Abhidhamma is exceedingly abstruse, and the elder has expounded this alone to me at great length; of what use is he to us?" Provoked, he took his retinue with him and went to the Elder Ānanda. Said the Elder Ānanda, "What is it, lay disciple?" Atula replied, "Reverend sir, we approached the Elder Revata for the purpose of hearing the Dhamma and got not so much as a syllable from him. Provoked at this, we went to the Elder Sāriputta and he expounded to us at great length the Abhidhamma alone with all its subtleties. 'Of what use is he to us?' we thought to ourselves and provoked at him also, we came here. Teach the Dhamma to us, reverend sir." – "Well then," replied the Elder Ānanda, "sit down and listen." Thereupon the Elder Ānanda expounded the Dhamma to them very briefly, and making it very easy for them to understand.

But they were provoked at the Elder Ānanda also, and going to the Teacher, saluted him, and sat down respectfully on one side. Said the Teacher to them, "Lay disciples, why have you come here?" – "To hear the Dhamma, reverend sir." – "But you have heard the Dhamma." – "Reverend sir, first we went to the Elder Revata, and he had nothing to say to us; provoked at him, we approached the Elder Sāriputta, and he expounded the Abhidhamma to us at great length; but we were unable to understand his discourse, and provoked at him we approached the Elder Ānanda; the Elder Ānanda, however, expounded the Dhamma to us very briefly, therefore we were provoked at him also and came here."

The Teacher heard what they had to say and then replied, "Atula, from days of old until now it has been the invariable practice of men to blame him who said nothing, him who said much, and him who said little. There is no one who deserves unqualified blame and no one who deserves unqualified praise. Even kings are blamed by some and praised by others. Even the great earth, even the sun and moon, even a Supremely Enlightened Buddha, sitting and speaking in the midst of the fourfold assembly,[1] some blame and others praise. For blame or praise bestowed by utter simpletons is a matter of no account. But he whom a man of learning and intelligence blames or praises—he is blamed or praised indeed." So saying, he pronounced the following stanzas:

227. From days of old it has been, Atula—
This is not only of today:
They blame one who keeps silent,
They blame one who speaks much,
They blame one who says little too—
There is no one in the world unblamed.

228. There never was, and never will be,
Nor is there found at present
A person blamed exclusively
Nor yet one wholly praised.

---

1. Of monks, nuns, laymen, and laywomen.

229. But if the wise praise a man,
     After observing him day by day—
     One of flawless conduct, astute,
     In wisdom and virtue well-composed—

230. Who can blame that worthy one
     Like ornament of finest gold?
     Even the devas praise him,
     By Brahmā, too, he is praised.

12. Ciñcā the Brahmin Girl

THE PERSON OF FALSE SPEECH — TRANSGRESSOR OF ONE PRINCIPLE.... This instruction was given by the Teacher while he was in residence at Jetavana with reference to Ciñcā Mānavikā.

For in the first period after the Enlightenment the disciples of the Master multiplied and innumerable gods and men entered on the plane of the noble ones.[1] And as the glory of his virtues became widely known, rich gain and high honour were bestowed upon him. But as for the sectarians, lost to them were gain and honour alike, even as fireflies lose their brilliance before the coming of the sun. And they gathered in the street and cried out, "Is the monk Gotama the only Buddha? We also are Buddhas! Does that alone which is given to him yield abundant fruit? That which is given to us brings abundant fruit also. Therefore give alms to us; bestow honour upon us." With such words as these did they appeal to the multitude, but for all their appeal they got neither gain nor honour. Accordingly they met together in secret and considered within themselves, "By what means can we cast reproach upon the monk Gotama in public and so put an end to the gain and honour bestowed upon him?"

Now at that time there lived in Sāvatthī a certain wandering nun named Ciñcā Mānavikā. She possessed surpassing beauty and loveliness; a very celestial nymph was she; from her body proceeded forth rays of light. Now a certain harsh counsellor made this proposal, "With the assistance of this woman we shall be able to cast reproach upon the monk Gotama, and so put an end to the gain and honour bestowed upon him." – "That is the way!" exclaimed the sectarians, agreeing to his proposal.

Ciñcā Mānavikā went to the monastery of the sectarians, saluted them, and stood waiting; but the sectarians had nothing to say to her. Thereupon she said, "What fault do you find in me?" This question she repeated three times; then she said, "Noble sirs, I appeal to you for an answer. Noble sirs, what fault do you find in me? Why do you not speak to me?" – "Sister," replied the sectarians, "Don't you know the monk Gotama, who goes about doing us harm,

---

1. Meaning that they attained the paths and fruits up to arahantship.

60

depriving us of gain and honour alike?" – "No, noble sirs, I do not know him; but is there anything I can do to help you in this matter?" – "Sister, if you wish us well, summon up your resources, contrive to cast reproach upon the monk Gotama, and so put an end to the gain and honour bestowed upon him." – "Very well, noble sirs," replied Ciñcā Mānavikā. "I will take all the responsibility; have no anxiety as to the outcome." So saying, she departed.

From that time on, she employed all of her skill in the arts of a woman to effect her purpose. When the residents of Sāvatthī were returning from Jetavana after listening to the Dhamma, she would put on a cloak the colour of cochineal, and bearing perfumes and garlands in her hands, would walk in the direction of Jetavana. "Where are you going at this time of day?" people would ask her. "What business of yours is it where I am going?" she would reply. She would spend the night near Jetavana at the monastery of the sectarians, and early the following morning, when throngs of lay disciples were coming out of the city for the purpose of rendering the morning greeting to the Teacher, she would wend her way back and re-enter the city. "Where have you spent the night?" people would ask her. "What business of yours is it where I have spent the night?" she would reply.

After the lapse of a month and a half, whenever they asked her this question, she would reply, "I spent the night at Jetavana alone with the monk Gotama in the Perfumed Chamber." And by her answer she caused doubts and misgivings to spring up in the minds of those who were still worldlings. And they said to themselves, "Is this true, or is it false?" When three or four months had gone by she wrapped her belly about with bandages, to create the impression that she was pregnant, and dressing herself in a scarlet cloak, she went about, saying, "I have conceived a child by the monk Gotama." Thus did she deceive utter simpletons.

When eight or nine months had gone by, she fastened a disc of wood to her belly, drew a cloak over it, produced swellings all over her body by pounding her hands and feet and back with the jaw-bone of an ox, and pretending to be physically exhausted, went one evening to the Hall of Truth and stood before the Tathāgata. There, in his gloriously adorned Seat of Truth, sat the Tathāgata teaching the Dhamma. And standing there before him, Ciñcā Mānavikā opened her lips and reviled him, saying, "Mighty

61

monk, mighty is the throng to which you teach the Dhamma; sweet is your voice, soft are your lips. Nevertheless you are the one by whom I have conceived a child, and the time of my delivery is near at hand. But in spite of all this, you make no effort to provide a lying-in chamber for me, nor do you offer to provide me with ghee and oil and such other things as I need. And failing yourself to attend to your duty, neither do you say to any one of your supporters, the king of Kosala, or Anāthapiṇḍika, or Visākhā, your eminent female lay disciple, 'Do for this young woman what should be done for her.' You know well enough how to take your pleasure, but you do not know how to look after the child you have begotten." Thus did she revile the Tathāgata in the midst of the congregation, even as a woman with a mass of dung in her hand might seek to defile the face of the moon.

The Tathāgata stopped his discourse, and like a lion's roar, cried out, "Sister, as to whether what you have said is true or false, that is something which only you and I know." – "Yes, mighty monk, but who is to decide between the truth and the falsehood of what is known only to you and to me?" At that moment Sakka's seat showed signs of heat. Thereupon Sakka pondered the cause and became aware of the following, "Ciñcā Mānavikā is falsely accusing the Tathāgata." Thereupon Sakka said to himself, "I will clear up this matter," and forthwith set out with four deities. The deities turned themselves into little mice. With one bite of their teeth these little mice severed the cords with which the disc of wood was fastened to the belly of the woman. At that moment the wind blew up the cloak which was wrapped about her, and the disc of wood fell upon her feet, cutting off the toes of both her feet.

Thereupon the multitude cried out, "A hag is reviling the Supremely Enlightened One." They spat on her head, and taking clods of earth and sticks in their hands, drove her out of the Jetavana. As she passed out of sight of the Tathāgata, the great earth split apart, an abyss opened under her feet, and flames shot up from the Avīci hell. Thus was she swallowed up, enveloped as it were in a scarlet blanket such as is presented by wealthy families, and reborn in the Avīci hell. From that time the gain and honour of the sectarians decreased, but the offerings presented to the Master increased more and more.

On the following day the monks began a discussion in the Hall of Truth: "Brethren, Ciñcā Mānavikā, because she falsely accused the Possessor of Eminent Virtues, the Foremost Recipient of Offerings, the Supremely Exalted, came to utter ruin." The Teacher approached and asked, "Monks, what are you sitting here now talking about?" When they told him, he said, "Monks, this is not the first time she has falsely accused me and come to utter ruin; she did the same thing in a previous state of existence also." Having thus spoken, he said:

> Unless a king discern clearly
> Fault on the part of another,
> After himself investigating carefully all the facts,
> Both small and great,
> He should not inflict punishment.

So saying, he related in detail this Mahā Paduma Jātaka (Jāt. No. 472).

Story of the Past: The Lewd Woman and the Youth

At that time, it appears, Ciñcā Mānavikā was reborn as one of the chief consorts of the king, fellow-wife of the mother of the Future Buddha, Prince Mahā Paduma. She invited the Great Being[2] to lie with her, and when he refused to do so, disfigured her own body with her own hands, feigned sickness, and told the king, "Your son brought me to this pass because I would not lie with him." The king, hearing this, was filled with rage, and straightaway flung the Great Being down Robbers' Cliff. The deity dwelling in the mountain chasm cared for him and placed him safe and sound within the hood of the king of the dragons. The king of the dragons carried him to the abode of the dragons and honoured him by conferring upon him half his kingly power. After the Great Being had dwelt there for a year, he conceived a desire to adopt the life of an ascetic. Accordingly he went to the Himalaya country, adopted the life of an ascetic, and in the course of time developed the direct knowledges by the practice of deep meditation.

Now a certain forester happened to see him there and reported the matter to the king. Thereupon the king went to him, exchanged

---

2. The Bodhisatta or future Buddha in his earlier existences.

friendly greetings with him, learned what had happened, and offered to bestow his kingdom upon the Great Being. The Great Being, however, declined his offer and admonished him as follows, "For my part, I have no desire to rule. But as for you, you should keep unimpaired the ten royal virtues,[3] avoid evil deeds, and rule your kingdom justly." Thereupon the king arose from his seat in tears and went back to the city. On the way there he asked his ministers, "Through whose fault was I separated from one endowed with such uprightness?" – "Your chief consort was to blame for this, your majesty." Thereupon the king had her taken by the heels and flung head first down Robbers' Cliff. And entering his city, from then on he ruled his kingdom justly. At that time Prince Mahā Paduma was the Great Being, and the fellow-wife of his mother was Ciñcā Mānavikā. (*End of Story of the Past.*)

When the Teacher had made this matter clear, he said, "Monks, in the case of those who have abandoned one thing – the speaking of truth – who have become confirmed in falsehood, who have rid themselves of (the chance of a happy) next world, there is no evil deed which they will not commit." So saying, he pronounced the following stanza:

176. The person of false speech—
     Transgressor of one principle,[4]
     Rejecter of the other world:
     There is no evil he cannot do.

---

3. Giving, virtuous conduct, renunciation, uprightness, gentleness, austerity, non-anger, harmlessness, patience, non-opposition (to the will of the people).

4. Truthfulness is the one necessary principle (*dhamma*).

13. The Black Ogress

NOT BY ENMITY AT ANY TIME.... This instruction was given by the Teacher while he was in residence at Jetavana with reference to a certain barren woman.

It appears that a certain householder's son, on the death of his father, did all the farm and household work by himself alone and took care of his mother as well. Now his mother said to him, "Dear son, I will fetch you a young wife." – "Dear mother, do not speak like that. My sole desire is to take care of you so long as you shall live." – "Dear son, you alone are doing the farm and household work, and I am not satisfied to have it so; let me fetch you a young wife." He protested time and again, and then held his peace.

The mother left the house, intending to go to a certain family and fetch home the daughter of that family. Her son asked her, "To what family are you going?" – "To such and such a family." He would not let her go to the family she had in mind, but told her of a family he liked better. So she went to the family he fancied, selected a wife for her son, and having set the day, installed her in her son's house. The woman turned out to be barren.

Then said the mother to the son, "Son, you had me fetch you a wife you yourself selected. Now she turns out to be barren. Without children a family dies out, and the line is not continued. Therefore let me fetch you another young wife." – "Enough said, dear mother," replied the son; but the mother repeated her request time and again. The barren wife heard the talk and thought to herself, "It is certain that sons cannot disobey the words of their mothers and fathers. Now if she fetches him a wife who is fruitful, they will treat me like a slave. Suppose I were to fetch him a young woman of my own selection?"

So the barren wife went to a certain family and selected a young woman for him. But she immediately encountered the opposition of the young woman's parents, who said to her, "Woman, what are you saying?" The barren wife replied, "I am a barren woman, and without children a family dies out. If your daughter gives birth to a son, she will be mistress of the family and the wealth thereof. Therefore give your daughter to me for my husband."

She finally prevailed upon them to grant her request, and taking the young woman with her, installed her in her husband's house.

Then this thought occurred to her, "If my rival gives birth to a son or daughter, she alone will be mistress of the household. I must see to it that she shall not give birth to a child." So the barren wife said to her rival, "As soon as you have conceived a child in your womb, please let me know." – "Very well," replied her rival. In accordance with her promise, as soon as she had conceived, she told her fellow-wife.

Now the barren wife was accustomed to give her rival a meal of rice-porridge regularly every day with her own hand. So along with the food she gave her a drug to cause abortion. The result was that her rival had a miscarriage. Again the second time the fruitful wife conceived a child and informed the barren wife, and again her fellow-wife did as before and brought about a miscarriage.

The women who lived in the neighbourhood asked the fruitful wife, "Is not your rival putting an obstacle in your way?" When she told them the facts, they said to her, "You foolish woman, why did you do this? This woman was afraid you would get the upper hand, so she mixed a preparation to bring about a miscarriage and gave it to you. Do not tell her again." Accordingly the third time the fruitful wife said nothing to her rival. But the barren wife, seeing her belly, said to her, "Why did you not tell me that you had conceived a child?" Said the fruitful wife, "It was you who brought me here, and twice you have caused me to suffer a miscarriage; why should I tell you?"

"Now I am lost," thought the barren wife. From that time on she watched to catch her rival off her guard. When the baby in the womb was fully matured, she took advantage of an opportunity, mixed a drug, and gave it to her. But because the baby in the womb was fully mature, an abortion was out of the question, and the result was that the child lodged across the neck of the womb. Immediately the mother suffered acute pains and feared that her hour had come.

"You have killed me!" she cried. "It was you alone that brought me here; it was you alone that killed my three children. Now I also am going to die. When I have passed out of this existence, may I be reborn as an ogress able to devour your children." And having made this earnest wish, she died, and was reborn in that very house as a cat. The husband seized the barren wife, and saying to her, "It was you who destroyed my family," beat her soundly with elbows, knees, and otherwise. As the result of the beating she received, she sickened and died, and was reborn in that very house as a hen.

So the fruitful wife was reborn as a cat, and the barren wife was reborn as a hen. The hen laid eggs, and the cat came and ate them. This happened three times. Said the hen, "Three times you have eaten my eggs, and now you are seeking an opportunity to eat me too. When I have passed out of this existence, may I be able to eat you and your offspring." And having made this earnest wish, she passed out of that existence, and was reborn as a leopardess. The cat was reborn as a doe.

So the barren wife, at the end of her existence as a hen, was reborn as a leopardess; and the fruitful wife, at the end of her existence as a cat, was reborn as a doe. Thrice the doe brought forth young, and thrice the leopardess went and devoured the doe's offspring. When the doe came to die, she said, "Thrice this beast has devoured my offspring, and now she intends to devour me too. When I have passed out of this existence, may I be able to devour her and her offspring." And having made this earnest wish, she was reborn as an ogress. When the leopardess passed out of that existence, she was reborn in Sāvatthī as a young woman of station.

So the fruitful wife, at the end of her existence as a doe, was reborn as an ogress; and the barren wife, at the end of her existence as a leopardess, was reborn in Sāvatthī as a young woman of station. When the latter grew up, she was married and went to live with her husband's family in a little settlement near the gate of the city. After a time she gave birth to a son. The ogress disguised herself as a dear friend of the young woman and went to see her. "Where is my friend?" said the ogress. "In the inner room; she has just given birth to a child." – "Did she give birth to a son or a daughter? I should like to see her." So saying, the ogress went in. While pretending to be looking at the child, she seized him, devoured him, and then went out. Again a second time she devoured a child of the young wife in the same way.

The third time the young wife was pregnant she addressed her husband, "Husband, in this place an ogress has devoured two sons of mine and escaped. This time I intend to go to the house of my parents to give birth to my child."

Now at this time the ogress was away doing her turn at drawing water. (For Vessavaṇa's ogresses take their turn at drawing water from Lake Anotatta, passing it along from the source.[1] At the expiration of four or five months they are released; the others die from exhaustion.) The moment the ogress was released from her turn at drawing water, she went quickly to the young wife's house and inquired, "Where is my friend?" – "Where you will not see her. There is an ogress that devours every child she bears in this house, and therefore she has gone to the house of her parents." – "She may go wherever she likes, but she will not escape from me." Spurred on by an impulse of hatred, the ogress dashed towards the city.

On the day appointed for the naming of the child, the mother bathed him, gave him a name, and then said to her husband, "Husband, now we will go back to our own home." Accordingly she took the boy in her arms and set out with her husband along the path leading through the grounds of the monastery. When they reached the monastery pool, the young wife gave the boy to her husband and bathed in the pool. When she had finished her bath, her husband bathed in the pool. While the husband was bathing, the wife remained near, giving suck to her child.

Just then the ogress drew near. The young wife saw her coming and recognized her. Immediately she screamed with a loud voice, "Husband! Husband! Come quickly! Come quickly! Here is that ogress!" Not daring to wait until her husband came, she turned and dashed into the monastery.

Now at this time the Teacher was teaching the Dhamma in the midst of the Order. The young wife laid her boy at the feet of the Tathāgata and said, "I give you this child; spare the life of my son." The deity Sumana, who resided in the gate, prevented the ogress from entering. The Teacher addressed the Elder Ānanda, saying, "Go, Ānanda, summon that ogress within." The Elder

---

1. Vessavaṇa is one of the divine kings in the heaven of the Four Great Kings. He rules over the ogres and ogresses.

summoned her within. The young wife said, "Here she comes, reverend sir." Said the Teacher, "Let her come; make no noise."

When the ogress came and stood before him, the Teacher said: "Why have you done so? Had you not come face to face with a Buddha like me, you would have cherished hatred towards each other for an aeon, like the snake and the mongoose, who trembled and quaked with enmity, like the crows and the owls. Why do you return hatred for hatred? Hatred is quenched by love, not by hatred." And when he had thus spoken, he pronounced the following stanza:

> 4. Not by enmity at any time
> Are those with enmity allayed:
> They are allayed by amity—
> This is an ancient principle.

At the conclusion of the stanza the ogress was established in the fruit of stream-entry.

The Teacher said to the woman, "Give your child to this ogress." – "I am afraid to, reverend sir." – "Fear not, you have no reason to be alarmed because of her." The young wife gave her child to the ogress. The ogress kissed and caressed him, gave him back again to his mother, and began to weep. The Teacher asked her, "Why do you weep?" – "Reverend sir, in the past I have managed somehow or other to get a living, but I have never had enough to eat. Now how am I to live?" Then the Teacher comforted her, saying, "Do not worry." And turning to the mother, he said, "Take this ogress home with you, let her live in your own house, and feed her with the choicest rice-porridge."

So the young wife took the ogress home with her, lodged her on the back veranda, and fed her with the choicest rice-porridge. Now when the rice was threshed and the flail was raised, she feared that it would strike her head. So she said to her friend, "I shall not be able to live here any longer; lodge me elsewhere." She was lodged successively in the flail-hut, the water hut, the bakehouse, the storeroom for nimbs, the dust-heap, and the village gate. But she refused to live in any of these places, saying, "Here the flail rises as if it would split my head in two; here boys empty out slops; here dogs lie down; here boys attend to nature's needs; here they throw away sweepings; here village boys practise fortune-telling." So they lodged her in a quiet place by herself outside of the village, and there they brought her the choicest rice-porridge.

The ogress said to her friend, "This year there will be abundance of rain; therefore plant your crops in a moist place." Other people's crops were destroyed either by excessive moisture or by drought, but the crops of the young wife flourished above measure.

People asked the young wife, "Woman, your crops are destroyed neither by excessive moisture nor by drought. When you plant your crops, you seem to know in advance whether the season will be wet or dry. How is this?" The young wife replied, "I have a friend, an ogress, who tells me whether the season will be wet or dry; and I plant my crops according to her directions on high or low ground. Don't you see? Every day the choicest rice-porridge and other kinds of food are carried out of our house and offered to her. If you also carry the choicest rice-porridge and other kinds of food to her, she will look after your crops also."

Straightaway all the residents of the city rendered honour to her. On her part, from that time forth, she looked after the crops of all. And she received abundant gifts and a large retinue. Subsequently she established the eight tickets for food, which are kept up even to this present day.

14. The Five Laymen

THERE IS NO FIRE LIKE LUST.... This instruction was given by the Teacher while he was in residence at Jetavana with reference to five lay disciples.

The story goes that these five men went to the monastery desiring to hear the Dhamma, and having saluted the Teacher, sat down respectfully on one side. Now in the case of the Buddhas, no such thought ever enters their mind as the following: "This man is a khattiya, this man is a brahmin, this is a rich man, this is a poor man; I will teach the Dhamma to this man in such a way as to exalt him; I will not do so, however, in the case of this other man." It matters not with reference to what subject the Buddhas teach the Dhamma. They place reverence for the Dhamma before all else, and teach the Dhamma as though they were bringing down the celestial river from the sky.

But though the Tathāgata taught the Dhamma in this way to the five men who sat about him, one of the five, even as he sat there, fell asleep, another sat and dug the earth with his finger, another sat and shook a tree, another gazed at the sky. Only one listened attentively to the Dhamma. As the Elder Ānanda stood there fanning the Teacher, he observed the conduct of the five men and said to the Teacher, "Reverend sir, you are teaching the Dhamma even as thunders the thunder which accompanies a heavy rain, but even as you teach the Dhamma, these men sit doing this and that." – "Ānanda, do you not know these men?" – "No, reverend sir, I do not."

"Of these five men, he that sits there sound asleep was reborn as a snake in five hundred states of existence, and in each of these states of existence he laid his head in his coils and fell asleep; therefore at the present time also he is sound asleep; not a sound I make enters his ear."

"But, reverend sir, tell me, was this in successive states of existence or at intervals?" – "Ānanda, at one time this man was reborn as a human being, at another time as a god, and at another time as a snake. Indeed it would be impossible, even with the knowledge of omniscience, to determine exactly the number of

71

times he has undergone rebirth at intervals. But in five hundred successive states of existence he was reborn as a snake and fell asleep; not even yet is he sated with sleep.

"The man who sits there scratching the earth with his finger was reborn in five hundred successive states of existence as an earthworm and burrowed into the earth; hence he digs the earth at the present time also, and fails to hear my voice.

"The man who sits there shaking a tree was reborn in five hundred successive states of existence as a monkey, and from sheer force of habit acquired in previous states of existence, he still continues to shake a tree, and the sound of my voice does not enter his ears.

"The brahmin who sits there gazing at the sky was reborn in five hundred successive states of existence as an astrologer, and therefore today also he gazes at the sky just the same, and the sound of my voice does not enter his ears.

"The man who sits there listening attentively to the Dhamma was reborn in five hundred successive states of existence as a brahmin versed in the Three Vedas, devoted to the repetition of the sacred texts, and therefore listens attentively today also, as though he were putting together a sacred text."

"But, reverend sir, your teaching of the Dhamma cleaves the skin and penetrates to the marrow of the bones. Why is it that while you are teaching the Dhamma, they do not listen attentively?" – "Ānanda, you evidently imagine that my Dhamma is easy to listen to." – "Why, reverend sir, do you mean that it is difficult to listen to?" – "Precisely so, Ānanda." – "Why is that, reverend sir?" – "Ānanda, these living beings, during countless thousands of cycles of time, never heard of the Buddha, the Dhamma, and the Order, and therefore are unable now to listen to this Dhamma which I teach. In the round of existences without conceivable beginning, these living beings have been accustomed to listen to the speech of animals in its countless forms. Therefore they spend their time in places where men drink and amuse themselves, and therefore sing and dance; it is impossible for them to listen to the Dhamma." – "But, reverend sir, for what reason is it that they are unable to listen to the Dhamma?"

The Teacher answered him as follows: "Ānanda, they are unable to do so by reason of lust, by reason of hatred, by reason of delusion. For there is no fire like the fire of lust, consuming living beings as it does, without leaving so much as ashes behind. To be sure, the world-conflagration which closes an epoch burns up the world without leaving anything behind, but this is a fire which breaks out only on the appearance of the seven suns, and this fire burns only at times and at seasons. But as for the fire of lust, there is no time when the fire of lust does not burn. Therefore I say that there is no fire like the fire of lust, no grip like hatred, no snare like delusion, and no river like craving." So saying, the Teacher pronounced the following stanza:

251. There is no fire like lust,
    No captor like aversion;
    Unequalled is delusion's net,
    No river like craving.

15. King Pasenadi of Kosala

A DULLARD DROWSY WITH MUCH GLUTTONY.... This instruction was given by the Teacher while he was in residence at Jetavana with reference to King Pasenadi of Kosala.

At a certain period of his life this king used to eat boiled rice cooked by the bucketful, and sauce and curry in proportion. One day after he had his breakfast, unable to shake off the drowsy feeling occasioned by overeating, he went to see the Teacher and paced back and forth before him with a very weary look. Overcome by drowsiness, unable to lie down and stretch himself out, he sat down on one side. Thereupon the Teacher asked him, "Did you come, great king, before you were well rested?" – "Oh no, reverend sir," replied he king, "but I always suffer greatly after eating a meal." Then said the Teacher to him, "Great king, overeating always brings suffering in its train." So saying, he pronounced the following stanza:

> 325. A dullard drowsy with much gluttony,
> Engrossed in sleep, who wallows as he lies,
> Like a great porker stuffed with fattening food,
> Comes ever and again unto the womb.[1]

At the conclusion of the lesson the Teacher, desiring to help the king, pronounced the following stanza:

> If a man is ever mindful,
> If moderate in taking food,
> His sufferings will be but slight,
> He ages slowly, preserving his life.

The Teacher taught this stanza to Prince Uttara and said to him, "Whenever the king sits down to eat, you must recite this stanza to him, and by this means you must cause him to diminish his food." In these words the Teacher told him just what means to employ. The prince did as he was directed. After a time the king was content with a pint-pot of rice at most, and became lean and cheerful. He established intimate relations with the Teacher and

---

1. The translation of Ven. Ñāṇamoli Thera from *The Guide* (PTS 1962).

for seven days gave "the gifts beyond compare."[2] When the Teacher pronounced the words of rejoicing for the gifts presented to him by the king, the assembled multitude obtained great spiritual advantage.

---

2. "The gifts beyond compare" are described in the Dhammapada Commentary in *Buddhist Legends*, 3:24ff.

16. Great-wealth the Treasurer's Son

HAVING LED NEITHER THE HOLY LIFE NOR RICHES WON WHILE YOUNG.... This instruction was given by the Teacher while he was in residence at Isipatana with reference to Great-wealth, Mahādhana, the treasurer's son.

Great-wealth, it appears, was reborn at Benares in a household worth eighty crores.[1] Now his mother and father thought to themselves, "We have a vast store of wealth in our house, and there is no necessity that our son should do anything else than enjoy himself according to his own good pleasure." Accordingly they had him instructed in singing and in the playing of musical instruments, and that was all the instruction he received. Likewise in that same city, in a household worth eighty crores of treasure, a daughter was reborn. The same thought occurred to her mother and father also, and they had her instructed only in dancing and singing. When the two reached the proper age, they were married with the customary ceremonies. In the course of time both their parents died, and then there were twice eighty crores of treasure in the same house.

It was the custom of the treasurer's son to go thrice a day to wait upon the king. One day a company of knaves who lived in that city thought to themselves, "If this treasurer's son would only get drunk, it would be a fine thing for us. Let us show him how to get drunk." Accordingly they procured strong drink, put roast meat, salt, and sugar in the skirts of their clothing, and taking roots and bulbs, seated themselves in a convenient place, watching the path by which he would approach from the royal palace. When they saw him approaching, they began to drink strong drink, placed particles of salt and sugar in their mouths, and took the roots and bulbs in their teeth and chewed them. And they said, "Live for a hundred years, master treasurer's son! With your help may we be enabled to eat and drink to our heart's content!" Hearing their words, the youth asked the little page who followed him, "What are these men drinking?" – "A certain drink, master." – "Does it

---

1. This is a way of saying "multi-millionaire."

taste good?" – "Master, in this world of the living there is no kind of drink to be had comparable to this." – "In that case," said the youth, "I must have some, too." So he caused the page to bring him first a little, and then a little more, and all this he drank.

Now in no long time those knaves discovered that he had taken up the habit of drinking. Then they flocked around him. As time went on, the crowd that surrounded him increased in numbers. He would spend a hundred or two hundred pieces of money at a time on strong drink. It became a habit with him after a time, wherever he happened to be, to pile up a heap of coins and call out as he drank, "Take this coin and fetch me flowers! Take this coin and fetch me perfumes! This man is clever at dicing, and this man at dancing, and this man at singing, and this man at the playing of musical instruments! Give this man a thousand and this man two thousand!" Thus did he spend his money.

In no long time he squandered all the eighty crores of treasure that formerly belonged to him. Then those knaves said to him, "Master, your wealth is all spent." – "Has my wife no money?" – "Yes, master, she has." – "Well then, fetch that too." And he spent his wife's money in precisely the same way. As time went on, he sold his fields and his parks and his gardens and his carriages. He even disposed of the vessels he used at meals, of his coverlets and his cloaks and couches. All that belonged to him, he sold, and the proceeds he spent in riotous living. In old age he sold his house, the property of his family. And those to whom he sold his house took possession of it and straightaway put him out. Thereupon, taking his wife with him, he found lodging near the house-wall of other people's houses. With a broken potsherd in his hand, he would go about begging alms. Finally he began to eat the leavings of other people's food.

One day he stood at the door of a rest house, receiving leavings of food presented to him by young novices. The Teacher saw him and smiled. Thereupon the Elder Ānanda asked him why he smiled. The Teacher explained the reason for his smile by saying, "Ānanda, just look here at Great-wealth, the treasurer's son! In this very city he has squandered twice eighty crores of treasure. Now, accompanied by his wife, he is begging alms. For if in the prime of life this man had not squandered his wealth, but had applied himself to business, he would have become the principal treasurer in this very city; and if he had retired from the world and become a monk, he would have attained arahantship, and his wife would have been established in the fruit of the third path. If in middle life he had not squandered his wealth, but had applied himself to business, he would have become the second treasurer; and if he had retired from the world and become a monk, he would have attained the fruit of the third path, and his wife would have been established in the fruit of the second path. If in the latter years of his life he had not squandered his wealth, but had applied himself to business, he would have become the third treasurer; and if he had retired from the world and become a monk, he would have attained the fruit of the second path, and his wife would have been established in the fruit of stream-entry. But now he has fallen away from the wealth of a layman and he has likewise fallen away from the estate of an ascetic. He has become like a heron in a dried-up pond." So saying, he pronounced the following stanzas:

155. Having led neither the holy life
      Nor riches won while young,
      They linger on like aged cranes
      Around a fished-out pond.

156. Having led neither the holy life
      Nor riches won while young,
      They lie around like worn-out bows
      Sighing about the past.

Part III

The Buddha Teaches Dhamma

17. Māra the Evil One

HAPPY ARE COMPANIONS WHEN THE NEED ARISES.... This instruction was given by the Teacher while he was dwelling in a forest-hut in the Himalaya country with reference to Māra.

Tradition has it that at this time kings who exercised rule oppressed the subjects over whom they ruled. As the Exalted One saw men punished and persecuted under the rule of these wicked kings, he was moved to compassion. And he considered thus within himself, "Is it not possible to exercise sovereignty without killing or causing to kill, without conquering or causing to conquer, without sorrow or causing sorrow, with justice and righteousness?" Now Māra the Evil One perceived within himself the thought that was passing through the mind of the Exalted One, and he reflected thus, "The monk Gotama is considering within himself, 'Is it not possible to exercise sovereignty?' It must be that he now desires to exercise sovereignty. And this thing which is called sovereignty is an occasion of heedlessness. If he does exercise sovereignty, I may be able to catch him off his guard. I will therefore go and arouse his ambition."

Accordingly Māra the Evil One approached the Teacher and said, "Reverend sir, let the Exalted One exercise sovereignty; let the Happy One exercise sovereignty, without killing or causing to kill, without conquering or causing to conquer, without sorrow or causing sorrow, with justice and righteousness." Said the Teacher to Māra, "Evil One, what do you see in me that makes you speak thus to me?" Said Māra to the Teacher, "Reverend sir, the Exalted One has developed to the full the four bases of spiritual power. For should the Exalted One resolve, 'Let the Himālaya, king of mountains, be turned to gold,' that mountain would turn to gold. I, too, will do with this wealth all those things which can be done with wealth. Thus you shall rule justly and righteously." Then said the Teacher:

> "A mountain made of gold,
> Of only gold alone,
> Given to one – not enough!
> Knowing this, live steadily.

Having seen where suffering has its cause,
How can a person turn away to pleasures?
Knowing the 'assets'[1] as attachments in the world,
Let such a one by training subdue them."

With these stanzas the Teacher aroused and alarmed Māra the Evil One. Then he said to him, "I will admonish you yet again, Evil One. I have nothing in common with you. Thus do I admonish you." So saying, he pronounced the following stanzas:

331. Happy are companions when the need arises,
Contentment is happiness with just this and that;
Happy is merit when life is at an end,
Abandoning all suffering is happiness.

332. Happiness is it to serve one's mother here,
To serve one's father, too, is happiness;
Happiness is serving ascetics here.
To serve brāhmaṇas[2] is happiness.

333. Virtue till old age is happiness;
Happiness is faith planted firmly;
Happy is the gaining of wisdom,
Not doing evil – that is happiness.

---

1. *Upadhi*, the substrata of the mind ensuring continued rebirth: the five aggregates (*khandha*), sense pleasures (*kāma*), defilements (*kilesā*), and intentional action (*kamma*).

2. Here "*brāhmaṇas*" means arahants.

18. The Buddha Settles a Quarrel

WE LIVE INDEED SO HAPPILY.... This instruction was given by the Teacher while he was in residence among the Sākiyas with reference to the cessation of a quarrel among kinsmen.

The story goes that the Sākiyas and the Koliyas caused the waters of the river Rohiṇī to be confined by a single dam between the city of Kapilavatthu and the city of Koliya and cultivated the fields on both sides of the river.[1] Now in the month Jeṭṭhamūla the crops began to droop, whereupon the labourers employed by the residents of both cities assembled. Said the residents of the city of Koliya, "If this water is diverted to both sides of the river, there will not be enough both for you and for us too. But our crops will ripen with a single watering. Therefore let us have the water."

The Sākiyas replied, "After you have filled your storehouses, we shall not have the heart to take ruddy gold and emeralds and black pennies, and baskets and sacks in our hands, and go from house to house seeking favours at your hands. Our crops also will ripen with a single watering. Therefore let us have this water." – "We will not give it to you." – "Neither will we give it to you." Talk waxed bitter, until finally one arose and struck another a blow. The other returned the blow and a general fight ensued, the combatants making matters worse by aspersions on the origins of the two royal families.

Said the labourers employed by the Koliyas, "You who live in the city of Kapilavatthu, take your children and go where you belong. Are we likely to suffer harm from the elephants and horses and shields and weapons of those who, like dogs and jackals, have cohabited with their own sisters?" The labourers employed by the Sākiyas replied. "You lepers, take your children and go where you belong. Are we likely to suffer harm from the elephants and horses and shields and weapons of destitute outcasts who have lived in jujube-trees like animals?" Both parties of labourers went and reported the quarrel to the ministers who had charge of the work, and the ministers reported the matter to the royal households.

---

1. The Sākiyas were the Buddha's kinsfolk, who lived at Kapilavatthu. The Koliyas were close relations on his mother's side.

Thereupon the Sākiyas came forth armed for the battle and cried out, "We will show what strength and power belong to those who have cohabited with their sisters." Likewise the Koliyas came forth armed for battle and cried out, "We will show what strength and power belong to those who dwell in jujube-trees."

As the Teacher surveyed the world at dawn and beheld his kinsmen, he thought to himself, "If I refrain from going to them, these men will destroy each other. It is clearly my duty to go to them." Accordingly he flew through the air quite alone to the spot where his kinsmen were gathered together, and seated himself cross-legged in the air over the middle of the river Rohiṇī. When the Teacher's kinsmen saw the Teacher, they threw away their weapons and did reverence to him. Said the Teacher to his kinsmen, "What is all this quarrel about, great king?" – "We do not know, reverend sir." – "Who then would be likely to know?" – "The commander-in-chief of the army would be likely to know." The commander-in-chief of the army said, "The viceroy would be likely to know." Thus the Teacher put the question first to one and then to another, asking the slave-labourers last of all. The slave-labourers replied, "The quarrel is about water, reverend sir."

Then the Teacher asked the king, "How much is water worth, great king?" – "Very little, reverend sir." – "How much are khattiyas[2] worth, great king?" – "Khattiyas are beyond price, reverend sir." – "It is not fitting that because of a little water you should destroy khattiyas who are beyond price." They were silent. Then the Teacher addressed them and said, "Great kings, why do you act in this manner? Were I not here present today, you would set flowing a river of blood. You have done what should not be done. You live in strife, I live free from strife. You live afflicted with the sickness of the evil passions, I live free from disease. You live in eager pursuit of the five kinds of sensual pleasure, but I live free from eager pursuit." So saying, he pronounced the following stanzas:

197. We live indeed so happily
     Unhating amidst the haters;
     Among those who hate
     We dwell free from hate.

2. The princely caste, later the stock from which royal families sprang.

198. We live indeed so happily
     Unailing amidst the ailers;
     Among those who are ailing
     We dwell free from illness.

199. We live indeed so happily
     Ungreedy amidst the greedy;
     Among those who are greedy
     We dwell free from greed.

19. A Certain Brahmin

FROM CRAVING SPRINGS GRIEF.... This instruction was given by the Teacher while he was in residence at Jetavana with reference to a certain brahmin.

The story goes that this brahmin, who was a holder of false views, went one day to the bank of the river to clear his field. The Teacher, seeing that he was ripe for stream-entry, went to the place where he was. The brahmin, although he saw the Teacher, paid him no mark of respect, but remained silent. The Teacher was the first to speak and said, "Brahmin, what are you doing?" – "Clearing my field, Sir Gotama." The Teacher said no more and went his way. On the following day the brahmin went to plough his field. The Teacher went to him and asked, "Brahmin, what are you doing?" – "Ploughing my field, Sir Gotama." The Teacher, hearing his reply, went his way. On several days in succession the Teacher went to the brahmin and asked the same question. Receiving the answers, "Sir Gotama, I am planting my field, I am weeding my field, I am guarding my field," the Teacher went his way. One day the brahmin said to the Teacher, "Sir Gotama, you have been coming here ever since I cleared my field. If my crop turns out well, I will divide it with you. I will not myself eat without giving to you. Henceforth you shall be my partner."

As time went on, his crop prospered. One day he said to himself, "My crop has prospered; tomorrow I will set the reapers to work." So he made ready for the reaping. But a severe rainstorm raged that night and beat down all his crops; the field looked as if it had been cut clean. The Teacher, however, knew from the very first that his crop would not prosper. Early in the morning the brahmin said to himself, "I will go look at my field." But when he reached the field and saw that it had been swept clean, he thought with deep grief, "The monk Gotama has visited this field from the day when I first cleared it, and I have said to him, 'If this crop of mine prospers, I will divide it with you. I will not myself eat without giving to you. Henceforth you shall be my partner.' But the desire of my heart has not been fulfilled." And he refused to eat and took to his bed.

Now the Teacher stopped at the door of his house. When the brahmin heard that the Teacher had arrived, he said, "Bring my partner in and give him a seat here." His servants did so. When the Teacher had taken his seat, He asked, "Where is the brahmin?" – "He is lying in his room." – "Summon him." When the brahmin had come in response to the summons and had seated himself on one side, the Teacher said to him, "What is the matter, brahmin?" – "Sir Gotama, you have visited me from the day when I first cleared my field, and I have said to you, 'If my crop prospers, I will divide it with you.' But the desire of my heart has not been fulfilled. Therefore sorrow has come upon me, and my food no longer agrees with me." Then the Teacher said to him, "But brahmin, do you know from what cause sorrow has come upon you?" – "No, Sir Gotama, that I do not know. But do you know?" The Teacher replied, "Yes, brahmin. Whether sorrow or fear arises, it arises solely from desire." So saying, he pronounced the following stanza:

216. From craving springs grief,
From craving springs fear:
For one quite free of craving
There is no grief – how fear?

20. A Certain Head of Family

FROM ENDEARMENT SPRINGS GRIEF.... This instruction was given by the Teacher while he was in residence at Jetavana with reference to a certain head of a family.

The story goes that this layman, on losing his son, was so overwhelmed with grief that he went every day to the burning-ground and wept, being unable to restrain his grief. As the Teacher surveyed the world at dawn, he saw that the layman had the faculties requisite for stream-entry. So when he came back from his alms round, he took one attendant monk and went to the layman's door. When the layman heard that the Teacher had come to his house, he thought to himself, "He must wish to exchange the usual compliments of health and civility with me." So he invited the Teacher into his house, provided him with a seat in the house court, and when the Teacher had taken his seat, he approached him, saluted him, and sat down respectfully on one side.

At once the Teacher asked him, "Layman, why are you sad?" – "I have lost my son; therefore I am sad," replied the layman. Said the Teacher, "Grieve not, layman. That which is called death is not confined to one place or to one person, but is common to all creatures who are born into the world. Not one is permanent. Therefore one should not give oneself up to sorrow, but should rather thoroughly recollect, even as it is said, 'That which is subject to death has died, that which is subject to destruction is destroyed.' For wise men of old did not sorrow over the death of a son, but applied themselves diligently to meditation upon death, saying to themselves, 'That which is subject to death has died, that which is subject to destruction is destroyed." The layman asked the Teacher, "Reverend sir, who were they that did this? When was it that they did this? Please tell me about it." So to make the matter clear, the Teacher related the following Story of the Past:

> Man quits his mortal frame when joy in life is past,
> Even as a snake is wont its worn-out slough to cast.
> While he burns he does not know
> The lamentation of his kin, their woe.

Because of that I do not mourn,
Destined to birth he's gone to be born.

Uncalled he hither came, unbidden soon to go;
Even as he came, he went. What cause is here for woe?
While he burns he does not know
The lamentation of his kin, their woe.
Because of that I do not mourn,
Destined to birth he's gone to be born.

Though I should fast and weep, how would it profit me?
My kith and kin, alas! would more unhappy be.
While he burns he does not know
The lamentation of his kin, their woe.
Because of that I do not mourn,
Destined to birth he's gone to be born.

As children cry in vain to grasp the moon above,
So mortals idly mourn the loss of those they love.
While he burns he does not know
The lamentation of his kin, their woe.
Because of that I do not mourn,
Destined to birth he's gone to be born.

A broken pot of earth, ah! who can piece again?
So too to mourn the dead is nought but labour vain.
While he burns he does not know
The lamentation of his kin, their woe.
Because of that I do not mourn,
Destined to birth he's gone to be born.

When the Teacher had related in detail this Uraga Jātaka (No.
354), he continued as follows: "In times past wise men did not do
as you are doing on the death of a son. You have abandoned your
customary occupations, have deprived yourself of food, and spend
your time in lamentation. Wise men of old did not do so. On the
contrary, they applied themselves diligently to meditation upon
death, would not allow themselves to grieve, ate their food as
usual, and attended to their customary occupations. Therefore do
not grieve at the thought that your dear son is dead. For whether
sorrow or fear arises, it arises solely because of one that is dear."

So saying, the Teacher pronounced the following stanza:

212. From endearment springs grief;
From endearment springs fear;
For one quite free of endearment
There is no grief – how fear?

At the conclusion of this instruction the head of family was established in the fruit of stream-entry; the assembled company also profited by the teaching.

21. Merchant Great-wealth

HERE SHALL I SPEND THE RAINS.... This instruction was given by the Teacher while he was in residence at Jetavana with reference to Merchant Great-wealth, Mahādhana.

The story goes that he loaded five hundred carts with cloths dyed with safflower and set out from Benares to trade. When, on his return to Sāvatthī, he reached the bank of the river, he thought, "Tomorrow I will cross the river," and unyoked his carts right there and spent the night. During the night a severe storm came up and it rained all night long. For seven days the river was in flood; for seven days the citizens kept holiday. The result was that the merchant had no opportunity to dispose of his crimson cloths. Thought the merchant to himself, "I have come a long distance and if I go back again, I shall be delayed; right here will I dwell during the rain, during the winter and summer, doing my work and selling these cloths."

As the Teacher made his alms round through the city, he became aware of the merchant's intention and smiled. Thereupon the Elder Ānanda asked him why he smiled. The Teacher replied, "Ānanda, did you see Merchant Great-wealth?" – "Yes, reverend sir." – "Not realizing that the end of his life is near, he has made up his mind to dwell right here during this entire year for the purpose of selling his goods." – "But, reverend sir, is the end of his life at hand?" – "Yes, Ānanda; he will live only seven days longer and then he will fall into the mouth of death." So saying, the Teacher pronounced the following stanzas:

> Today the effort must be made:
> Tomorrow death may come, who knows?
> No bargain with Mortality
> Can keep him and his hordes away.
> But one who dwells thus ardently,
> Relentlessly, by day, by night,
> Him, the Hermit Stilled has called,
> The ideal lover of solitude.[1]

---

1. These verses (found in full in Majjhima Nikaya No.131) combine the renderings of Ven. Ñāṇamoli Thera and Ven. Bhikkhu Ñāṇananda. See *Ideal Solitude* (BPS Wheel No. 188) by Bhikkhu Ñāṇananda.

"Reverend sir, I will go tell him." – "By all means go, Ānanda." The elder went to the enclosure formed by the carts and made his round for alms. The merchant reverently presented him with food. Then the elder said to the merchant, "How long a time do you expect to remain here?" – "Reverend sir, I have come a long distance, and if I go back again, I shall suffer delay; I shall remain here during this entire year, and when I have sold my goods, I shall go on." – "Layman, though the end of one's life is near, yet it is hard to realize; one should be heedful." – "Why, reverend sir, is the end of my life at hand?" – "Yes, layman, it is; only seven days more will your life continue."

His heart stirred with deep emotion, the merchant invited the Order of Monks presided over by the Buddha to be his guests. For seven days he gave alms and finally took the Teacher's bowl to permit him to pronounce the words of thanksgiving. Said the Teacher, in pronouncing the words of thanksgiving, "Disciple, a wise man should never allow himself to think, 'Right here will I dwell during the rain, during the winter, and during summer. I will do this work and I will do that work.' Rather a man should meditate on the end of his own life." So saying the Teacher pronounced the following stanza:

286. "Here shall I spend the rains,
     Here the winter, here the summer,"
     Thus speculates the fool
     The danger he does not know.

At the conclusion of the lesson the merchant was established in the fruit of stream-entry; the assembled company also profited by the lesson.

The merchant accompanied the Teacher on his way for a short distance and then turned back. "I feel as if I have some trouble in my head," said he, and laid himself on his bed. No sooner had he lain down than he died, and was reborn in the world of the Tusita gods.

22. The Brahmin Who Asked About Loss

BETTER THE CONQUEST OF ONESELF.... This instruction was given by the Teacher while he was in residence at Jetavana with reference to a brahmin who asked about loss.

The story goes that this brahmin considered within himself, "Does the Supremely Enlightened One know gain alone or does he know loss also? I will ask him." Accordingly he approached the Teacher and asked him, "Reverend sir, tell me, please, do you know gain alone, and not loss?" – "Brahmin, I know both gain and loss." – "Well, then, tell me about loss." At once the Teacher pronounced the following stanza:

> Unprofitable is sleeping after sunrise, idleness,
> A hot temper, and addiction to drink,
> Travelling far by oneself,
> Seeking after other men's wives;
> Seek after these things, brahmin, and you will gain
> That which will be of no advantage to you.

When the brahmin heard this, he applauded the Teacher, saying, "Well said, well said, teacher of the multitude, leader of the multitude! You know indeed both gain and loss." – "Indeed, brahmin, there is none other that knows loss so well as I." Then the Teacher considered within himself what motive actuated the brahmin, and asked him, "Brahmin, how do you make your living?" – "By gambling, Sir Gotama." – "But who wins, you or the other man?" – "Sometimes I win and sometimes the other man wins." Then said the Teacher, "Brahmin, a trifling matter is the victory of him who defeats another; there is no superior advantage in such a victory. But he who overcomes his defilements and so conquers self, wins a better victory, for such a victory no one can turn into defeat." So saying, he showed the connection, and teaching the Dhamma, pronounced the following stanzas:

> 104. Better the conquest of oneself
> Than that of other people;
> The man who has trained himself
> In conduct ever well-restrained—

105. Neither deva nor minstrel divine,
Nor Māra together with Brahmā,
Can overthrow the victory
Of such a man as this.

Part IV

Noble Attainments

23. The Maiden Rohiṇī

ONE SHOULD GIVE UP ANGER.... This instruction was given by the Teacher while he was in residence at Banyan Grove with reference to the maiden Rohiṇī.

The Maiden with Blotches on her Face

The story goes that once upon a time the Venerable Anuruddha went with his retinue of five hundred monks to Kapilavatthu. When the elder's kinsfolk heard that he had arrived, all except his sister, a maiden named Rohiṇī, went to the monastery where the elder was in residence and paid their respects to him. The elder asked his kinsfolk, "Where is Rohiṇī?" – "At home, reverend sir." – "Why didn't she come here?" – "Reverend sir, she is suffering from an eruption of the skin, and on this account was ashamed to come." The elder caused her to be summoned, saying, "Summon her immediately." Rohiṇī fastened a covering of cloth about her face and went to the elder.

When she came into his presence, the elder asked her, "Rohiṇī, why didn't you come here before?" – "Reverend sir, I am suffering from an eruption of the skin, and on this account I was ashamed to come." – "But ought you not to perform works of merit?" – "What can I do, reverend sir?" – "Cause an assembly-hall to be erected." – "What funds have I to use for this purpose?" – "Have you not a set of jewels?" – "Yes, reverend sir, I have." – "How much did it cost?" – "It must have cost ten thousand pieces of money." – "Well then, spend this in building an assembly-hall." – "Who will build it for me, reverend sir?" The elder looked at her kinsfolk who stood near and said, "This shall be your duty." – "But, reverend sir, what will you do?" – "I shall stay right here; therefore bring her the building materials." – "Very well, reverend sir," said they, and brought them.

The elder superintended the arrangements for the erection of the assembly-hall. Said he to Rohiṇī, "Cause an assembly-hall two storeys in height to be erected and as soon as the planks are put in place above, you take your stand below, sweep constantly, prepare seats, and keep the water-vessels filled with water." – "Very well, reverend sir," replied Rohiṇī. So she spent her set of jewels in the erection of an assembly-hall two storeys in height. As soon as the planks were put in place above, she took her stand below, swept, and performed the other duties, and monks sat therein constantly. Even as she swept the assembly-hall, the eruption subsided.

When the assembly-hall was completed, she invited the Order of Monks presided over by the Buddha; and when the Order of Monks presided over by the Buddha had taken their seats, filling the assembly-hall, she offered them choice food, both hard and soft. When the Teacher finished his meal, he asked, "Whose is this offering?" – "Your sister Rohiṇī's, reverend sir." – "But where is she?" – "In the house, reverend sir." – "Summon her." She was unwilling to go. But in spite of her unwillingness, the Teacher caused her to be summoned all the same.

When she had come and saluted him and taken her seat, the Teacher said to her, "Rohiṇī, why didn't you come before?" – "Reverend sir, I was suffering from an eruption of the skin and was ashamed to come." – "But do you know the reason why this eruption of the skin broke out on your body?" – "No, reverend sir, I do not." – "It was because of anger that this eruption of the skin broke out on your body." – "Why, reverend sir, what did I do?" – "Well then, listen," said the Teacher. So saying, he told her the following story.

Story of the Past: The Jealous Queen and the Nautch-girl

In times long past, the chief consort of the king of Benares took a dislike to one of the king's nautch-girls and said to herself, "I will make her suffer." So she procured a number of large ripe scabs, reduced them to powder, and summoning that nautch-girl to her, contrived secretly to place the powdered scabs in her bed and cloak and her goats' hair coverlet. Then, as if in fun, she sprinkled some of the powder on her body. Immediately the girl's body became covered with pimples and boils so as to have a horridly angry look, and she went about scratching herself. When she lay down on her bed, there, too, the powdered scabs ate her up, and she suffered yet harsher pain. The chief consort at that time was Rohiṇī. (*End of Story of the Past.*)

When the Teacher had related this Story of the Past, he said, "Rohiṇī, that was the evil deed which you committed at that time. Anger or jealousy, however slight, is always unbecoming." So saying, he pronounced the following stanza:

221. One should give up anger and abandon pride
And all the fetters one should overcome;
Suffering does not fall on one desiring naught,
Clinging not to mind or body.

At the conclusion of the lesson many obtained the fruit of stream-entry and the fruits of the second and third paths. Rohiṇī also was established in the fruit of stream-entry and at that moment her body took on a golden hue.

Sequel: The Celestial Nymph

Rohiṇī passed from that state of existence and was reborn in the world of the Thirty-three Gods at the meeting-point of the boundaries of four deities. She was fair to look upon and possessed the perfection of beauty. When the four deities looked upon her, desire arose within them, and they began to quarrel over her, saying, "She was reborn within my boundary, she was reborn within my boundary." Finally they went to Sakka king of gods and said to him, "Sire, a dispute has arisen among us over this nymph; decide the dispute for us."

When Sakka looked at the nymph, desire arose within him also. Said he, "What manner of thoughts have arisen within you since you saw this nymph?" The first deity said, "As for me, the thoughts which have arisen within me have no more been able to subside than a battle drum." The second said, "My thoughts have run wild like a mountain torrent." The third said, "From the time I first saw this nymph, my eyes have popped out like the eyes of a crab." The fourth said, "My thoughts have no more been able to stand still than a banner raised on a shrine." Then Sakka said to them, "Friends as for you, your thoughts are on fire. For my part, if I can have this nymph I shall live, but if I cannot have her, I shall surely die."

The deities replied, "Great king, there is no need of your dying." So saying, they yielded the nymph to Sakka and went their way. She was Sakka's darling and delight. If she ever said, "Let us go engage in such and such sport," he could not refuse her.

24. The Weaver's Daughter

THIS WORLD IS INDEED BLIND.... This instruction was given by the Teacher while he was in residence at Aggāḷava Shrine with reference to a certain weaver's daughter.

For one day, when the Teacher came to Ālavi, the residents of Ālavī invited him to a meal and gave alms. At the end of the meal the Teacher spoke the words of thanksgiving, saying: "Practise meditation on death, saying to yourselves, 'Uncertain is my life. Certain is my death. I shall surely die. Death will be the termination of my life. Life is unstable. Death is sure.' For they that have not practised meditation on death will tremble and fear when their last hour comes, and will die screaming screams of terror, even as a man without a stick, on seeing a snake, is stricken with fear. But those who have practised meditation on death will have no fear when their last hour comes, but will be like a steadfast man who, seeing a snake even afar off, takes it up with his stick and tosses it away. Therefore practise meditation on death."

With a single exception all those who heard this discourse remained absorbed in their worldly duties as before. Only a single weaver's daughter, about sixteen years of age, said to herself, "Marvellous indeed is the speech of the Buddhas; it behooves me to practise meditation on death." And she did nothing else but practise meditation on death day and night. The Teacher left Āāavi and went to Jetavana. Then that maiden for three years developed just the meditation on death.

Now one day, as the Teacher surveyed the world at early dawn, he perceived that this maiden had entered the net of his knowledge. When he saw her, he considered within himself, "What will happen?" And he became aware of the following, "From the day when this maiden heard my discourse on the Dhamma, she has practised meditation on death for three years. I will now go to Ālavī and ask this maiden four questions. On each of the four points she will answer me correctly, and I will congratulate her. I will then pronounce the stanza, *This world is indeed blind.* At the conclusion of the stanza she will be established in the fruit of stream-entry. By reason of her, my discourse will be profitable to the multitude besides." So the Teacher, with his retinue of five hundred monks, departed from Jetavana, and in due course arrived at the Aggāḷava monastery.

When the people of Āḷavī heard that the Teacher had come, they went to the monastery and invited him to be their guest. That maiden also heard that he had come, and her heart was filled with joy at the thought, "Here has come, so people say, one that is my father, my master, my teacher, one whose countenance is like the full moon, the mighty Gotama Buddha." And she reflected, "Now, for the first time in three years, I am to see the Teacher, the hue of whose body is as the hue of gold; now I am to be permitted to behold his body, whose hue is as the hue of gold, and to hear him preach the sublime Dhamma, containing within itself all sweetness."

But her father, on his way to the workshop, said to her, "Daughter, a garment for a customer is on the loom, and a span of it is yet incomplete. I must finish it today. Quickly replenish the shuttle and bring it to me." Thought the maiden, "It was my desire to hear the Teacher preach the Dhamma, but my father has thus addressed me. Shall I hear the Teacher preach the Dhamma, or replenish the shuttle and carry it to my father?" Then this thought occurred to her, "If I should fail to bring my father the shuttle, he would strike me and beat me. Therefore I will first replenish the shuttle and give it to him, and wait until afterwards to hear the Dhamma." So she sat down on a stool and replenished the shuttle.

The people of Āḷavi waited upon the Teacher and provided him with food, and when the meal was over, took his bowl and stood waiting for him to speak the words of rejoicing (with the merits of the donors). Said the Teacher, "I came here on a journey of thirty leagues for the sake of a certain maiden. As yet she finds no opportunity to be present. When she finds the opportunity to be present, I will speak the words of rejoicing." Having so said, he sat down and remained silent. Likewise his hearers also remained silent. (When the Teacher is silent, neither men nor gods dare utter a sound.)

When the maiden had replenished the shuttle, she put it in her basket and set out in the direction of her father's workshop. On her way she stopped in the outer circle of the congregation and stood gazing at the Teacher. The Teacher also lifted up his head and gazed at her. By his manner of gazing at her she knew, "The

101

Teacher, sitting in such a congregation, signifies by gazing at me that he desires me to come, that his sole desire is that I come into his very presence." So she set her shuttle-basket on the ground and went into the presence of the Teacher.

(But why did the Teacher gaze at her? The following thought, we are told, occurred to him, "If this maiden leaves, she will die as a worldling and her future state will be uncertain. But if she comes to me, she will depart established in the fruit of stream-entry, and her future state will be certain, for she will be reborn in the world of the Tusita gods." We are told that there was no escape from death for her that day.)

At the mere hint of his look she approached the Teacher, and penetrating the rays of six-coloured light that shone from his body, she paid obeisance to him and stood respectfully at one side. No sooner had she paid obeisance to the Teacher and taken her stand beside him, seated in silence in the midst of the assemblage there gathered together, than he thus addressed her, "Maiden, from where do you come?" – "I do not know, reverend sir." – "Where are you going?" – "I do not know, reverend sir." – "Do you not know?" – "I know, reverend sir." – "Do you know?" – "I do not know, reverend sir." Thus the Teacher asked her four questions. The multitude were offended and said, "Look, this daughter of a weaver talks as she pleases with the Supremely Enlightened One. When he asked her, 'From where do you come?' she should have answered, 'From the weaver's house.' And when he asked her, 'Where are you going?' she should have answered, 'To the weaver's workshop.' "

The Teacher put the multitude to silence and asked her, "Maiden, when I asked you, 'From where do you come?' why did you say, 'I do not know'?" She answered, "Reverend sir, you yourself know that I came from the house of my father, a weaver. So when you asked me, 'From where do you come?' I knew very well that your meaning was, 'From where did you come when you were reborn here?' But as for me, from where I came when I was reborn here, that I do not know." Then the Teacher said to her, "Well said, well said, O maiden! You have answered correctly the question I asked you."

Thus did the Teacher congratulate her, and having done so, he asked her yet another question, "When I asked you, 'Where are you going?' why did you say, 'I do not know'?" – "Reverend sir, you yourself know that I was going to the weaver's workshop with my shuttle-basket in hand. So when you asked me, 'Where are you going?' I knew very well that your meaning was, 'When you pass away, where will you be reborn?' But as for me, where I shall be reborn when I have passed from this present existence, that I do not know." Then the Teacher said to her, "You have answered correctly the question I asked you."

Thus did the Teacher congratulate her the second time, and having so done, asked her yet another question, "When I asked you, 'Do you not know?' why did you say, 'I know'?" – "Reverend sir, this I know, that I shall surely die; and therefore I said so." Then the Teacher said to her, "You have answered correctly the question I asked you."

Thus did the Teacher congratulate her the third time, and having done so, he asked her yet another question, "When I asked you, 'Do you know?' why did you say, 'I do not know'?" – "This only do I know, reverend sir, that I shall surely die; but at what time I shall die, whether in the night or in the daytime, whether in the morning or at some other time, that I do not know; and therefore I said so." Then said the Teacher to her, "You have answered correctly the question I asked you."

Thus did the Teacher congratulate her the fourth time, and having so done, addressed the assemblage as follows: "Those among you who failed to understand the words she spoke, you only were offended. For those who lack the eye of understanding, they only are blind; those who possess the eye of understanding, they only see." So saying, he pronounced the following stanza:

174. This world is indeed blind
     Few are those who deeply see.
     Like birds escaping from a net
     Few will go to heaven.

At the conclusion of the discourse that maiden was established in the fruit of stream-entry.

Then the maiden took her shuttle-basket and went to her father. He was asleep even as he sat at the loom. Not observing that he was asleep, she presented the shuttle-basket. As she did so, the basket hit the tip of the loom and fell with a clatter. Her father awoke, and accidentally, as a result of taking hold of the loom, gave it a pull, whereupon the tip of the loom swung around and struck the maiden in the breast. Then and there she died and was reborn in the world of the Tusita gods. Her father looked at her as she lay there, her whole body spotted with blood, and saw that she was dead.

Straightaway there arose within him intense grief. Wailing, "There is none other that can extinguish my grief," he went to the Teacher and told him what had happened. "Reverend sir," said he, "extinguish my grief." The Teacher comforted him, saying, "Grieve not, disciple, for in the round of existences without conceivable beginning, you have even thus, over the death of your daughter, shed tears more abundant than the water contained in the four great oceans." In this way the Teacher discoursed on the round of existences without conceivable beginning. The disciple's grief was assuaged, and he requested the Teacher for the going forth. Afterwards he gained acceptance into the Order and in no long time attained arahantship.

25. A Certain Layman

HUNGER IS THE GREATEST DISEASE.... This instruction was given by the Teacher while he was in residence at Āḷavī with reference to a certain lay disciple.

For one day, as the Teacher seated in the Perfumed Chamber at Jetavana surveyed the world at dawn, he beheld a certain poor man at Āḷavī. Perceiving that he possessed the faculties requisite for attaining the fruit of stream-entry, he surrounded himself with a company of five hundred monks and went to Āḷavī. The inhabitants of Āḷavī straightaway invited the Teacher to be their guest. That poor man also heard that the Teacher had arrived and made up his mind to go and hear the Teacher teach the Dhamma. But that very day an ox of his strayed off. So he considered within himself, "Shall I seek that ox, or shall I go and hear the Dhamma?" And he came to the following conclusion, "I will first seek that ox and then go and hear the Dhamma." Accordingly, early in the morning, he set out to seek his ox.

The residents of Āḷavī said provided seats for the Order of Monks presided over by the Buddha, served them with food, and after the meal took the Teacher's bowl, that he might pronounce the words of rejoicing. Said the Teacher, "He for whose sake I came here on a journey of thirty leagues has gone into the forest to seek his ox which was lost. I will not teach the Dhamma until he returns." And he remained silent.

While it was still day, that poor man found his ox and straightaway drove the ox back to the herd. Then he thought to himself, "Even if I can do nothing else, I will at least pay my respects to the Teacher." Accordingly, although he was oppressed with the pangs of hunger, he decided not to go home, but went quickly to the Teacher, and having paid obeisance to the Teacher, sat down respectfully on one side. When the poor man came and stood before the Teacher, the Teacher said to the steward of the alms, "Is there any food left over by the Order of Monks?". – "Reverend sir, it is all there." – "Well then, serve this poor man with food." So when the steward had provided that poor man with a seat in a place indicated by the Teacher, he served him dutifully with rice-porridge and other food, both hard and soft. When the poor man had eaten his meal he rinsed his mouth. (We are told that with this single exception there is no other instance on record in the Three Piṭakas of the Tathāgata's having thus inquired about the supply of food.)

As soon as the poor man's physical sufferings had been relieved his mind became tranquil. Then the Teacher taught the Dhamma in orderly sequence, expounding one after another the Four Noble Truths. At the conclusion of the lesson, the poor man was established in the fruit of stream-entry. Then the Teacher pronounced the words of thanksgiving, and having done so, arose from his seat and departed. The multitude accompanied him a little way and then turned back.

The monks who accompanied the Teacher were highly indignant and said, "Just consider, brethren, what the Teacher did. Nothing of the sort ever happened before. But today, seeing a certain poor man, the Teacher inquired about the supply of food and directed that food to be given to another." The Teacher turned around, stopped, and said, "Monks, what are you saying?" When he heard what they were saying, he said to them, "It is even so, monks. When I came here on a journey of thirty leagues, a long and difficult journey, my sole reason for coming was the fact that I saw that this lay disciple possessed the faculties requisite for the attainment of the fruit of stream-entry. Early in the morning, oppressed with the pangs of hunger, this man went to the forest and spent the day in the forest seeking his ox which was lost. Therefore I thought to myself, 'If I preach Dhamma to this man while he is suffering from the pangs of hunger, he will not be able to comprehend it.' Therefore I did what I did. Monks, there is no affliction like the affliction of hunger." So saying, he pronounced the following stanza:

203. Hunger is the greatest disease,
Conditioned things are the greatest suffering.
For one who has known this as it is
Nibbāna is the bliss supreme.

26. Kāla, Anāthapiṇḍika's Son

BETTER THAN SOLE SOVEREIGNTY OVER THE EARTH.... This instruction was given by the Teacher while he was in residence at Jetavana with reference to Kāla, son of Anāthapiṇḍika.

Tradition has it that Kāla, although the son of so distinguished a father, a treasurer endowed with faith, never showed any desire to visit the Teacher, or to see him when he came to his father's house, or to hear the Dhamma, or to perform services for the Order. Moreover, whenever his father said to him, "Dear son, do not do this," he paid no attention to what he said. Now his father thought to himself, "If this son of mine adopts such an attitude as this and acts accordingly, the Avīci hell will be his end. But it would not look well for me if my son went to hell before my very eyes. Now there is no living being here in the world who may not be broken by gifts; I will therefore break him with gifts." So he said to his son, "Dear son, take upon yourself the precepts of Uposatha day,[1] go to the monastery, listen to the Dhamma, and then return. If you will do so, I will give you a hundred pieces of money." – "Will you really give me this, dear father?" – "That I will, dear son."

After his father had repeated his promise three times, Kāla took upon himself the precepts of Uposatha day and went to the monastery. But not caring to listen to the Dhamma, he lay down to sleep in a pleasant place and returned home early in the morning. Thereupon his father said, "My son has undertaken the precepts of Uposatha day; bring him rice-porridge and other food straightway." So saying, his father caused food to be brought and given to him. But Kāla said, "Unless I receive the money, I will not eat." So saying, he steadfastly refused whatever was brought to him. His father, who could not endure forcing him to eat, ordered that the money be presented to his son. The son took the purse of money into his hands and ate the food that was brought to him.

On the following day the treasurer sent him forth, saying to him, "Dear son, I will give you a thousand pieces of money if you

---

1. The Eight Precepts for a lay person's special practice on the full and new moon days. See *Mirror of the Dhamma* (BPS Wheel No. 54) and *Lay Buddhist Practice* (BPS Wheel No. 206/207).

will stand before the Teacher, learn a single verse of the Dhamma, and then return to me." Accordingly Kāla went to the monastery and took his stand before the Teacher. But no sooner had he mastered a single verse than he desired to run away. The Teacher therefore caused him to misunderstand the true meaning of the verse. Kāla, failing to understand the verse, said to himself, "I will master the following verse." Therefore he remained and continued to listen. (Those who listen to the Dhamma with a firm resolution to learn, listen attentively; and to those who thus listen, the Dhamma gives the fruit of stream-entry and the remaining fruits.) Kāla listened to the Dhamma with a firm resolution to learn; but the Teacher, as before, caused him to misunderstand the true meaning. "I will master the following verse," said Kāla. So he remained and listened and was established in the fruit of stream-entry.

On the following day he accompanied the Order of Monks presided over by the Buddha to Sāvatthī. When the great treasurer saw him, he said to himself, "Today the demeanour of my son pleases me." And straightaway the following thought occurred to the son, "I hope my father will not give me the money today in the presence of the Teacher. I hope he will conceal the fact that it was for the sake of money that I took upon myself the precepts of the Uposatha day." (But the Teacher knew all the same that it was for the sake of money that Kāla took upon himself the Uposatha precepts on the preceding day.)

The great treasurer presented rice-porridge to the Order of Monks presided over by the Buddha and then presented the same to his son. Kāla sat down in silence, drank the porridge, ate the hard food, and then ate the boiled rice. When the Teacher had finished his meal, the great treasurer placed the purse containing a thousand pieces of money before his son and said, "Dear son, you will remember that I persuaded you to take upon yourself the Uposatha precepts and to go to the monastery by promising to give you a thousand pieces of money; here are your thousand pieces of money." When Kāla saw the thousand pieces of money presented to him in the very presence of the Teacher, he was greatly embarrassed and said, "I do not care for the money." – "Take the money, dear son," said the father. But the son refused to touch it.

Then his father saluted the Teacher and said, "Reverend sir, today the demeanour of my son pleases me." – "How is that, great treasurer?" – "The day before yesterday I sent him to the monastery, saying to him, 'I will give you a hundred pieces of money.' Yesterday he refused to eat because I did not give him the money; but today, when I give him the money, he refuses to touch it." The Teacher replied, "It is even so, great treasurer. Today, in attaining the fruit of stream-entry your son has attained that which surpasses the attainment of a Universal Monarch, the attainment of the world of the gods, the attainment of the world of Brahmā." So saying, he pronounced the following stanza:

178. Better than sole sovereignty over the earth,
   Better than going to heaven,
   Better than lordship over all worlds
   Is the fruit of entering the stream.

27. A Brahmin of Sāketa

THOSE INOFFENSIVE SAGES.... This instruction was given by the Teacher while he was in residence at Añjanavana near Sāketa with reference to a question asked by the monks.

The story goes that once upon a time, as the Exalted One, accompanied by the Order of Monks, was entering Sāketa for alms, a certain old brahmin who lived in Sāketa passed out of the city, and seeing the Master of the Ten Powers entering within the gate, fell down before his feet, and grasping him firmly by the ankles, said to him, "Dear son, is it not the duty of sons to care for their mother and father when they have grown old? Why is it that for so long a time you have not shown yourself to us? This is the first time I have seen you. Come look upon your mother." And taking the Teacher with him, he escorted him into his house. When the Teacher had entered the house, he sat down on the seat prepared for him, together with the Order of Monks.

The brahmin's wife also approached the Teacher, and falling before his feet, said, "Dear son, where have you been all this time? Ought not mothers and fathers to be cared for when they have grown old?" And she directed her sons and daughters to salute the Teacher, saying, "Go and salute your brother." Delighted at heart, the brahmin and his wife offered food to the Order of Monks presided over by the Buddha, saying, "Reverend sir, take all of your meals right here." The Teacher replied, "The Buddhas never take their meals regularly in the same place." Then said the brahmin and his wife, "Well then, reverend sir, be good enough to send to us all those who come to you and invite you to be their guest."

From that time forward, the Teacher sent to the brahmin and his wife all those who came to him with an invitation to be their guest, saying, "Go tell the brahmin." Such persons would then go and say to the brahmin, "We would invite the Teacher for tomorrow," and the brahmin on the following day would take from his own house vessels of boiled rice and curries, and go to the place where the Teacher sat. In case the Teacher was invited nowhere else, he always took his meal in the house of the brahmin. Both the brahmin and his wife gave alms regularly to the Tathāgata, listened to the Dhamma, and in the course of time obtained the fruit of the third path.

The monks began a discussion in the Hall of Truth: "Friends, the brahmin knows perfectly well that the Tathāgata's father is Suddhodana and that his mother is Mahāmāyā. But although he knows this, both he and his wife address the Tathāgata as 'our son,' and the Teacher acquiesces in this form of address; what can be the explanation of this?" The Teacher overheard their talk and said, "Monks, both the brahmin and his wife are addressing their own son when they say to me, 'Our son.'" Having said this, he related the following story.

Story of the Past

"Monks, in times past this brahmin was my father for five hundred successive existences, my uncle for five hundred existences, and my grandfather for five hundred existences; likewise the brahmin's wife was my mother for five hundred existences, my aunt for five hundred existences, and my grandmother for five hundred existences. Thus I was brought up by this brahmin during fifteen hundred states of existence, and by the wife of this brahmin during fifteen hundred states of existence." Having thus explained that he had been their son during three thousand states of existence, he pronounced the following stanzas:

> If the mind rests satisfied, and the heart reposes confidence
> in a man,
> One may repose confidence in that man, though it be the
> first time one has seen him.
> Through previous association or present advantage,
> That old love springs up again like the lotus in the water.
> *(End of the Story of the Past.)*

For the entire period of three months during which the Teacher spent the rains-residence, he resorted only to that family for his meals and at the end of the three months they attained arahantship and passed into Nibbāna. People rendered high honours to their bodies, placed both bodies on one hearse, and carried them out. The Teacher, surrounded by a retinue of five hundred monks, accompanied the

111

bodies to the burning ground. Hearing the report, "They were the mother and father of the Buddha," a great multitude went forth from the city. The Teacher entered a certain hall near the burning ground and remained there. People saluted the Teacher, saying to him, "Reverend sir, do not grieve because your mother and father are dead," and held amiable conversation with him. Instead of repulsing them by saying, "Speak not thus," the Teacher surveyed the thoughts of the company and preaching the Dhamma with reference to that particular occasion, recited the Jarā Sutta, as follows:[1]

Short indeed is this life –
Within a hundred years one dies,
And if anyone lives longer,
Then he dies of decay.

People grieve for what is 'mine':
Indeed possessions are not permanent,
And this is subject to destruction—
See this and homeless dwell!

In death it is abandoned
Yet men think 'it is mine';
Knowing this, the wise devoted to me
Should not stoop down to making 'his own.'

As a man awake sees not
The things he met in sleep,
So, too, the beloved one is not seen,
Having departed and done his time.

People now are seen and heard
And thus are called by name,
But alone shall the name remain
For the departed to be spoken of.

The greedy in mine-making do not give up
Sorrow, lamentation, avarice;
Therefore sages, leaving possesions,
Have wandered about, Seers of the Secure.

---

1. Suttanipāta IV,6. The complete sutta is not given in the text but has been inserted here.

For a bhikkhu practising seclusion,
Keeping company with the secluded mind,
All are agreed and say of him,
'He should not show himself again in becoming!'

The sage is unsupported in all circumstances;
Nothing he makes dear nor what is not dear;
Sorrow and avarice stain him not
Just as water stays not upon a leaf.

As a water-drop upon a lotus plant,
As water does not stain a lotus flower,
Even so the sage is never stained
By what has been seen, heard, and sensed by him.

Certainly the wise man does not conceive
By what has been seen, heard, and sensed,
Nor through another does he wish for purity
For he is not attached nor yet is he displeased.

The monks, not knowing that the brahmin and his wife had
attained Nibbāna, asked the Teacher, "Reverend sir, what will be
their future state?" The Teacher replied: "Monks, in the case of
such as they, arahants and sages, there is no future state. Such as
they attain the Eternal, the Deathless, Great Nibbāna." So saying,
he pronounced the following stanza:

225. Those inoffensive sages
    In body ever restrained
    Go to the Everlasting State
    Where gone they grieve no more.

28. Santati the King's Minister

THOUGH HE BE ADORNED, IF HE LIVES AT PEACE.... This instruction was given by the Teacher while he was in residence at Jetavana with reference to the king's minister Santati.

For once upon a time Santati returned from suppressing disorder on King Pasenadi Kosala's frontier, and the king was so pleased that he turned over his kingdom to him for seven days and gave him a woman who danced and sang. For seven days Santati steeped himself in liquor, and on the seventh day, adorned with all adornments, he mounted the back of the state elephant and set out for the bathing place. As he passed out of the gateway, he saw the Teacher entering the city for alms. Remaining seated as he was on the back of the elephant, he nodded his head by way of salute to the Teacher and passed on.

The Teacher smiled. "Why do you smile, reverend sir?" asked the Elder Ānanda. Said the Teacher, explaining the reason for his smile, "Ānanda, just look at the king's minister Santati! This very day, adorned as he is with all adornments, he will come into my presence, and at the conclusion of a stanza consisting of four lines he will attain arahantship. He will then assume a sitting posture at a height of seven palm-trees above the earth and will then and there pass into Nibbāna."

The populace heard the words that passed between the Teacher and the elder. Those of the crowd who held false views thought to themselves, "Look at the way the monk Gotama acts! Whatever comes into his head he speaks with his mouth! This very day, so he says, that drunken sot, adorned as he is with all adornments, will come into his presence and listen to the Dhamma and pass into Nibbāna! But that is precisely what will not happen; this very day we shall catch him in a lie." On the other hand those of right view thought to themselves, "The Buddhas are of great might! Today we shall get the chance to see both the grace of the Buddha and the gracefulness of Santati the king's minister."

Santati spent a portion of the day at the bathing place sporting in the water, and then entered his pleasure garden and sat down in his drinking hall. Straightaway a woman came down to the centre of

114

the stage and began to display her skill in dancing and singing. Now she had fasted for seven days that she might display more perfect grace of body; and the result was that on that particular day, as she was displaying her skill in dancing and singing, knife-like pains arose in her belly and as it were cut the flesh of her heart asunder. And then and there with open mouth and open eyes she died.

Santati the king's minister said, "Look to the lady!" – "She is dead, master," was the reply. As soon as Santati heard those words, he was overwhelmed with mighty sorrow; and in an instant the liquor he had drunk during the preceding week vanished away like a drop of water on a red-hot potsherd. He said to himself, "With the single exception of the Teacher, who is able to extinguish my sorrow?"

So in the evening, surrounded by his force of men, he went to the Teacher, and having saluted him, spoke as follows, "Reverend sir, such and such sorrow has come upon me. I have come to you because I know that you will be able to extinguish my sorrow. Be my refuge." Then the Teacher said to him, "You have indeed come into the presence of one who is able to extinguish your sorrow. On the numberless occasions when this woman has died in this very manner and you have wept over her, you have shed tears more abundant than all the water contained in the four great oceans." So saying, he pronounced the following stanza.

> Whatever in the past was produced by excellence
> Let there be for you no ownership afterwards,
> And if in the present you will not grasp at all
> You will fare on to the perfect peace.

At the conclusion of the stanza, Santati the king's minister attained arahantship. Thereupon he surveyed his own aggregate of life, and perceiving that he had but a little while to live, he said to the Teacher, "Reverend sir, permit me to attain (final) Nibbāna." The Teacher, although he himself knew what had been Santati's meritorious deed in a previous state of existence, thought to himself, "Those of wrong views who have gathered themselves together for the purpose of catching me in a lie will not succeed in doing so; and those of right view who have assembled with the thought in their minds, 'We shall behold the grace of the Buddha and the gracefulness of Santati the king's minister,' when they hear about

115

the meritorious deed he performed in a previous state of existence, will increase in esteem for works of merit."

Therefore the Teacher said to Santati the king's minister, "Well then, rehearse to us all the meritorious deeds you did in a previous state of existence. Do not, however, rehearse it to us standing on the ground, but rehearse it to us poised in the air at a height of seven palm trees above the ground."

"Very well," replied Santati. So saluting the Teacher, he rose into the air to the height of one palm tree and then descended to the ground. Then he saluted the Teacher once more, and rising gradually to the height of seven palm trees above the ground, he seated himself cross-legged in the air, and said, "Listen, reverend sir, to the meritorious deed I performed in a previous state of existence." So saying, he related the following story.

Story of the Past: The Preacher and the King

"Ninety-one cycles of time ago, in the dispensation of the Buddha Vipassī, I was reborn in a certain household in a city named Bandhumatī. And the following thought occurred to me, 'What labour will do away with the want and sufferings of others?' While I was pondering this thought, I observed the labours of those who went about proclaiming the Dhamma, and from that time forth I laboured at that very task. I incited others to perform works of merit, and I performed works of merit myself. On Uposatha days I took upon myself the Uposatha precepts; I gave alms; I listened to the Dhamma. And I went about proclaiming, 'There are no jewels comparable to the Three Jewels named the Buddha, the Dhamma, and the Order; therefore do honour to the Three Jewels.'

"Now the great King Bandhumatī, father of the Buddha, hearing my voice, sent for me and asked me, 'Friend, on what business are you going about?' I replied, 'Your majesty, I am going about proclaiming the virtues of the Three Jewels, and inciting the populace to perform works of merit.' – 'What vehicle do you use on your travels?' asked the king. I replied, 'I travel about on my two legs, your majesty.' Thereupon the king said, 'Friend, it is not fitting that you should go about in that fashion. Deck yourself with this garland of flowers and seat yourself on the back of a horse and go about in this fashion.' So saying, he gave me a garland of flowers

116

similar in appearance to a string of pearls, and at the same time he gave me a horse.

"After the king had done me this kindness, I went about as before proclaiming the Dhamma. Thereupon the king summoned me again and asked me, 'Friend, on what business are you going about?' – 'The same as before, your majesty,' I replied. 'Friend,' said the king, 'a horse is not good enough for you; sit herein as you go about.' So saying, he presented me with a chariot drawn by four Sindh horses. Again, the third time the king heard my voice, whereupon he sent for me and asked me, 'Friend, on what business are you going about?' – 'The same as before, your majesty,' I replied. 'Friend,' said the king, 'a chariot is not good enough for you.' And forthwith he presented me with great wealth and a splendid set of jewels, and at the same time he gave me an elephant. Accordingly I decked myself with all my jewels and seated myself on the back of the elephant, and in this manner for eighty thousand years I went about performing the meritorious work of proclaiming the Dhamma.[1] And during all that time there was diffused from my body the fragrance of sandal and from my mouth the fragrance of the lotus. This was my meritorious deed in a previous state of existence." (*End of Story of the Past.*)

As Santati the king's minister thus related the story of his meritorious deed in a previous state of existence, sitting cross-legged in the air, he applied himself to meditation on the element of fire; and having thus induced a state of deep meditation, he entered therein and straightaway attained Nibbāna. Instantly flames of fire burst from his body and consumed his flesh and blood, and his relics floated down like jasmine flowers. The Teacher spread out a pure white cloth, and his relics fell upon it. Then the Teacher deposited them at a crossing of four highways, caused a stupa to be erected over them, and said, "By doing reverence to these relics the populace will earn much merit."

The monks started up a discussion in the Hall of Truth, "Santati the king's minister attained arahantship at the conclusion of the stanza, and though adorned and dressed in state, sitting cross-legged in the air, he attained Nibbāna. Ought one to speak of him

---

1. In the time of this Buddha human beings are reputed to have lived very long.

as a monk or as a brahmin?" At that moment the Teacher entered and asked the monks, "Monks, what is it that engages your attention as you sit here all gathered together?" When they told him, he said, "Monks, it is proper to speak of my son as a monk, and it is equally proper to speak of him as a brahmin." So saying he preached the Dhamma by pronouncing the following stanza:

142. Though he be adorned, if he lives at peace,
　　　Calm, tamed, restrained, and pure,
　　　Having laid down the rod towards all beings:
　　　He is a brahmin, an ascetic, a monk.

29. The Elder Bāhiya Dārucīriya

THOUGH A THOUSAND VERSES ARE MADE OF MEANINGLESS LINES.... This instruction was given by the Teacher while he was in residence at Jetavana with reference to the Elder Bāhiya Dārucīriya, Bāhiya of the Bark Garment.[1]

For once upon a time a party of men set out to sea in a ship. When they were well out to sea, the ship sprang a leak. Thereupon all of the men, with a single exception, became food for fishes and tortoises. Only one man, who seized a plank and struggled with all his might, succeeded in reaching land near Suppāraka Port. When he came to land, he lacked both under and upper garments. So for lack of anything better, he wrapped himself with dry twigs and sticks and bark, and obtaining a postsherd from the royal household, went to Suppāraka Port. All who saw him gave him broth, rice-porridge, and other kinds of food, and did reverence to him, saying, "This is an arahant."

He thought, "If I clothe myself in under and upper garments of fine texture, I shall no longer receive gain and honour." Therefore he avoided such garments, using only the bark of trees to clothe himself. As many persons greeted him with the salutation "Arahant! Arahant!" the following consideration presented itself to his mind, "Am I perhaps one of those who are arahants in this world, or who have entered the path leading to arahantship?" Thereupon a certain thought occurred to a deity who was a former blood-relative of his.

Story of the Past

By "former blood-relative" is meant one who formerly practised meditation with him. It appears that in former times, when the dispensation of the Buddha Kassapa was disappearing from the earth, seven monks, observing a change for the worse in the conduct of novices and others, their emotions deeply stirred, said to themselves, "So long as our dispensation has not yet disappeared, we will establish ourselves in it." So after reverencing their golden shrine, they entered the forest, and seeing a certain mountain, they

---

1. This story is an elaborated version of Udāna I, 10.

said, "Let those who still cherish attachment for the life of this world turn back; let those who have rid themselves of such attachment ascend this mountain." Thereupon they set up a ladder, and all of them ascended the mountain, whereupon they kicked the ladder down and devoted themselves to meditation. After but a single night had passed, one of them, the elder of the assembly, attained arahantship.

The elder of the assembly chewed a toothstick of serpent-creeper at Lake Anotatta, rinsed his mouth, brought food from North Kuru, and said to those monks, "Friends, chew this toothstick, rinse your mouths, and then eat this food." But this they refused to do, saying, "But, reverend sir, did we make the following agreement, 'All shall eat the food brought by him who first attains arahantship'?" – "We made no such agreement, friends." – "Well then, if, like you, we also develop something special, we will bring food for ourselves and eat it." On the second day the second elder attained the fruit of the third path, whereupon he likewise brought food to the monks and invited them to eat it. But they said, "But, reverend sir, did we agree not to eat the food brought by the chief elder, but to eat that which should be brought by a subordinate elder?" – "We did not so agree, friends." – "In that case, if, like you, we also develop something special, we shall be able by our own unaided efforts to provide ourselves with food, and we shall so provide ourselves with food." Thus did they refuse to eat the food he had brought.

Of the seven monks, the elder of the assembly who had attained arahantship attained (final) Nibbāna; he who had attained the fruit of the third path was reborn in the Brahma-world; and the remaining five, unable to develop something special, wasted and withered away, died on the seventh day, and were reborn in the world of the gods. In the period of this present Buddha they passed from that state of existence and were reborn in various households. One of them was King Pukkusāti, one was Kumāra Kassapa, one was Dārucīriya, one was Dabba Mallaputta, and one was the monk Sabhiya. The term "former blood-relative" therefore refers to the monk who was reborn in the Brahma-world. (*End of Story of the Past.*)

The Story of Bāhiya Dārucīriya (concluded)

To this denizen of the Brahma-world, then, occurred the following thought, "This man was associated with me in setting up the ladder and in the ascent of the mountain and in the practice of meditation; but now he has adopted false views, and by his present course of conduct he is in danger of perdition; I will stir him up." Accordingly he approached him and spoke thus, "Bāhiya, you are not an arahant, nor have you entered the path that leads to arahantship; moreover, the course that you have adopted is not such that you will thereby attain arahantship or enter the path that leads to arahantship." As Mahā Brahmā, poised in the air, spoke these words, Bāhiya looked upon him and thought to himself, "Oh, what a plight I am in! I thought to myself, 'I am an arahant'; but that spirit says to me, 'You are not an arahant, nor have you entered the path that leads to arahantship.' Is there perhaps any other arahant in the world?"

Accordingly Bāhiya asked the spirit, "Deity, are there perhaps now in the world arahants or those who have entered the path leading to arahantship?" Then the deity informed him as follows, "Bāhiya, there lies to the north a city named Sāvatthī; and there, at the present time, dwells he that is the Exalted One, the Arahant of arahants, the Supremely Enlightened One; and he that is the Exalted One, the Arahant of arahants, preaches the truth of arahantship."

As Bāhiya listened in the night time to the speech of the deity, he became deeply moved in his heart; and instantly departing from Suppāraka, within a single night he arrived at Sāvatthī.[2] At the moment when he arrived, the Teacher had entered the city for alms. When Bāhiya had finished breakfast, he observed many monks taking their exercise in the open air by walking up and down, and he asked them, "Where is the Teacher now?" Said the monks, "He has just entered Sāvatthī for alms." Then the monks asked Bāhiya, "But from where have you come?" – "I have come from Suppāraka." – "When did you leave Suppāraka?" – "Yesterday evening." – "You have come a long way. Just sit down, bathe your feet, anoint them with oil, and rest a while. When the Teacher returns, you will see him." – "Reverend sir, I do not know when the Teacher may die, or when I may die myself. I came here in the space of but a single night, neither stopping nor sitting down anywhere to rest. I have

---

2. This is quick work on foot. The distance could be 2000 miles!

come on a journey of a hundred and twenty leagues. As soon as I have seen the Teacher, I will rest."

When he had thus spoken, his body trembling all over, he entered Sāvatthī and beheld the Exalted One making his round for alms with the incomparable grace of a Buddha. He said to himself, "At long last I see Gotama, the Supremely Enlightened One." And from the point where he had first seen him, he proceeded with his body inclined in an attitude of profound reverence; even as he stood in the street, he paid obeisance to him, and took him firmly by the ankles, and spoke thus to him, "Let the Exalted One teach me the Dhamma; let the Happy One teach me the Dhamma, that it may for a long time lead to my welfare and salvation."

But the Teacher turned him away, saying, "You come at the wrong time, Bāhiya; I have entered among the houses for alms." When Bāhiya heard these words, he said, "Reverend sir, as I have passed through the round of existences, previously I have received solid food, but I do not know the hour when you or I shall die; then teach me the Dhamma." But the Teacher turned him away the second time as before. (This, we are told, was the thought that occurred to him: "From the time this man first saw me, his whole body has been suffused with joy; from the great shock of joy he has received, though he should listen to the Dhamma, he would not be able to comprehend it. Let him remain for a time in a state of placid equanimity.") Therefore the Teacher turned him away twice. When Bāhiya put his request the third time, the Teacher, remaining where he was in the street, said to him:

"Herein, Bāhiya, you should train yourself thus: 'In the seen will be merely what is seen; in the heard will be merely what is heard; in the sensed will be merely what is sensed; in the cognized will be merely what is cognized.' In this way you should train yourself, Bāhiya.

"When, Bāhiya, in the seen is merely what is seen … in the cognized is merely what is cognized, then Bāhiya, you will not be 'with that' (wrong view, passion etc.); when Bāhiya, you are not 'with that,' then Bāhiya, you will not be 'in that situation' (of being empassioned by passion, enraged be hate, deluded by delusion); when Bāhiya, you are not 'in that situation,' then Bāhiya, you will be neither 'here' (in this world) nor 'beyond' (in the next life) nor 'in between both' (going from one to another). Just this is the end of suffering."[3]

Even as Bāhiya listened to the Teacher's discourse, he threw off all the taints and attained arahantship together with the analytical knowledges. Straightaway he asked the Teacher to admit him to the Order. The Teacher asked him, "Have you bowl and robe complete?" – "I have not bowl and robe complete," replied Bāhiya. Then the Teacher said to him, "Well then, seek bowl and robe." So saying, the Teacher went his way.

As Bāhiya was seeking bowl and robe, a certain ogress in the form of a heifer approached, struck him with her left shoulder, and deprived him of life. The Teacher, after making his round for alms and after eating his breakfast, came forth with a large company of monks and saw the body of Bāhiya lying prostrate on the dust-heap. Straightaway he commanded the monks as follows, "Monks, bring a litter which stands at the door of a certain house, carry the body of this man out of the city, burn it, and erect a mound over the remains." The monks did so, and having so done, returned to the monastery, approached the Teacher, told him what they had done, and inquired about the future state of the dead man.

Thereupon the Teacher announced that he had attained Nibbāna, and assigned him pre-eminence, saying, "Monks, pre-eminent among my disciples and monks who are quick to learn the truth is Bāhiya Dārucīriya." Then the monks asked him, "Reverend sir, you say, 'Bāhiya Dārucīriya has attained arahantship', when did he attain arahantship?" – "Monks, it was when he heard me preach the Dhamma." – "But when did you preach the Dhamma to him?" – "While I was making my rounds for alms, standing in the middle of the street." – "Was not the discourse you delivered standing in the middle of the street an extremely short one, reverend sir? How was it that he developed something special after hearing so very little?" Then the Teacher said to them, "Monks, do not measure my Dhamma as being 'little' or 'much.' There is no virtue even in many thousands of stanzas. A single line of a stanza which contains the truth is better." And when he had thus spoken, he showed the connection, and teaching the Dhamma, he pronounced the following stanza:

101. Though a thousand verses
Are made of meaningless lines,

---

3. Based on a translation by John Ireland appearing in *Pāli Buddhist Review* 2,3

30. Uggasena the Treasurer's Son

LET GO WHAT IS BEFORE, LET GO WHAT IS BEHIND .... This instruction was given by the Teacher while he was in residence at Veḷuvana with reference to Uggasena.

The story goes that once a year, or once every six months, five hundred acrobats used to visit Rājagaha and give performances for seven days before the king. By these performances they earned much gold and money; in fact there was no end to the gifts tossed at them from time to time. The people stood on beds piled on top of beds and watched the acrobats perform their feats.

One day a certain female acrobat climbed a pole, turned somersaults thereon, and balancing herself on the tip of the pole, danced and sang as she trod the air. Now on this occasion, a certain treasurer's son, accompanied by a companion, stood on top of a pile of beds watching her. The grace and skill with which she managed her hands and feet attracted his attention, and he straightaway fell in love with her. He went home and said, "If I can have her, I shall live; but if I cannot have her, I shall die right here." So saying, he flung himself down on his bed and refused to take food.

His mother and father asked him, "Son, what is wrong with you?" The son replied, "If I can have that acrobat's daughter, I shall live; if I cannot have her, I shall die right here." Said his mother and father, "Do not act in this way. We will bring you another maiden, our equal in birth and wealth." But he made the same reply as before and remained lying in bed. His father argued with him at length but was unable to make him see things in a better light. Finally he sent for his son's friend, gave him a thousand pieces of money, and sent him off, saying to him, "Tell the acrobat to take this money and give his daughter to my son."

"I will not give my daughter for money," replied the acrobat, "but if it be true that he cannot live without my daughter, then let him travel about with us; if he will do this, I will give him my daughter." The mother and father communicated this information to their son. The son immediately said, "Of course I will travel about with them." His mother and father begged him not to do so, but he paid no attention to anything they said, and went and joined the acrobats.

124

The acrobat gave him his daughter in marriage, and travelled about with him through villages, market-towns, and royal cities, giving exhibitions everywhere. In no long time the female acrobat, after living with her husband, gave birth to a son. As she played with the boy, she would address him as "son of a cart-driver" or "son of a fetcher-of-wood and drawer-of-water," or "son of a know-nothing." It appears that the husband used to attend to everything relating to their carts. Wherever they halted, he would fetch grass for the oxen. Wherever they gave an exhibition, he would procure whatever apparatus was required, set it up, and remove it.

It was with reference to duties such as these performed by her husband that this woman employed such terms as these in playing with her son. The husband came to the conclusion that the songs she sang were about himself, and asked her, "Do you refer to me?" – "Yes, I refer to you." – "In that case I will run away and leave you." – "What difference does it make to me whether you go away or not?" replied the wife. And over and over again she sang the same song. It appears that by reason of the beauty she possessed and the large amount of money she earned, she was utterly indifferent to him.

"Why is it that she is so proud?" thought the husband to himself. Straightaway he perceived within himself, "It is because of her skill as an acrobat." So he thought to himself, "Very well! I will learn acrobatic feats myself." Accordingly he went to his father-in-law and learned all the feats that he knew. And he exhibited his art in villages, market-towns, and royal cities, one after another, until finally he came to Rājagaha. And he caused proclamation to be made throughout the city, "Seven days from today Uggasena the treasurer's son will exhibit his art to the residents of the city." The residents of the city caused platform above platform to be erected and assembled on the seventh day. Uggasena climbed a pole sixty cubits in height and balanced himself on the top of it.

On that day, as the Teacher surveyed the world at dawn, he perceived that Uggasena had entered the net of his knowledge. And he considered within himself, "What will become of him?" Straightaway he became aware of the following, "The treasurer's son will balance himself on the tip of the pole for the purpose of displaying his skill, and a great multitude will assemble for the purpose of witnessing his exhibition. At this point I will pronounce a stanza consisting of four verses. Hearing this stanza, 84,000 living beings will obtain comprehension of the Dhamma, and Uggasena himself will be established in arahantship." So on the following day, taking note of the time, the Teacher set out, attended by the Order of Monks, and entered the city of Rājagaha for alms.

A moment before the Teacher entered the city, Uggasena motioned to the multitude as a sign for applause, and balancing himself on the tip of the pole, turned seven somersaults in the air, alighted on his feet, and balanced himself once more on the tip of the pole. At that moment the Teacher entered the city, and so contrived that the multitude looked not at Uggasena, but at himself. When Uggasena looked at the audience and perceived that they were not looking at him at all, he was overwhelmed with disappointment. Thought he, "Here is a feat which it has taken me a year to perfect, but when the Teacher enters the city, the audience, instead of looking at me, looks at the Teacher. My exhibition has failed completely." The Teacher, perceiving the thought that was passing through his mind, addressed the Elder Moggallāna, "Go inform the treasurer's son that the Teacher desires him to exhibit his skill." The elder went and stood at the base of the pole, and addressing the treasurer's son, pronounced the following stanza:

"Please look, Uggasena, acrobat of mighty strength.
Perform for the crowd; make the people laugh."

When Uggasena heard the words of the elder, he was delighted at heart. "Doubtless the Teacher desires to witness my skill," he thought. And even as he balanced himself on the tip of the pole, he pronounced the following stanza:

"Please look, Moggallāna, mighty in wisdom and power.
I perform for the crowd; I make the people laugh."

So saying, he sprang into the air from the top of the pole, turned fourteen somersaults in the air, and alighting on his feet, balanced himself once more on the tip of the pole. The Teacher said to him, "Uggasena, a man that is wise should let go attachment for the aggregates in the past, the present, and the future; even so should he win release from birth, decay, disease, and death." So saying, he pronounced the following stanza:

126

348. Let go what is before, let go what is behind,
   Let go the middle and get beyond becoming:
   Thus with a mind released in every way
   To birth and decay you shall come no more.

At the conclusion of the lesson 84,000 living beings obtained comprehension of the Dhamma. The treasurer's son, even as he stood poised on the tip of the pole, attained arahantship together with the higher powers.

The treasurer's son straightaway descended from the pole, advanced to the Teacher, saluted him respectfully and requested the Teacher to admit him to the Order. The Teacher stretched out his right hand and said to him, "Come, monk!" At that moment he was supernaturally provided with the eight requisites, and had the appearance of an elder of sixty rains. The monks asked him, "Friend Uggasena, had you no fear as you descended from that pole sixty cubits in height?" Uggasena replied, "Friends, I have no fear." The monks said to the Teacher, "Reverend sir, Uggasena says, 'I have no fear'; he says that which is not true, utters falsehood." Said the Teacher, "Monks, those monks who, like my son Uggasena, have severed the attachments, have no fear or perturbation." So saying, he pronounced the following stanza:

397. He who having severed
   All the fetters trembles not,
   Gone beyond ties, free from bonds—
   That one I call a brāhmaṇa.

Again one day the monks began the following discussion in the Hall of Truth: "Friends, how did it happen that a monk, endowed as was this monk with the faculties requisite for the attainment of arahantship, travelled about with acrobats for the sake of an acrobat's daughter? And how did it happen that he was endowed with the faculties requisite for the attainment of arahantship?" The Teacher drew near and asked them, "Monks what is the subject you are discussing as you sit here all gathered together?" When they told him, he said, "Monks, both of these things happened through one and the same circumstance." And to make the matter clear, he related the following story.

127

Story of the Past: A Joke in Earnest

The story goes that in times long past, while the golden shrine for the relics of the Buddha Kassapa was being built, the children of certain respectable families living in Benares loaded carts with an abundant supply of food and set out for the shrine to do the work of labourers. As they proceeded, they saw along the way a certain elder entering the city for alms. Now a certain young woman looked at the elder and said to her husband, "Husband, our noble elder is entering the city for alms, and there is an abundant supply of food both hard and soft in our cart. Fetch his bowl, and let us give him food." Her husband fetched the elder's bowl, and when they had filled it with food both hard and soft, they placed it in the hands of the elder, and both husband and wife made the following earnest wish, "Reverend sir, may we be partakers of the Truth you have seen."

Now this elder was an arahant, and therefore looked into the future to see whether their earnest wish would be fulfilled. And perceiving that it would be fulfilled, he smiled. The woman noticed the smile and said to her husband, "Husband, our noble elder smiled; he must be some actor." Her husband replied, "He must be indeed, my dear wife," and passed on. This was their deed in a former birth. (*End of Story of the Past.*)

Remaining in this state of existence during the term of life allotted to them, they were reborn in the world of the gods, and passing from that state of existence in the dispensation of the present Buddha, that woman was reborn in the household of an acrobat, the man in the household of a treasurer. Because he returned the reply, "He must be indeed, my dear wife," he travelled about with actors; and because he gave a portion of food to an elder who was an arahant, he attained arahantship. The acrobat's daughter said to herself, "Whatever future state my husband shall attain, that will I also attain." So saying, she went forth into homelessness and became established in arahantship.

Part V

What Novices Can Do

31. The Elder Sangharakkhita's Nephew

FARING FAR, WANDERING ALONE.... This instruction was given by the Teacher while he was in residence at Sāvatthī with reference to Sangharakkhita.

The story goes that a certain youth of respectable family living at Sāvatthī, after hearing a discourse of the Teacher, made his renunciation and went forth, obtained acceptance as a monk, and in but a few days attained arahantship. He was known as the Elder Sangharakkhita. When a nephew of the Elder Sangharakkhita came of age, he went forth under the elder, and after obtaining acceptance entered upon the rains residence at a certain monastery.[1]

Receiving two robes such as are worn by monks during the period of the rains, one seven cubits long, the other eight cubits long, he decided to present the robe eight cubits long to his preceptor and to keep the robe seven cubits long for himself. When he had completed the rains residence, he set out for the purpose of seeing his preceptor and journeyed from place to place, receiving alms along the way.

He arrived at the monastery before the elder arrived. Entering the monastery, he swept the elder's day-quarters, set out water for bathing the feet, prepared a seat, and then sat down, watching the road by which the elder would approach. When he saw the elder approach, he advanced to meet him, took his bowl and robe, seated the elder with the words, "Please be seated, reverend sir," took a palm-leaf fan and fanned him, gave him water to drink, and bathed his feet. Finally he brought forth the robe, laid it at the elder's feet, and said, "Reverend sir, please wear this robe." Having done so, he resumed fanning him. Said the elder to the nephew, "Sangharakkhita, I have a complete set of robes; you wear this robe yourself." – "Reverend sir, from the moment I received this robe I set my heart on giving it to you alone. Please make use of it." – "Never mind, Sangharakkhita, my set of robes is complete; you wear this robe yourself." – "Reverend sir, please do not refuse the robe, for if you wear it, great will be the fruit I shall receive thereby."

---

1. The "going forth" (*pabbajjā*) is the novice ordination. "Acceptance" (*upasampadā*) is full ordination as a bhikkhu.

Although the younger monk repeated his request several times, the elder refused to accept the present of the robe. So, as the younger monk stood there fanning the elder, he thought to himself, "While the elder was a layman, I stood in the relation of nephew to him. Since he has been a monk, I have been his fellow-resident. But in spite of this he is not willing as my preceptor to share my possessions. If he is not willing to share my possessions with me, why should I longer remain a monk? I will become a householder once more." Then the following thought occurred to him, "It is a hard thing to live the household life. Suppose I become a householder once more; how shall I gain a living?" Finally the following thought occurred to him:

"I will sell this robe eight cubits long and buy a she-goat. Now she-goats are very prolific, and as fast as the she-goat brings forth young, I will sell them, and in this way accumulate some capital. As soon as I have accumulated some capital, I will take a wife. My wife will bear me a son, and I will name him after my uncle. I will put my son in a go-cart, and taking son and wife with me, will go to pay my respects to my uncle. As I journey by the way, I will say to my wife, 'Just bring me my son; I wish to carry him.' She will reply, 'Why should you carry this boy? Come, push this go-cart.' So saying, she will take the boy in her arms, thinking to herself, 'I will carry him myself.' But lacking the necessary strength to carry him, she will let him fall in the path of the wheels, and the go-cart will run over him. Then I will say to her, 'You would not even give me my own son to carry, although you were not strong enough to carry him yourself. You have ruined me.' So saying, I will bring down my stick on her back."

Thus pondered the younger monk as he stood fanning the elder. As he concluded his reflections, he swung his palm-leaf fan and brought it down on the head of the elder. The elder considered within himself, "Why did Sangharakkhita strike me on the head?" Immediately becoming aware of every single thought that had passed through the mind of his nephew, he said to him, "Sangharakkhita, you did not succeed in hitting the woman; but what has an old monk done to deserve a beating?" The younger monk thought to himself, "Oh, I am ruined! My preceptor, it appears, knows every thought that has passed through my mind. What have I to do with the life of a monk any longer?" Straightaway he

132

threw his fan away and started to run off. But the young monks and novices ran after him, caught him, and led him to the Teacher.

When the Teacher saw those monks, he asked them, "Monks, why have you come here? Have you captured a monk?" – "Yes, reverend sir. This young monk became discontented and ran away, but we captured him and have brought him to you." – "Monk, is what they say true?" – "Yes, reverend sir." – "Monk, why did you commit so grievous a fault? Are you not the son of a Buddha of strenuous effort? And once having gone forth in the dispensation of a Buddha like me, though you failed through self-conquest to win for yourself the attainments of stream-entry or once-returning or non-returning, even so why did you commit so grievous a fault as this?"

"I am discontented, reverend sir." – "Why are you discontented?" In reply the younger monk related the whole story of his experiences, from the day he received the robes worn by monks in residence to the moment when he struck the elder on the head with his palm-leaf fan. "Reverend sir," said he, "That is why I ran away." Said the Teacher, "Come, monk; be not disturbed. The mind has a way of dwelling on subjects that are far off. One should strive to free it from the bonds of lust, hatred, and delusion." So saying, he pronounced the following stanza:

37   Faring far, wandering alone,
       Formless and lying in a cave –
       Those who restrain the mind
       Are freed from Māra's bonds.

32. The Elder Tissa's Novice

PEACEFUL IS HIS MIND.... This instruction was given by the Teacher while he was in residence at Jetavana with reference to the novice of the Elder Tissa.

The story goes that a certain youth of good family, residing at Kosambī, went forth and obtained acceptance as a monk in the dispensation of the Teacher. After his acceptance, he was known as Elder Kosambivāsī Tissa. After he had kept the rains at Kosambī, his supporter brought a set of three robes and offerings of ghee and jaggery[1] and laid them at his feet. The elder said to him, "What are these, lay disciple?" – "Reverend sir, have you not kept residence with me during the season of the rains? Those who keep residence in our monastery always receive these offerings; please accept them, reverend sir." – "Never mind, lay disciple, I have no need of them." – "Why is that, reverend sir?" – "I have no novice to make things allowable for me, friend."[2] – "Reverend sir, if you have no novice to make things allowable, my son will become your novice."

The elder graciously accepted the offer. The lay disciple brought his own son, but seven years old, to the elder, and committed him into the elder's hands, saying "Please give him the going forth, reverend sir." The elder moistened the boy's hair, taught him the formula of meditation on the first five of the constituent parts of the body,[3] and gave him the going forth. The instant the razor touched his hair, he attained arahantship together with the analytical knowledges.

The elder, having given him the going forth, remained there for a fortnight. Then, deciding to visit the Teacher, he directed the novice to take the requisites, and set out on his journey. On the way he entered a certain monastery. The novice obtained lodging for the elder and looked after it for him.

---

1. Brown palm sugar, usually in soft cakes, allowed to monks as a refreshment.

2. It is one of the novice's duties to offer such medicines to monks who themselves may not keep them longer than seven nights.

3. Head hairs, body hairs, nails, teeth, skin. These are traditionally taught as a meditation subject on the occasion of the novice ordination.

While he was thus engaged, it grew dark and he was therefore unable to provide a lodging for himself. When the time came
for the novice to wait upon the elder, the novice approached the
elder and sat down. The elder asked the novice, "Novice, have
you not neglected to provide yourself with a lodging?" – "Reverend sir, I have had no opportunity to look after a lodging for
myself." – "Well then, remain with me. It will inconvenience you
to lodge outside in the place reserved for visitors." So saying, the
elder, taking him with him, entered his own lodging. Now the
elder had not yet attained the fruit of stream-entry, and as soon as
he lay down, fell asleep. Thereupon the novice thought to himself,
"Today is the third day during which I have occupied the same
lodging with my preceptor. If I lie down to sleep, the elder will
commit the offense of sleeping in common.[4] Therefore I will spend
the night sitting up." So assuming a cross-legged posture near the
bed of his preceptor, he spent the night sitting up.

The elder rose at dawn and said to himself, "I must cause the
novice to go out." So he took a fan which was placed at the side of
the bed, struck the mat of the novice with the tip of the palm-leaf,
and then, tossing the fan into the air, said, "Novice, go out" (so as
to avoid the above offence). The handle of the fan struck the novice
in the eye and straightaway put out his eye. "What did you say,
reverend sir?" said the novice. "Rise and go out," was the reply.
The novice, instead of saying, "Reverend sir, my eye has been put
out," covered his eye with one hand and went out. Moreover, when
it was time for him to perform his duties as novice, he did not say,
"My eye has been put out," nor did he remain seated, but covering his eye with one hand and taking a handbroom in the other,
he swept out the privy and the washroom, after which, setting out
water for washing the face, he swept out the elder's cell.

When he advanced to present the toothstick to the elder, he
presented it to him with only one hand. His preceptor said to him,
"This novice is not properly trained. Is it proper for a novice to
present a toothstick to teachers and preceptors with one hand?"[5] –
"Reverend sir, I know perfectly well what is the proper form, but

---

4. The fifth offence of expiation (*pācittiya*): "Should any bhikkhu sleep for more
than two or three nights along with one not fully ordained (as a bhikkhu), this entails
expiation."

5. Respectful offering is done with both hands.

135

one of my hands is engaged." – "What is the matter, novice?" Then the novice told him the whole story, beginning at the beginning. When the elder heard his story, he was deeply moved and said to himself, "Oh, what a grave deed I have done!" Then he said to the novice, "Pardon me, most excellent youth; I did not know this. Be my refuge." And extending his clasped hands in an attitude of reverent salutation, he crouched on the ground before the feet of the seven-year-old novice. Then said the novice to him, "It was not for this purpose, reverend sir, that I spoke. I said this for the purpose of sparing your feelings. You are not to blame in this matter and neither am I. The round of existences alone is to blame for this. It was because I wished to spare you remorse that I did not tell you the real facts."

The novice tried to comfort the elder, but he would not be comforted. Overcome with remorse, he took the novice's requisites and proceeded to the Teacher. As the Teacher sat, he observed him approaching. The elder went to the Teacher, saluted him, and exchanged friendly greetings with him. The Teacher asked him, "Monk, is everything well with you? I trust that you have suffered no excessive discomfort." The elder replied, "All is well with me, reverend sir. I have suffered no excessive discomfort. But here is a young novice whose good qualities surpass anything I have ever seen."

"Why, what has he done, monk?" Thereupon the elder told him the whole story, beginning at the beginning and concluding as follows, "Reverend sir, when I asked him to pardon me, he said this to me, 'You are not to blame in this matter and neither am I. The round of existences alone is to blame for this. Be not disturbed.' Thus he tried to comfort me, appearing to cherish neither anger nor hatred towards me. His good qualities surpass anything I have ever seen." Said the Teacher to the elder, "Monk, those who have rid themselves of the taints cherish neither anger nor hatred towards anyone. On the contrary, their senses are in a state of calm and their thoughts are in a state of calm." So saying, he joined the connection, and teaching the Dhamma, pronounced the following stanza:

96. Peaceful is his mind,
Peaceful too his speech and action,
Who, truly knowing, is released,
Perfectly tranquil and wise.

33. Paṇḍita the Novice

IRRIGATORS LEAD THE WATERS.... This instruction was given by the Teacher while he was in residence at Jetavana with reference to the novice Paṇḍita.

Story of the Past: Sakka and the Poor Man

In times past, they say, Kassapa the Supremely Enlightened One, accompanied by a retinue of twenty thousand monks freed from the taints, paid a visit to Benares. Thereupon the residents, mindful of the fame they should acquire thereby, united in bands of eight or ten and presented the visiting monks with the customary offerings. Now it happened one day that the Teacher, in rejoicing with the merits of the donors at the end of the meal, spoke as follows: "Lay disciples, here in this world one man says to himself, 'It is my bounden duty to give only that which is my own. Why should I urge others to give?' So he himself gives alms, but does not urge others to give. That man, in his future states of existence, receives the blessing of wealth, but not the blessing of a following. Another man urges others to give, but does not himself give. That man receives in his future states of existence the blessing of a following, but not the blessing of wealth. Another man neither himself gives nor urges others to give. That man, in his future states of existence, receives neither the blessing of wealth nor the blessing of a following, but lives as an eater of remnants. Yet another man not only himself gives, but also urges others to give. That man, in his future states of existence, receives both the blessing of wealth and the blessing of a following."

Now a certain wise man who stood there heard this and thought to himself, "I will straightaway act so as to obtain both blessings for myself." Accordingly he paid obeisance to the Teacher and said, "Reverend sir, tomorrow receive alms from me." – "How many monks do you wish me to bring?" – "How many monks are there in your following, reverend sir?" – "Twenty thousand monks." – "Reverend sir, tomorrow bring all your monks and receive alms from me." The Teacher accepted his invitation.

The man entered the village and announced, "Men and women, I have invited the Order of Monks presided over by the Buddha to take a meal here tomorrow; each and all of you give to as many monks as you are able." Then he went about inquiring how many each could provide for. "We will supply ten"; "We will supply twenty"; "We will supply a hundred"; "We will supply five hundred," they replied, each giving in proportion to their means. All of the pledges he wrote down in order on a leaf.

Now at that time there lived in this city a certain man who was so poor that he was known as Prince of Paupers, Mahāduggata. The solicitor, meeting him face to face, said also to him, "Sir Mahāduggata, I have invited the Order of Monks presided over by the Buddha for tomorrow's meal; tomorrow the residents of the city will give alms. How many monks will you provide for?" – "Sir, what have I to do with monks? Monks need rich men to provide for them. But as for me, I possess not so much as a small measure of rice wherewith to make porridge tomorrow; what have I to do with monks?"

Now it behooves a man who urges others to give to be circumspect; therefore when the solicitor heard the poor man plead his poverty as an excuse, instead of remaining silent, he spoke to him as follows, "Sir Mahāduggata, there are many people in this city who live in luxury, eating rich food, wearing soft clothes, adorned with all manner of adornments, and sleeping on beds of royal splendour. But as for you, you work for your living and yet get scarcely enough to fill your belly. That being the case, does it not seem to you likely that the reason why you yourself get nothing is that you have never done anything for others?" – "I think so, sir." – "Well, why do you not do a work of merit right now? You are young, and you have plenty of strength; is it not your bounden duty while you are earning a living to give alms according to your ability?" Even as the solicitor spoke, the poor man was overcome with emotion and said, "Write my name on the leaf for one monk; no matter how little I may earn, I will provide food for one monk." The solicitor said to himself, "What is the use of writing one monk on the leaf?" and omitted to write down the name.

Mahāduggata went home and said to his wife, "Wife, tomorrow the residents of the village will provide food for the Order of Monks. I, also, was requested by the solicitor to provide food for one monk; therefore we also will provide food for one monk to-morrow." His wife, instead of saying to him, "We are poor; why did you promise to do so?" said, 'Husband, what you did was quite right. We are poor now because we have never given anything; we will both work for hire and give food to one monk." So both of them went out to look for work.

A rich merchant saw Mahāduggata and said to him, "Sir Mahāduggata, do you wish to work for hire?" – "Yes, your honour." – "What kind of work can you do?" – "Whatever you would like to have done." – "Well then, we are going to entertain three hundred monks; come, split wood." And he brought an axe and a hatchet and gave them to him. Mahāduggata put on a stout girdle and, exerting himself to the utmost, began to split wood, first tossing the axe aside and taking the hatchet, and then tossing the hatchet aside and taking the axe. The merchant said to him, "Sir, today you work with unusual energy; what is the reason for it?" – "Master, I expect to provide food for one monk." The merchant was pleased at heart and thought to himself, "It is a difficult task this man has undertaken; instead of remaining silent and refusing to give because of his poverty, he says, 'I will work for hire and provide food for one monk.' "

The merchant's wife also saw the poor man's wife and said to her, "Woman, what kind of work can you do?" – "Whatever you wish to have done." So she took her into the room where the mortar was kept, gave her a winnowing-fan, a pestle, and so on, and set her at work. The woman pounded the rice and sifted it with as much joy and pleasure as if she were dancing. The merchant's wife said to her, "Woman, you appear to take unusual joy and pleasure in doing your work; what is the reason for it?" – "Lady, with the wages we earn at this work we expect to provide food for one monk." When the merchant's wife heard this, she was pleased and said to herself, "What a difficult task it is that this woman is doing!"

When Mahāduggata had finished splitting the wood, the merchant gave him four measures of rice as pay for his work and four more as an expression of goodwill. The poor man went home and said to his wife, "The rice I have received for my work will serve as a supply of provisions for us. With the pay you have earned procure curds, oil, wood, relishes, and utensils." The merchant's wife gave the woman a cup of ghee, a vessel of curds, an assortment of relishes, and a measure of clean rice. The husband and wife between them therefore received nine measures of rice.

Filled with joy and satisfaction at the thought that they had received food to bestow in alms, they rose very early in the morning. Mahāduggata's wife said to him, "Husband, go seek leaves for curry and fetch them home." Seeing no leaves in the shop, he went to the bank of the river. And there he went about picking up leaves, singing for joy at the thought, "Today I shall have the privilege of giving food to the noble monks."

A fisherman who had just thrown his big net into the water and was standing close by thought to himself, "That must be the voice of Mahāduggata." So he called him and asked, "You sing as though you were overjoyed at heart; what is the reason?" – "I am picking up leaves, friend." – "What are you going to do?" – "I am going to provide food for one monk." – "Happy indeed the monk who shall eat your leaves!" – "What else can I do, master? I intend to provide for him with the leaves I have myself gathered." – "Well then, come here." – "What do you wish me to do, master?" – "Take these fish and tie them up in bundles to sell for a shilling, sixpence and a penny."

Mahāduggata did as he was told, and the residents of the city bought them for the monks they had invited. He was still engaged in tying up bundles of fish when the time came for the monks to go on their rounds for alms, whereupon he said to the fisherman, "I must go now, friend; it is time for the monks to come." – "Are there any bundles of fish left?" – "No, friend, they are all gone." – "Well then, here are four redfish which I buried in the sand for my own use. If you intend to provide food for the monks, take them with you." So saying he gave him the redfish.

Now as the Teacher surveyed the world on the morning of that day, he observed that Mahāduggata had entered the net of his knowledge. And he considered within himself, "What is going to happen? Yesterday Mahāduggata and his wife worked for hire that they might provide food for one monk. Which monk will he obtain?" And he came to the following conclusion, "The residents will obtain monks to entertain in their houses according to the names written on the leaf; no other monk will Mahāduggata obtain, but only me." Now the Buddhas are said to show particular tenderness to poor men. So when the Teacher, very early in the morning, had attended to his bodily needs, he said to himself, "I will bestow my favour on Mahāduggata." And he went into the Perfumed Chamber and sat down.

When Mahāduggata went into his house with the fish, the Yellowstone Throne of Sakka, king of the gods, showed signs of heat.[1] Sakka looked about and said to himself, "What can be the reason for this?" And he considered within himself, "Yesterday Mahāduggata and his wife worked for hire that they might provide food for one monk; which monk will he obtain?" Finally he came to the following conclusion, "Mahāduggata will obtain no other monk than the Buddha, who is sitting in the Perfumed Chamber with this thought in his mind, 'I will bestow my favour on Mahāduggata.' Now it is Mahāduggata's intention to offer the Tathāgata a meal of his own making, consisting of porridge and rice and leaf-curry. Suppose I were to go to Mahāduggata's house and offer to act as cook?"

Accordingly Sakka disguised himself, went to the vicinity of his house, and asked, "Would anyone like to hire a man to work for him?" Mahāduggata saw him and said to him, "Sir, what kind of work can you do?" – "Master, I am a man-of-all-work; there is nothing I do not know how to do. Among other things I know how to cook porridge and boil rice." – "Sir, we need your services, but we have no money to pay you." – "What work is it you have to do?" – "I wish to provide food for one monk and I should like to have someone prepare the porridge and rice." – "If you intend to provide food for a monk, it will not be necessary for you to pay me. Is it not proper that I should perform a work of merit?" – "If that is the case, very well, sir; come in." So Sakka entered the poor man's house, had him bring the rice and other articles of food, and then dismissed him, saying, "Go and fetch the monk allotted to you."

Now the solicitor of alms had sent to the houses of the residents the monks according to the names on the leaf. Mahāduggata met him and said to him, "Give me the monk allotted to me." The solicitor immediately recollected what he had done and replied, "I forgot to allot you a monk." Mahāduggata felt as if a

---

1. Sakka's throne becomes hot as a portend of some event of momentous virtue about to occur in the human world.

sharp dagger had been thrust into his belly. Said he, "Sir, why are you ruining me? Yesterday you urged me to give alms. So my wife and I worked all day for hire, and today I got up early in the morning to gather leaves, went to the bank of the river, and spent the day picking up leaves. Give me one monk!" And he wrung his hands and burst into tears.

People gathered about and asked, "What is the matter Mahāduggata?" He told them the facts, whereupon they asked the solicitor, "Is it true, as this man alleges, that you urged him to hire himself out for service to provide food for a monk?" – "Yes, noble sirs." – "You have done a grave wrong in that, while making arrangements for so many monks, you failed to allot this man a single monk." The solicitor was troubled by what they said and said to him, "Mahāduggata, do not ruin me. You are putting me to great inconvenience. The residents have taken to their several houses the monks allotted to them according to the names written on the leaf, and there is no monk in my own house whom I can take away and give to you. But the Teacher is even now sitting in the Perfumed Chamber, having just bathed his face; and without are seated kings, royal princes, commanders-in-chief, and others, waiting for him to come forth, that they may take his bowl and accompany him on his way. Now the Buddhas are accustomed to show particular tenderness to a poor man. Therefore go to the monastery, pay obeisance to the Teacher, and say to him, 'I am a poor man, reverend sir. Bestow your favour on me.' If you have merit, you will undoubtedly obtain what you seek."

So Mahāduggata went to the monastery. Now on previous occasions he had been seen at the monastery as an eater of remnants of food. Therefore the kings, royal princes, and others said to him, "Mahāduggata, this is not meal time. Why do you come here?" – "Sirs," he replied, "I know it is not meal time; but I have come to pay obeisance to the Teacher." Then he went to the Perfumed Chamber, laid his head on the threshold, paid respectful obeisance to the Teacher, and said, "Reverend sir, in this city there is no man poorer than I. Be my refuge; bestow your favour on me."

The Teacher opened the door of the Perfumed Chamber, took down his bowl, and placed it in the poor man's hands. It was as though Mahāduggata had received the glory of a Universal Monarch. Kings, royal princes, and others gasped at each other. Now when the Teacher presents his bowl to a man, no one dares take it from him by force. But they spoke thus, "Sir Mahāduggata, give us the Teacher's bowl; we will give you all this money for it. You are a poor man; take the money. What need do you have of the bowl?" Mahāduggata said, "I will give it to no one. I have no need of money; all that I desire is to provide food for the Teacher." All without exception begged him to give them the bowl, but failing to get it, desisted.

The king thought to himself, "Money will not tempt Mahāduggata to give up the bowl, and no one can take from him the bowl which the Teacher has given to him of his own free will. But how much will this man's alms amount to? When the time comes for him to present his alms, I will take the Teacher aside, conduct him to my house, and give him the food I have made ready." This was the thought in his mind even as he accompanied the Teacher.

Now Sakka, king of gods, prepared porridge, rice, leaf-curry, and other kinds of food, made ready a seat worthy of the Teacher, and sat down awaiting the arrival of the Teacher. Mahāduggata conducted the Teacher to his house and invited him to enter. Now the house in which he lived was so low that it was impossible to enter without bowing the head. But the Buddhas never bow their heads in entering a house. When they enter a house, the earth sinks or the house rises. This is the fruit of the generous alms they have given. And when they have departed and gone, all becomes as before. Therefore the Teacher entered the house standing quite erect, and having entered, sat down on the seat prepared by Sakka. When the Teacher had seated himself, the king said to Mahāduggata, "Sir Mahāduggata, when we begged you to give us the Teacher's bowl, you refused to do so. Now let us see what sort of alms you have prepared for the Teacher."

At that moment Sakka uncovered the dishes and showed the porridge, rice, and other kinds of food. The perfume and fragrance that arose enveloped the whole city. The king surveyed the porridge, rice, and other foods, and said to the Exalted One, "Reverend sir, when I came here, I thought to myself, 'How much will Mahāduggata's alms amount to? When he presents his alms, I will take the Teacher aside, conduct him to my house, and give him the food I have myself prepared.' But as a matter of fact, I have never yet seen such provisions as these. If I remain here, Mahāduggata will be annoyed; therefore I will depart." And having paid obeisance to the Teacher, he departed. Sakka presented the porridge and other food to the Teacher and faithfully ministered to his needs. After the Teacher had eaten his meal, he returned thanks, rose from his seat, and departed. Sakka made a sign to Mahāduggata, who thereupon took the Teacher's bowl and accompanied him.

Sakka turned back, stopped at the door of Mahāduggata's house, and looked up at the sky. Thereupon there came down from the sky a rain of the seven kinds of jewels. The jewels filled all the vessels in his house and the very house itself. When there was no room left in the house, they took the children in their arms, carried them outside, and stood there. When Mahāduggata returned from accompanying the Teacher and saw the children standing outside the house, he asked, "What does this mean?" – "Our whole house is filled with the seven kinds of jewels, so much that there is no room to go in." Mahāduggata thought to himself, "Today I have received the reward of the alms I have given." Thereupon he went to the king, made obeisance to him, and when the king asked him why he had come, he said, "Your majesty, my house is filled with the seven kinds of jewels; accept this wealth." The king thought, "This very day have the alms given to the Buddhas reached their consummation." And he said to the man, "What must you have to remove the jewels?" – "Your majesty, it will require a thousand carts to remove all of this wealth." The king sent out a thousand carts and had the wealth removed and dumped in the palace court. It made a heap as high as a palm tree.

The king assembled the citizens and asked them, "Is there anyone in this city who possesses so much wealth as this?" – "There is not, your majesty." – "What ought to be done for a man possessed of so much wealth as this?" – "He should be given the post of treasurer, your majesty." The king bestowed high honour upon him and gave him the post of treasurer. Then he pointed out the site of a house occupied by a former treasurer, and said to him, "Have the bushes that are growing there removed, build a house and reside in it."

As the ground was being cleared and levelled, urns of treasure came to light with their brims touching each other. When

Mahāduggata reported this to the king, the latter said, "It is through your merit that these urns have come to light; you alone shall have them." When Mahāduggata had completed the house, he gave alms for seven days to the Order of Monks presided over by the Buddha. Thereafter, having lived out his allotted term of life in the performance of works of merit, Mahāduggata was reborn at the end of his life in the world of the gods. After enjoying celestial glory for the space of the interval between the appearances of two Buddhas, he passed from that state of existence in the dispensation of the present Buddha, and was conceived in the womb of the daughter of a rich merchant of Sāvatthī, a supporter of the Elder Sāriputta. (*End of Story of the Past.*)

Story of the Present: Paṇḍita the Novice

When the mother and father of the merchant's daughter learned that she had conceived a child in her womb, they saw to it that she received the treatment necessary for the protection of the embryo. After a time the longing of pregnancy came upon her and she thought to herself, "Oh, that I might make offerings of the choicest portions of redfish to the five hundred monks headed by the Marshal of the Dhamma.[2] Oh, that I might put on yellow robes, sit down in the outer circle of the seats, and partake of the food left uneaten by these monks!" She expressed her longing to her mother and father and fulfilled her longing, whereupon it subsided. Thereafter she held seven festivals more, and provided the five hundred monks headed by the Marshal of the Dhamma with the choicest portions of redfish. This was the fruit of his offering of the choicest portions of redfish in his former existence as the poor man, Mahāduggata.

Now on the day appointed for the naming of the child the mother said to the Elder Sāriputta, "Reverend sir, confer the moral precepts on your servant." Said the elder, "What is the name of this child?" – "Reverend sir, from the day this child came into existence in my womb, those of this household who were stupid and deaf and dumb became wise; therefore the name of my child shall be Young Wiseman, Paṇḍita Dāraka." The elder then conferred the moral precepts on the child.

---

2. Ven. Sāriputta Thera.

145

Now from the day of his birth his mother resolved, "I will not interfere with the desire of my son." When he was seven years old, he said to his mother, "I desire to become a monk under the elder." She replied, "Very well, dear child; long ago I made up my mind not to interfere with your desire." So she invited the elder to her house, provided him with food, and said to him, "Reverend sir, your servant desires to become a monk; I will bring him to the monastery this evening." Having seen the elder off, she gathered her kinsfolk together and said to them, "This very day I shall render the honours appropriate to the occasion of my son's leaving the life of a layman." So she prepared rich gifts, and taking the child to the monastery, committed him to the hands of the elder, saying, "Reverend sir, give him the going forth."

The elder spoke to him of the difficulties of going forth. The boy replied, "I will carry out your admonitions, reverend sir." "Well then," said the elder, "Come!" So saying, he wetted his hair, taught him the formula of meditation on the first five of the constituent parts of the body,[3] and gave him the going forth. His mother and father remained at the monastery for seven days, making offerings consisting wholly of the choicest portions of redfish to the Order of Monks headed by the Buddha. Having done so, they returned home.

On the eighth day the elder took the novice with him to the village. He did not, however, accompany the monks. Why was this? Not yet had the novice acquired a pleasing manner of taking his bowl and robe; not yet had he acquired a pleasing manner of walking, standing, sitting, and lying. Besides, the elder had duties to perform at the monastery. So when the Order of Monks had entered the village for alms, the elder went the rounds of the entire monastery, swept the places that had not been swept, filled the empty vessels with water for drinking and refreshment, and restored to their proper places the beds, chairs, and other articles of furniture that had been left in disorder. Having done so, he entered the village. It was because he did not wish to give the sectarians, who might enter the empty monastery, a chance to say, "Behold the habitations of the disciples of the Monk Gotama!" that he cleaned up the entire monastery before entering the village.

3. See p.134, n.3.

Therefore on that particular day, having instructed the novice how to take his bowl and robe, he entered the village somewhat later than usual.

As the novice proceeded with his preceptor, he saw a ditch by the roadside. "What is that, reverend sir?" he asked. "That is called a ditch, novice." – "What do they use it for?" – "They use it to lead the water this way and that, for irrigating their grain fields." – "But, reverend sir, has the water mind or bile?"[4] – "It has not, friend." – "But, reverend sir, can they lead anything like this, which lacks reason, to whatever place they desire?" – "Yes, friend." The novice thought to himself, "If they can lead even such a thing as this, which lacks mind, to whatever place they wish, why cannot also they that have mind bring their own mind under their own control and cause it to do the monks' duty?"[5]

Proceeding farther, he saw arrow-makers heating reeds and sticks over the fire and straightening them by sighting with them out of the corner of their eye. "What are these men, reverend sir?" he asked. "They are arrow-makers, friend." – "What are they doing?" – "They are heating reeds and sticks over the fire and straightening them." – "Have these reeds a mind, reverend sir?" – "They are without mind, friend." The novice thought to himself, "If they can take reeds, which are without mind, and straighten them by heating them over the fire, why cannot also they that have mind bring their own mind under control and cause it to do the monks' duty?"

Proceeding yet farther, he saw carpenters fashioning spokes, rims, naves, and other parts of wheels. "Reverend sir, what are these men?" he asked. "These men are carpenters, friend." – "What are they doing?" – "Out of pieces of wood they make wheels and other parts of carts and other vehicles, friend." – "But do these objects possess mind, reverend sir?" – "No, friend, they are without mind." Then this thought occurred to the novice, "If they can take these logs of wood lacking mind and make wheels and so forth out of them, why cannot also they that have mind bring their own mind under control and cause it to do the monks' duty?"

---

4. "Mind or bile" (*cittaṃ vā pittaṃ vā*): an idiomatic phrase in Pāli with rhyming words, which English cannot imitate.

5. The monks' duty is the attainment of arahantship.

Having seen all these things, the novice said to the elder, "Reverend sir, if you will be so good as to take your bowl and robe, I should like to turn back." The elder, not allowing himself to think, "This young novice who has just gone forth addresses me thus!" said, "Bring them, novice," and took his bowl and robe. The novice paid obeisance to the elder and turned back, saying, "Reverend sir, when you bring me food, be kind enough to bring me only the choicest portions of redfish." – "Where shall we get them, friend?" – "Reverend sir, if you cannot obtain them through your own merit, you will succeed in obtaining them through my merit."

The elder thought to himself, "Should this young novice sit outside, some danger may befall him." Therefore he gave him a key and said to him, "Open the door of the hut where I reside, go in, and remain there." The novice did so. Sitting down, he investigated with wisdom his own physical body and thoroughly comprehended his own personality. Through the power of his virtue Sakka's seat showed signs of heat. Sakka considered within himself, "What can be the cause of this?" and came to the following conclusion, "The novice Paṇḍita has given his preceptor his bowl and robe and turned back, saying, 'I will strive for the attainment of arahantship'; therefore I also ought to go there."

So Sakka addressed the Four Great Kings,[6] saying, "Drive away the birds that make their homes in the monastery park and guard the approaches from all quarters." And he said to the moon-deity, "Hold back the disk of the moon"; and to the sun-deity, "Hold back the disk of the sun." Having so said, he went in person to the place where hung the rope for opening and closing the door and stood on guard. There was not so much as the sound of a withered leaf in the monastery. The novice's mind was tranquil, and before his meal he knew thoroughly his own personality and obtained the three lower fruits.

The elder thought, "The novice is seated in the monastery, and I can obtain food in such and such a house to assist him in his preparation." So he went to the house of a certain supporter, whose love and respect for him he well knew. Now the members of this household had obtained some redfish that very day and were

6. The four deities that rule over the realm of the Four Great Kings, the lowest of the six sense-sphere heavens.

seated, watching for the elder to come. When they saw him coming, they said to him, "Reverend sir, it is good that you have come here." And they invited him in, gave him broth and hard food, and presented him with alms consisting of the choicest portions of redfish. The elder allowed the purpose of his visit to be known, whereupon the members of the household said to him, "Eat your meal, reverend sir, and you shall also receive food to take with you." So when the elder had finished his meal, they filled his bowl with food consisting of the choicest portions of redfish and gave it to him. The elder, thinking to himself, "The novice must be hungry," hastened back to the monastery with all speed.

Very early on the morning of that day the Teacher ate his meal and went to the monastery. And he considered within himself, "The novice Paṇḍita has given his preceptor his bowl and robe and turned back, saying, 'I will strive for the attainment of arahantship.' Will he reach the goal of his religious life?" Perceiving that he had attained the three lower fruits, he considered, "Has he or has he not the necessary factors to attain arahantship?" Perceiving that he had, he considered, "Will he or will he not be able to attain arahantship even before his meal?" And straightaway he perceived that he would.

Then the following thought occurred to him, "Sāriputta is hastening to the monastery with food for the novice and may perhaps interfere with his meditations. I will therefore sit down in the battlemented chamber on guard. When Sāriputta arrives, I will ask him four questions. While these questions are being answered, the novice will attain arahantship together with the analytical knowledges."

So he went and took his stand in the battlemented chamber, and when the elder arrived, the Teacher asked him four questions, each of which the elder answered correctly. These were the questions and answers. The Teacher asked Sāriputta, "Sāriputta, what have you got?" – "Food, reverend sir." – "What does food produce, Sāriputta?" – "Sensation, reverend sir." – "What does sensation produce, Sāriputta?" – "Material form, reverend sir." – "What does material form produce, Sāriputta?" – "Contact, reverend sir."[7]

---

7. There is a play on words here which English can only reproduce in a laboured way: "Sāriputta, what have you got?" – "*Sustenance*, reverend sir." – "What does *sustenance sustain?*" etc.

This is the meaning of these questions: When a hungry man eats food, the food banishes his hunger and brings a pleasurable sensation. As a result of the pleasurable sensation which comes to a man who is satisfied by the eating of food, his body takes on a beautiful colour; and for this reason it is said that sensation produces material form. Now when a man is satisfied by the material form which is the product of the food he has eaten, he is filled with joy and delight; and with the thought in his mind, "Now I have attained happiness," whether he lies down or sits down he obtains pleasurable contact.

While these four questions were being answered, the novice attained arahantship together with the analytical knowledges. Then the Teacher said to the elder, "Go, Sāriputta, give the food to your novice." The elder went and knocked at the door. The novice came out, took the bowl from the elder's hands, set it aside, and began to fan the elder with a palm-leaf fan. The elder said to him, "Novice, have your meal." – "But you, reverend sir?" – "I have eaten; you eat yours." Thus did a child seven years old, on the eighth day after going forth, like a freshly blossomed lotus, reflecting upon the subjects of reflection,[8] sit down for his meal.

When he had washed his bowl and put it away, the moon-deity released the moon and the sun-deity the sun; the Four Great Kings abandoned their watch over the four quarters; Sakka the king of the gods gave up his post at the rope of the door; and the sun vanished from mid-heaven and disappeared.

The monks were annoyed and said, "Unwonted darkness has come on; the sun has disappeared from mid-heaven, and the novice has only just eaten; what does this mean?" The Teacher, aware of what they were saying, came and asked, "Monks, what are you saying?"

They told him. He replied, "Yes, monks, while this novice, fruitful in good works, was striving for the attainment of arahantship, the moon-deity held back the disk of the moon and the sun-deity the disk of the sun; the Four Great Kings stood on guard over the four quarters in the monastery park; Sakka king of the gods kept watch over the rope of the door; and I myself,

---

8. This refers to the reflection upon the proper purpose of eating almsfood, part of the monk's discipline.

although a Buddha, was unable to remain in an attitude of repose, but went to the battlemented chamber and stood guard over my son. Wise men who observe ditch-diggers leading the water, arrow-makers straightening their arrows, and carpenters fashioning wood, meditate on these things, and so obtain mastery over themselves and attain arahantship." And joining the connection, he instructed them in the Dhamma by pronouncing the following stanza:

80.　Irrigators lead the waters,
　　　Arrow-makers bend the shafts,
　　　Carpenters shape the wood:
　　　Those who are wise tame themselves.

34. The Four Novices

AMONG THE HOSTILE UNHOSTILE.... This instruction was given by the Teacher while he was in residence at Jetavana with reference to four novices.

The story goes that the wife of a certain brahmin prepared food for four specially designated monks, and said to the brahmin, her husband, "Go to the monastery, have the steward pick out four old brahmins, and bring them here." The brahmin went to the monastery and said, "Have four brahmins picked out for me and give them to me."[1] There fell to him four seven-year-old novices who had attained arahantship: Saṅkicca, Paṇḍita, Sopāka, and Revata. The brahmin's wife had costly seats prepared and stood waiting. At sight of the novices, she was filled with rage, and sputtering as when salt is dropped on a brazier, she said to her husband, "You have gone to the monastery and brought back with you four youngsters not old enough to be your grandsons." She refused to let them sit on the seats which she had prepared, but spreading some low seats for them, said to them, "Sit here!" Then she said to her husband, "Brahmin, go and look out for some old brahmins and bring them here."

The brahmin went to the monastery, and seeing the Elder Sāriputta, said to him, "Come, let us go to our house," and took him back home with him. When the elder reached the house and saw the novices, he asked, "Have these brahmins received food?" – "No, they have received no food." Knowing that food had been prepared for just four persons, he said, "Bring me my bowl," and taking his bowl, departed. The brahmin's wife asked, "What did he say?" Her husband replied, "He said, 'These brahmins sitting here ought to receive food. Bring me my bowl.' So saying, he took his bowl and departed." Said the brahmin's wife, "It must be that he did not wish to eat; go quickly, look out for another brahmin and bring him here." The brahmin went back to the monastery, and seeing the Elder Moggallāna the Great, said the same thing to

---

1. It is very typical of a brahmin to wish to give only to other brahmins even if they are monks. But *brahmins*, in the Buddhist sense of the word, are arahants. They are also "old" (venerable) in the Buddhist sense due to their attainment.

him, and brought him back home with him. When the Elder Moggallāna the Great saw the novices, he said the same thing as had the Elder Sāriputta, and taking his bowl, departed. Then said the brahmin's wife to her husband, "These elders do not wish to eat; go to the brahmins' enclosure (around the brahmins' houses) and bring back with you a single old brahmin."

Now the novices had nothing to eat from early morning and sat there famished with hunger. By the power of their merit Sakka's seat showed signs of heat. Considering within himself what might be the cause, he perceived that the novices had sat there from early morning and that they were weak and exhausted. "It is my duty to go there," thought Sakka. So disguising himself as an old brahmin, worn out by old age, he went to the brahmins' enclosure and sat down in the most conspicuous seat of the brahmins. When the brahmin saw him, he thought to himself, "Now my wife will be delighted," and saying, "Come, let us go home," he took him and went back home with him. When the brahmin's wife saw him, her heart was filled with delight. She took rugs and mats which were spread over two seats, spread them over one, and said to him, "Noble sir, sit here."

When Sakka entered the house, he respectfully saluted the four novices, and finding a place for himself at the edge of the seats where the novices were sitting, sat down cross-legged on the ground.

When the brahmin's wife saw him, she said to the brahmin, "For sure, you have brought a brahmin, but you have brought back with you one old enough to be your father. He is going about saluting novices young enough to be his grandsons. What use have we for him? Put him out!"

The brahmin seized him first by the shoulder, then by the arm, finally by the waist, and tried his best to drag him out, but he refused to stir from where he sat. Then the brahmin's wife said to her husband, "Come, brahmin, you take hold of one arm and I will take hold of the other." So the brahmin and his wife both took hold of his two arms, belaboured him about the back, and dragged him through the door out of the house. Nevertheless, Sakka remained sitting in the same place in which he had sat before, waving his hands back and forth.

When the brahmin and his wife returned and saw him sitting in the very same place in which he had sat before, they screamed screams of terror and let him go. At that moment Sakka made known his identity. Then the brahmin and his wife gave food to their guests. When those five persons had received food, they departed. One of the novices broke through the circular peak of the house; the second broke through the front part of the roof; the third broke through the back part of the roof; the fourth plunged into the earth, while Sakka departed from the house by another route. Thus did those five persons depart from the house by five different routes. From that time on, so it is said, that house was known as the House with the Five Openings.

When the novices returned to the monastery, the monks asked them, "Friends, what was it like?" – "Please don't ask us," replied the novices. "The brahmin's wife fumed with rage the moment she saw us. She refused to allow us to sit on the seats which she had prepared and said to her husband, 'Make haste and bring an old brahmin.' Our preceptor came, and seeing us said, 'These brahmins who are sitting here ought to receive food.' So saying, he ordered his bowl to be brought to him and departed. Then the brahmin's wife said to her husband, 'Bring another old brahmin.' Then the brahmin brought the Elder Moggallāna the Great. When the Elder Moggallāna the Great saw us, he said the same thing as had the Elder Sāriputta and departed. Then the brahmin's wife said to her husband, 'These elders do not wish to eat; brahmin, go to the brahmins' enclosure and bring back a single old brahmin.' The brahmin went there and brought back Sakka, who came in the disguise of a brahmin. When Sakka arrived, the brahmin and his wife gave us food."

"But were you not angry with them for what they did?" – "No, we were not angry." When the monks heard their reply, they reported the matter to the Teacher, saying, "Reverend sir, when these monks say, 'We were not angry,' they say what is not true, they utter falsehood." Said the Teacher, "Monks, those who have rid themselves of the evil passions oppose not those by whom they are opposed." So saying, he pronounced the following stanza:

406. Among the hostile unhostile
Among the violent completely cool,
Detached amidst these who are attached –
That one I call a brāhmana.

154

Part VI

How Dhamma is Practised

35. Worthy of Reverence

FROM WHOMEVER ONE LEARNS THE DHAMMA.... This instruction was given by the Teacher while he was in residence at Jetavana with reference to the Elder Sāriputta.

, This venerable elder, we are told, first heard the Dhamma from the lips of the Elder Assaji; and from the day when he attained the fruit of stream-entry, in whatever quarter he heard that the Elder Assaji was residing, in that direction he would salute reverently with hands together, in that direction he would turn his head when he lay down to sleep. The monks said to each other, "Elder Sāriputta holds false views; on this very day he is going about doing reverence to the cardinal points." And they reported the matter to the Tathāgata.

The Teacher caused the elder to be summoned before him and asked him, "Sāriputta, is the report true that you are going about doing reverence to the cardinal points?" – "Reverend sir, you know me, and you yourself know whether or not I am going about doing reverence to the cardinal points." Then said the Teacher, "Monks, Sāriputta is not doing reverence to the cardinal points. The fact is that he first heard the Dhamma from the lips of the Elder Assaji, and from the day when he attained the fruit of stream-entry, he has reverenced his own teacher. For a monk should reverence the teacher through whom he has learned the Dhamma with the same degree of reverence with which a brahmin reverences the sacred fire." So saying, he taught the Dhamma, pronouncing the following stanza:

> 392. From whomever one learns the Dhamma—
> The Teaching of the Perfect Buddha—
> Devoutly one should honour him
> As a brahmin does the sacred fire.

36. The Elder Attadattha

ONE'S OWN GOOD ONE SHOULD NOT NEGLECT.... This instruction was given by the Teacher while he was in residence at Jetavana with reference to the Elder Attadattha ("Own Good").

For when the Teacher was about to pass into Nibbāna, he said to his disciples, "Monks, four months from now I shall attain final Nibbāna." Thereupon seven hundred monks who had not yet attained the fruit of stream-entry were deeply moved, and never leaving the Teacher's side, whispered to each other, "Brethren, what are we to do?" But the Elder Attadattha thought to himself, "The Teacher says that four months from now he is to attain final Nibbāna. Now I have not yet freed myself from the power of the evil passions. Therefore so long as the Teacher yet remains alive, I will strive with all my might for the attainment of arahantship." Accordingly the Elder Attadattha no longer went with the monks.

Now the monks said to him, "Brother, why is it that you thus avoid our company and do not talk with us?" And conducting the Elder Attadattha to the Teacher, they laid the matter before him, saying, "Reverend sir, this elder does thus and so." The Teacher asked the Elder Attadattha, "Why do you act thus?" The elder replied, "Reverend sir, you have said that four months from now you are to attain final Nibbāna; and I have determined that so long as you yet remain alive, I will strive with all my might for the attainment of arahantship."

The Teacher applauded him for his wise decision and said to the monks, "Monks, whosoever sincerely loves me should be like the Elder Attadattha. For truly they honour me not who honour me only with perfumes and garlands. They only honour me who practise the Dhamma according to Dhamma. Therefore others also should follow the example of the Elder Attadattha." So saying, he pronounced the following stanza:

> 166. One's own good one should not neglect
> For another's good however great:
> Knowing well one's own good
> Be intent on one's own good.

37. The Elder Ānanda's Question

THE PERFUME OF FLOWERS GOES NOT AGAINST THE WIND.... This instruction was given by the Teacher while he was in residence at Sāvatthī by way of reply to a question which the Elder Ānanda asked him.

We are told that one evening, absorbed in meditation, the elder pondered the following thought: "The Exalted One receives the three perfumes of superlative excellence: namely, the perfume of sandal, the perfume of roots, and the perfume of flowers. Each of these perfumes, however, goes only with the wind. Is there possibly a substance whose perfume goes against the wind, or is there possibly a substance whose perfume goes both with the wind and against the wind?" Then the following thought occurred to him: "What is the use of my trying to determine this question all by myself? I will ask the Teacher, and the Teacher alone." Accordingly he approached the Teacher and put the question to him. Therefore it is said:[1]

Now one evening the Venerable Ānanda arose from profound meditation and drew near to the place where the Exalted One was sitting, and when he had drawn near, he addressed the Exalted One as follows: "Reverend sir, there are these three substances whose perfume goes only with the wind and not against the wind. What are the three? The perfume of roots, the perfume of sandal, and the perfume of flowers. These, reverend sir, are the three substances whose perfume goes only with the wind and not against the wind. But, reverend sir, is there possibly a substance whose perfume goes with the wind, against the wind, and both with and against the wind?"

Said the Exalted One in answer to the question, "Ānanda, there is a substance whose perfume goes with the wind, against the wind, and both with and against the wind." – "But, reverend sir, what is that substance whose perfume goes with the wind, against the wind, and both with and against the wind?" – "Ānanda, if in any village or market-town in this world any human being, whether man or woman, seeks refuge in the Buddha, seeks refuge in the

---

1. The following is taken from Aṅguttara Nikāya 3:79.

Dhamma, seeks refuge in the Order; if they refrain from killing living beings, from taking that which is not given, from wrong conduct in sexual relations, and from lying, and avoid occasions of carelessness through the use of liquor or spirits or other intoxicants; if they are virtuous, if they live the life of a householder in righteousness, with a heart free from the stain of avarice, if they are liberal and generous, if they are open-handed, if they take delight in giving, if they are attentive to petitions, if they delight in the distribution of alms, in all parts of the world monks and brahmins utter their praise. If in such and such a village or market-town either a man or a woman seeks refuge in the Buddha ... if they take delight in the distribution of alms, deities and spirits utter their praise. If in such and such a village or market-town either a man or a woman seeks refuge in the Buddha ... if they take delight in the distribution of alms, such acts as these, Ānanda, are the substance whose perfume goes with the wind, whose perfume goes against the wind, whose perfume goes both with and against the wind." So saying, he pronounced the following stanzas:

54. The perfume of flowers goes not against the wind,
     Neither that of sandalwood, jasmine or *tagara*;
     But the perfume of the virtuous goes against the wind,
     The good person suffuses all directions.

55. Sandalwood or tagara,
     Lotus or the jasmine great—
     Of these various kinds of perfume
     Virtue's perfume is unexcelled.

38. Angry Bhāradvāja

ANGERLESS DOES HE ENDURE ABUSE.... This instruction was given by the Teacher while he was in residence at Veḷuvana with reference to Akkosa Bhāradvāja.[1]

For Akkosa Bhāradvāja had a brother named Bhāradvāja, whose wife, named Dhānañjānī, had attained the fruit of stream-entry. Whenever she sneezed or coughed or stumbled, she would breathe forth the solemn utterance, "Homage to the Exalted One, All-Worthy, Perfectly Enlightened!" One day, while distribution of food to brahmins was in progress, she stumbled, and immediately breathed forth that solemn utterance as usual with a loud voice.

The brahmin Bhāradvāja was greatly angered[2] and said to himself, "No matter where it may be, whenever this vile woman stumbles, she utters the praise of this shaveling monkling in this fashion." And he said to his wife, "Now, vile woman, I will go and worst that teacher of yours in an argument." She replied, "By all means go, brahmin; I have never seen the man who could worst the Exalted One in an argument. Nevertheless, go ask the Exalted One a question." The brahmin went to the Teacher, and without even saluting him, stood on one side and asked him a question, pronouncing the following stanza:

"What must one slay to live at ease?
What must one slay to grieve no more?
Of what one thing do you approve
The killing?—tell us, Gotama!"[3]

In answer, the Teacher pronounced the following stanza:

"To live at ease, anger must be slain.
With anger slain, one grieves no more.
Of anger with its poisoned root
And honeyed climax, brāhmaṇa,

---

1. This story combines Saṃyutta Nikāya 7:1 and 7:2.

2. Because all his brahmin guests were scandalized by the wife's praising   the Buddha and got up and left without touching the food, which perhaps they thought was ritually impure.

3. The brahmin may have wanted the Buddha to approve of ritual sacrifice.

161

The noble ones praise killing it:
When it is slain, one grieves no more.

Having serene confidence in the Teacher, the brahmin went forth and attained arahantship.

Now his younger brother, who was called Akkosa Bhāradvāja, heard the report, "Your brother has gone forth," and greatly angered, he went and abused the Teacher with wicked, ugly words. But the Teacher subdued him by employing the illustration of food given to guests: ["Do you sometimes have guests, brahmin?" – "Yes, Master Gotama, I sometimes do." – "Do you entertain them with various kinds of food?" – "Yes, I do." – "Now, if they do not accept your food, to whom does it then belong?" – "If they do not accept it, it again belongs to us." – "In the same way, brahmin, those words of scolding and abuse which you gave us, we do not accept; hence, brahmin, they belong to you."[4]]

Thereupon this brahmin too gained serene confidence in the Teacher, went forth and attained arahantship. Likewise Akkosa Bhāradvāja's two younger brothers, Sundari Bhāradvāja and Bilañjika Bhāradvāja, abused the Teacher, but the Teacher subdued them, and they too went forth and attained arahantship.

One day in the Hall of Truth the monks began the following discussion: "How wonderful are the virtues of the Buddhas! Although these four brothers abused the Teacher, the Teacher, without so much as saying a word, became their refuge." At that moment the Teacher drew near. "Monks," said he, "What is the subject that engages your attention now as you sit here all gathered together?" – "Such and such," replied the monks. Then said the Teacher, "Monks, because I possess the power of patience, because I am without defilements among those who are defiled, therefore I am truly the refuge of the multitude." So saying he pronounced the following stanza:

399. Angerless does he endure abuse,
Beating and imprisonment,
Patience his power and armed might—
That one I call a brāhmaṇa.

---

4. The bracketed passage is added from Saṃyutta Nikāya 7:2.

39. Patience Subdues Violence

ONE SHOULD NOT STRIKE A BRĀHMAŅA.... This instruction was given by the Teacher while he was in residence at Jetavana with reference to the Elder Sāriputta.

The story goes that once upon a time several men gathered together at a certain place and extolled the noble qualities of the elder, saying, "Oh, our noble master is endowed with patience to such a degree that even when men abuse him and strike him, he never gets the least bit angry!" Thereupon a certain brahmin who held false views asked, "Who is this that never gets angry?" – "Our elder." – "It must be that nobody ever provoked him to anger." – "That is not the case, brahmin." – "Well then, I will provoke him to anger." – "Provoke him to anger if you can!" – "Trust me," said the brahmin, "I know just what to do to him."

Just then the elder entered the city for alms. When the brahmin saw him, he stepped up behind him and struck him a tremendous blow with his staff on the back. "What was that?" said the elder, and without so much as turning around to look, continued on his way. The fire of remorse sprang up within every part of the brahmin's body. "Oh, how noble are the qualities with which the elder is endowed!" exclaimed the brahmin. And prostrating himself at the elder's feet, he said, "Pardon me, reverend sir." – "What do you mean?" asked the elder. "I wanted to try your patience and struck you." – "Very well, I pardon you." – "If, reverend sir, you are willing to pardon me, hereafter sit and receive your food only in my house." So saying, the brahmin took the elder's bowl, the elder yielding it willingly. The brahmin conducted him to his house and served him with food.

The bystanders were filled with anger. "This fellow," said they, "struck with his staff our noble elder, who is free from all offence; he must not be allowed to get away. We will kill him right here and now." And taking clods of earth and sticks and stones into their hands, they stood waiting at the door of the brahmin's house. As the elder rose from his seat to go, he placed his bowl in the hands of the brahmin. When the bystanders saw the brahmin going out with the elder, they said, "Reverend sir, order this brahmin

163

who has taken your bowl to turn back." – "What do you mean, lay disciples?" – "That brahmin struck you and we are going to treat him in as he deserves." – "What do you mean? Did he strike you or me?" – "You, reverend sir." – "If he struck me, he begged my pardon; go your way." So saying, he dismissed the bystanders, and permitting the brahmin to turn back, the elder went back again to the monastery.

The monks were highly offended. "What sort of thing is this!" they exclaimed. "A brahmin struck the Elder Sāriputta a blow, and the elder straightaway went back to the house of the very brahmin who struck him and accepted food at his hands! From the moment he struck the elder, for whom will he any longer have any respect? He will go about pounding everybody right and left." At that moment the Teacher drew near. "Monks," said he, "what is the subject that engages your attention now as you sit here all gathered together?" – "This was the subject we were discussing." Said the Teacher, "Monks, no brahmin ever strikes another brahmin;[1] it must have been a householder-brahmin who struck a monk-brahmin; for when a man attains the fruit of the third path, all anger is utterly destroyed in him." So saying, he expounded the Dhamma, pronouncing the following stanzas:

389. One should not strike a brāhmaṇa,
     Nor for that should he react.
     Shame on one who hits a brāhmaṇa,
     More shame on him should he react!

390. Nothing is better for the brāhmana
     Than restraining the mind from what is dear.
     When he turns away from the wish to harm
     Just thus does his suffering subside.

---

1. Note the play on the word "brahmin" again.

40. Sirimā

Behold this ornamented image.... This instruction was given by the Teacher while he was in residence at Veḷuvana with reference to Sirimā.

Sirimā, the story goes, was a very beautiful courtesan of Rājagaha who had, during a certain rainy season, offended against the female lay disciple Uttarā, wife of the treasurer's son Sumana and daughter of the treasurer Puṇṇaka. Desiring to be on good terms with her again, she went to her house when the Teacher and the Order of Monks were within, and after the Teacher had finished his meal, asked him for pardon. Now on that day the Master pronounced within the hearing of Sirimā the following words of rejoicing with the merits of the donors:

> 223. Conquer anger by non-anger;
> Conquer the evil with good;
> By giving conquer the miserly:
> By truth conquer the liar.

At the conclusion of the stanza Sirimā obtained the fruit of stream-entry. (This is a brief synopsis of the story; as for the complete story, it will be found related at length in the commentary on this stanza in the Chapter on Anger.)

Having thus attained the fruit of stream-entry, Sirimā invited the Master to be her guest, and on the following day presented rich offerings. From that time on she gave regularly eight food-tickets and from that time on eight monks came regularly to her house. "Accept ghee, accept milk," she would say, filling their bowls. What she gave to one monk would have sufficed for three or four; every day sixteen pieces of money were expended on the alms which were presented to the monks who visited her house.

Now one day a certain monk who had eaten the eight ticket-foods in her house went on a journey of three leagues and stopped at a certain monastery. In the evening, as he sat in the monastery, the monks asked him, "Friend, where did you obtain food just before you came here?" – "I have just eaten Sirimā's eight ticket-foods." – "Is the food which she gives pleasing to the taste, friend?"

– "It is impossible to describe her food; it is the choicest of choice food that she gives, and a single portion would suffice even for three or four. But good as her food is, she herself is still more pleasing to look upon; such and such are the marks of beauty which she possesses." Thus did the monk describe her marks of beauty.

A certain monk heard the visiting monk describe her marks of beauty, and in spite of the fact that he had never seen her, nevertheless fell in love with her. He said to himself, "I ought to go and see her." So having declared his seniority,[1] he asked the visiting monk some questions. The visiting monk replied, "Tomorrow, friend, stand at that house, and being the most senior in the Order there, you will receive the eight ticket-foods." The monk immediately took bowl and robe and went out. Early in the morning, as the dawn rose, he entered the ticket-hall, and being the most senior in the Order there, received the eight ticket-foods in the woman's house.

Now it so happened that on the day before, just as the last monk who had received food in her house went out, the female lay disciple became afflicted with a disease, and therefore removed her jewellery and lay down. When the monks came to receive the eight ticket-foods, her female slaves, seeing them, informed their mistress. Since she was unable to take their bowls in her own hands, provide them with seats, and wait upon them, she gave orders to her slaves, saying, "Women, take the bowls and provide the noble monks with seats; give them broth to drink and hard food to eat. When it is time to present boiled rice, fill their bowls and give them to the monks."

"Very well, noble lady," replied the slaves. So they invited the monks within, gave them broth to drink and hard food to eat, and when it was time to present boiled rice, they filled their bowls and gave them to the monks. When they had done so, they went and informed their mistress. She said, "Take me and carry me with you, that I may pay my respects to the noble monks." So they took her and carried her with them; and when they brought her into the presence of the monks, she paid obeisance to them, her body all of a tremble.

---

1. So that the visiting monk could know that he could be the leader of the Sangha.

When that monk looked upon her, he thought to himself, "Even in sickness this woman possesses wonderful beauty. What manner of beauty must she not possess when she is well and strong and adorned with all her adornments?" Thereupon human passion, accumulated during many millions of years, arose within him. He became indifferent to all about him and was unable to take food. He took his bowl and went back to the monastery; covering his bowl, he put it away, and spreading out a corner of his robe he lay down. A certain monk who was a companion of his tried to persuade him to eat, but without success, for he absolutely refused to take food.

On that very day in the evening Sirimā died. Thereupon the king sent word to the Teacher, "Reverend sir, Jīvaka's youngest sister, Sirimā, is dead." When the Teacher received that message, he sent back the following message to the king, "Sirimā's body should not be burned. Have her body laid in the burning-ground, and set a watch that crows and dogs may not devour it." The king did so. Three days passed, one after another. On the fourth day the body began to bloat, and from the nine openings of her body, which were just like sores, there oozed forth maggots. Her whole body looked like a cracked vessel of boiled rice.

The king caused a drum to go through the city and the following proclamation to be made: "Let all approach to behold Sirimā. Except watchmen of houses, all who refuse to do so shall be fined eight pieces of money." And he sent the following message to the Teacher: "Let the Order of Monks presided over by the Buddha approach to behold Sirimā." The Teacher made proclamation to the monks, "Let us go forth to behold Sirimā."

Now that young monk had lain for four days without touching food, paying no attention to anything anyone said to him; the rice in his bowl had rotted, and his bowl was covered with mildew. The rest of the monks who were his fellows approached him and said to him, "Brother, the Teacher is going forth to behold Sirimā." When the young monk, lying thus, heard the name Sirimā, he leaped quickly to his feet. Someone said to him, "The Teacher is going forth to behold Sirimā; will you also go?" – "Indeed I will go," he replied. And tossing the rice out of his bowl, he washed it and put it in his sling and then set out with the company of monks.

The Teacher, surrounded by the Order of Monks, stood on one side of the corpse; the Order of Nuns and the king's retinue and the company of lay disciples, both male and female, stood on the other side of the corpse, each company in its proper place. The Teacher then asked the king, "Great king, who is this woman?" – "Reverend sir, it is Jīvaka's sister, Sirimā." – "Is this Sirimā?" – "Yes, reverend sir." – "Well! Send a drum through the town and make proclamation: 'Those who will pay a thousand pieces of money for Sirimā may have her.' " Not a man said "hem" or "hum." The king informed the Teacher, "They will not take her, reverend sir."

"Well then, great king, put the price down." So the king had a drum beaten and the following proclamation made: "If they will give five hundred pieces of money, they may have her." But nobody would take her at that price. The king then proclaimed to the beating of a drum that anyone might have her who would give two hundred and fifty pieces of money, or two hundred, or a hundred, or fifty, or twenty-five, or ten, or five. Finally he reduced the price to a penny, then to a halfpenny, then to a farthing, then to an eighth of a penny. At last he proclaimed to the beating of a drum, "They may have her for nothing." Not a man said "hem" or "hum."

Then said the king to the Teacher, "Reverend sir, no one will take her, even as a gift." The Teacher replied, "Monks, you see the value of a woman in the eyes of the multitude. In this very city men used to pay a thousand pieces of money for the privilege of spending one night with this woman. Now there is no one who will take her as a gift. Such was her beauty who now has perished and gone. Behold, monks, this body diseased and corrupt." So saying, he pronounced the following stanza:

147. Behold this ornamented image,
     A mass of sores, a congeries,
     Miserable, full of desires,
     Where nothing is stable, nothing persists.

The bhikkhu, hearing this, attained the fruit of stream-entry.

41. A Certain Monk

THE MIND IS VERY HARD TO SEE.... This instruction was given by the Teacher while he was in residence at Jetavana with reference to a certain discontented monk.

We are told that while the Teacher was in residence at Sāvatthī, a certain treasurer's son approached an elder who resorted to his house for alms and said to him, "Reverend sir, I desire to obtain release from suffering. Tell me some way by which I can obtain release from suffering." The elder replied, "Good indeed, friend. If you desire release from suffering, give ticket-food, give fortnightly food, give lodgings during the season of the rains, give bowls and robes and the other requisites. Divide your possessions into three parts: with one portion carry on your business; with another portion support son and wife; dispense the third portion on alms to support the Teaching of the Buddha."

"Very well, reverend sir," said the treasurer's son, and did all in the prescribed order. Having done all, he returned to the elder and asked him, "Reverend sir, is there anything else I ought to do?" – "Brother, take upon yourself the Three Refuges and the Five Precepts." The treasurer's son did so, and then asked whether there was anything else he ought to do. "Yes," replied the elder, "take upon yourself the Ten Precepts." – "Very well, reverend sir," said the treasurer's son, and took upon himself the Ten Precepts. Because the treasurer's son had in this manner performed works of merit, one after another (*anupubbena*), he came to be called Anupubba. Again he asked the elder, "Reverend sir, is there anything else I ought to do?" The elder replied, "Yes, become a monk." The treasurer's son immediately went forth.

Now he had a teacher who was versed in the Abhidhamma and a preceptor who was versed in the Vinaya. After he had obtained acceptance as a monk, whenever he approached his teacher, the latter repeated questions found in the Abhidhamma, "In the dispensation of the Buddha it accords with Dhamma to do this; it does not accord with Dhamma to do that." And whenever he approached his preceptor, the latter repeated questions found in the Vinaya, "In the dispensation of the Buddha it accords with

Dhamma to do this; it does not accord with Dhamma to do that; this is proper; this is improper." After a time he thought to himself, "Oh, what a wearisome task this is! I became a monk in order to obtain release from suffering, but here there is not even room for me to stretch out my hands. It is possible, however, to obtain release from suffering even if one lives the household life. I had best become a householder once more."

From that time forth, discontented and dissatisfied, he no longer rehearsed the thirty-two constituent parts of the body and received instruction. He became emaciated; his skin shrivelled up; veins stood out all over his body; weariness oppressed him, and his body was covered with scabs. The young novices asked him, "Friend, how is it that wherever you stand, wherever you sit, you are sick with jaundice, emaciated, shrivelled up, your body covered with scabs? What have you done?" – "Friends, I am discontented." – "Why?" He told them his story, and they told his teacher and his preceptor, and his teacher and his preceptor took him with them to the Teacher.

Said the Teacher, "Monks, why have you come?" – "Reverend sir, this monk is dissatisfied in your dispensation." – "Monk, is what they say true?" – "Yes, reverend sir." – "Why are you dissatisfied?" – "Reverend sir, I became a monk in order to obtain release from suffering. My teacher has recited passages from the Abhidhamma, and my preceptor has recited passages from the Vinaya. Reverend sir, I have come to the following conclusion: 'Here there is not even room for me to stretch out my hands. It is possible for me to obtain release from suffering as a householder. I will therefore become a householder.' "

"Monk, if you can guard one thing, it will not be necessary for you to guard the rest." – "What is that, reverend sir?" – "Can you guard your mind?" – "I can, reverend sir." – "Well then, guard your mind alone." Having given this admonition, the Teacher pronounced the following stanza:

> 36. The mind is very hard to see,
> Subtle, falling on what it wants;
> Let the wise man guard his mind,
> A guarded mind brings happiness.

42. The Monk from the Vajji People

HARD IS THE GOING FORTH…. This instruction was given by the Teacher while he was in residence at Mahāvana near Vesālī with reference to a certain Vajjian prince who became a monk. The story concerning him is as follows:[1]

A certain Vajjian prince who had become a monk took up his residence at Vesālī in a certain forest grove. It so happened that at that time there was a festival in progress at Vesālī which lasted through the night. When this monk heard the noise and tumult of the beating of drums and the playing of musical instruments at Vesālī, he wept and lamented, and uttered on that occasion the following stanza:

> Alone we reside in the forest
> Like a log thrown away in the wood.
> On such a night as this is,
> Who is worse off than we?

It appears that this monk had formerly been a prince in the kingdom of the Vajjians, and that when his turn came to rule, he renounced his kingdom and became a monk. On the night of the full moon of the month Kattikā, the entire city of Vesālī was decked with flags and banners, making it co-terminous with the realms of the Four Great Kings, and the festival began. As the festival continued through the night, he listened to the noise of the beating of drums and the striking of other musical instruments and the sound of the playing of lutes. When the seven thousand and seven hundred and seven princes of Vesālī, and a like number of young princes and commanders-in-chief, all dressed and adorned in festive array, entered the street for the purpose of taking part in the festivities, he himself walked through his great meditation walk sixty cubits long, beheld the moon poised in mid-heaven, stopped near the seat at the end of the meditation walk, and surveyed his own person, for lack of festive garments and adornments resembling a log of wood thrown away in the forest. And then and there he thought to himself, "Is there any one worse off than we?"

---

1. This story is an expanded version of Saṃyutta Nikāya 9:9.

Under ordinary circumstances he possessed the merits and virtues of a forest dweller, but on this occasion was oppressed with discontent, and therefore spoke thus. Thereupon the forest spirit who inhabited that forest grove formed the resolution, "I will stir up this monk," and uttered in reply the following stanza:

> Alone you reside in the forest
> Like a log thrown away in the wood.
> Many do envy you just as hell-dwellers
> Envy those who go to heaven.

The discontented monk heard this stanza, and on the following day approached the Teacher, saluted him, and sat down respectfully on one side. Aware of what had happened, and desiring to make plain the hardships of the household life, the Teacher summed up the five kinds of suffering in the following stanza:[2]

302. Hard is the going forth, hard to delight in;
    Hard and painful is household life;
    Painful is association with unequals;
    Painful is it to be a wanderer.
    Therefore do not be a wanderer,
    Do not be afflicted with pain.

The bhikkhu concerned was established in arahantship.

---

2. (1) It is hard to give up one's wealth and go forth. (2) It is hard to delight in the going forth because of the difficulties of the alms round for instance, or because one lives in remote places. (3) The suffering of household life is familiar to all who have experienced it. (4) "Unequals" among laymen means those coming from different social backgrounds, etc.; among monks, those holding different views. (5) Wandering in the round of birth and death (*saṃsāra*) is always painful.

Part VII

The Attainments of Monks

43. The Elder Nanda

EVEN AS RAIN PENETRATES A HOUSE BADLY THATCHED.... This instruction was given by the Teacher while he was in residence at Jetavana with reference to the Elder Nanda.[1]

Nanda Becomes a Monk in Spite of Himself

For after the Teacher had set in motion the glorious Wheel of Dhamma, he retired to Rājagaha and took up residence at Veḷuvana. Thereupon his father, the great king Suddhodana, sent ten ambassadors to him, one after the other, each with a retinue of a thousand men, saying to them, "Bring my son here and show him to me before my face." After nine ambassadors had gone there, attained arahantship, and failed to return, the Elder Kāḷudāyī went and attained arahantship. And knowing that it was the proper time for the Teacher to go, he described the beauties of the journey and conducted the Teacher with his retinue of twenty thousand arahants to Kapilapura. And there, in the company of his kinsfolk, the Teacher, taking a shower of rain for his text, related the Vessantara Jātaka (J 547). On the following day he entered the city for alms. By the recitation of the stanza, "Be alert! Do not be negligent!" (Dhp 168) he established his father in the fruit of stream-entry and by the recitation of the stanza: "Live by good and righteous conduct" (Dhp 169) he established Mahā Pajāpatī in the fruit of stream-entry and his father in the fruit of the second path. And at the end of the meal, with reference to the praise bestowed on him by the Mother of Rāhula, he related the Canda Kinnara Jātaka (J 485).

On the following day, while the ceremonies of Prince Nanda's sprinkling, housewarming, and marriage were in progress, the Teacher entered the house for alms, placed his bowl in Prince Nanda's hands, and told him the things that bring true blessings. Then rising from his seat, he departed without taking his bowl from the hands of the prince. Out of reverence for the Tathāgata, Prince Nanda did not dare say, "Reverend sir, receive your bowl,"

---

1. This story is an elaboration of Udāna III, 2.

but thought within himself, "He will take his bowl at the head of the stairs." But even when the Teacher reached the head of the stairs, he did not take his bowl. Thought Nanda, "He will take his bowl at the foot of the stairs." But the Teacher did not take his bowl even there. Thought Nanda, "He will take his bowl in the palace court." But the Teacher did not take his bowl even there. Prince Nanda desired greatly to return to his bride, and followed the Teacher much against his own will. But so great was his reverence for the Teacher that he did not dare say, "Receive your bowl," but continued to follow the Teacher, thinking to himself, "He will take his bowl here! He will take his bowl there! He will take his bowl there!"

At that moment they brought word to his bride Belle-of-the-Country, Janapada-Kalyāṇī, "My lady, the Exalted One has taken Prince Nanda away with him; it is his purpose to deprive you of him." Thereupon Janapada-Kalyāṇī, with tears streaming down her face and hair half-combed, ran after Prince Nanda as fast as she could and said to him, "Noble sir, please return immediately." Her words caused a quaver in Nanda's heart; but the Teacher, without so much as taking his bowl, led him to the monastery and said to him, "Nanda, would you like to become a monk?" So great was Prince Nanda's reverence for the Buddha that he refrained from saying, "I do not wish to become a monk," and said instead, "Yes, I should like to become a monk." Said the Teacher, "Well then, make a monk of Nanda." Thus it happened that on the third day after the Teacher's arrival at Kapilapura he caused Nanda to be made a monk.

On the seventh day the Mother of Rāhula adorned Prince Rāhula and sent him to the Exalted One, saying, "Dear son, go look upon this monk, possessed of a retinue of twenty thousand monks, possessed of a body of the hue of gold, possessed of the beauty of form of Mahā Brahmā. This monk is your father. To him once belonged great stores of treasure. From the time of his Great Renunciation we have not seen him. Ask him for your inheritance, saying, 'Dear father, I am a royal prince, and so soon as I shall receive the ceremonial sprinkling I shall become a Universal Monarch. I have need of wealth; bestow wealth upon me; for to a son belongs the wealth which formerly belonged to his father.' "

Accordingly Prince Rāhula went to the Exalted One. The moment he saw him he conceived a warm affection for his father, and his heart rejoiced within him. And he said, "Monk, pleasant is your shadow," and said much else befitting his own station. When the Exalted One had finished his meal, he pronounced the words of rejoicing, arose from his seat, and departed. Prince Rāhula followed in the footsteps of the Exalted One, saying, "Monk, give me my inheritance; monk, give me my inheritance." The Exalted One did not repel the prince; even the attendants were unable to prevent the prince from accompanying the Exalted One. In this manner the prince accompanied the Exalted One to the grove. Then the thought occurred to the Exalted One, "The paternal wealth which this youth seeks inevitably brings destruction in its train. Behold, I will bestow upon him the sevenfold noble wealth[2] which I received at the foot of the Bodhi Tree; I will make him master of a wealth which transcends the world."

Therefore the Exalted One addressed the Venerable Sāriputta, "Well then, Sāriputta, make a monk of Prince Rāhula." When, however, Prince Rāhula had gone forth into homelessness, the king, his grandfather, was afflicted with great sorrow. Unable to endure his sorrow, he made known his sorrow to the Exalted One and made the following request of him, "It would be good, reverend sir, that the noble monks do not give novice ordination to any youth without the permission of his mother and father." The Exalted One granted him this request. Again one day, as the Exalted One sat in the royal palace after breakfast, the king, sitting respectfully at one side, said to the Exalted One, "Reverend sir, while you were practising your austerities, a certain deity approached me and said to me, 'Your son is dead.' But I refused to believe him and replied, 'My son will not die until he attains Enlightenment.' " Said the Exalted One, "Now will you believe? In a previous existence also, when a brahmin showed you bones and said to you, 'Your son is dead,' you refused to believe." And with reference to this incident he related the Mahā Dhammapāla Jātaka (J 447). At the conclusion of the story the king was established in the fruit of the third path.

---

2. These seven are: faith, virtue, shame (of evil-doing), fear (of the consequences), learning, generosity, wisdom.

Nanda and the Celestial Nymphs

When the Exalted One had thus established his father in the three fruits, he returned once more to Rājagaha, accompanied by the Order of Monks. Now he had promised Anāthapiṇḍika to visit Sāvatthī as soon as the great monastery of Jetavana should be completed, and receiving word shortly afterwards that the monastery had been completed, he went to Jetavana and took up his residence there. While the Teacher was thus residing at Jetavana, the Venerable Nanda, becoming discontented, told his troubles to the monks, saying, "Brethren, I am dissatisfied. I am now living the holy life, but I cannot endure to live it any longer. I intend to abandon the training and to return to the lower life, the life of a layman."

The Exalted One, hearing of this incident, sent for the Venerable Nanda and said this to him, "Nanda, is the report true that you spoke as follows to a large company of monks, 'Brethren, I am dissatisfied; I am now living the holy life, but I cannot endure to live it any longer; I intend to abandon the training and to return to the lower life, the life of a layman'?" – "It is quite true, reverend sir." – "But, Nanda, why are you dissatisfied with the holy life? Why cannot you endure to live the holy life any longer? Why do you intend to abandon the higher precepts and to return to the lower life, the life of a layman?" – "Reverend sir, when I left my house, my noble bride Janapada-Kalyāṇī, with hair half-combed, took leave of me, saying, 'Noble sir, please return immediately!' Reverend sir, it is because I keep remembering her that I am dissatisfied with the holy life; that I cannot endure to live the holy life any longer; that I intend to abandon the training and to return to the lower life, the life of a layman."

Then the Exalted One took the Venerable Nanda by the arm, and by supernormal power conducted him to the heaven of the Thirty-three. On the way, the Exalted One pointed out to Nanda, in a certain burnt field, seated on a burnt stump, a greedy monkey which had lost her ears and nose and tail in a fire. When they reached the heaven of the Thirty-three, he pointed out five hundred pink-footed celestial nymphs who came to wait upon Sakka, king of the gods. And when the Exalted One had shown the Venerable Nanda these two sights, he asked him this question: "Nanda, which do you regard as being the more beautiful and fair to look upon and handsome, your noble bride Janapada-Kalyāṇī or these five hundred pink-footed celestial nymphs?"

"Reverend sir," replied Nanda, "as far inferior as this greedy monkey which has lost her ears and nose and tail is to Janapada-Kalyāṇī, so is she to these five hundred pink-footed celestial nymphs. In comparison with these nymphs my noble bride does not count; she does not come within a fraction of them; she does not come within a fraction of a fraction of them; on the contrary, these five hundred pink-footed celestial nymphs are infinitely more beautiful and fair to look upon and handsome."

"Cheer up, Nanda!" replied the Exalted One. "I guarantee that you will win these five hundred pink-footed celestial nymphs." Said Venerable Nanda, "If, reverend sir, the Exalted One guarantees that I shall win these five hundred pink-footed celestial nymphs, in that case, reverend sir, I shall take the greatest pleasure in living the exalted life of a monk." Then the Exalted One, taking Nanda with him, disappeared from the heaven of the Thirty-three and reappeared at Jetavana. Now it was not long before the monks heard the following report: "It appears that it is in the hope of winning celestial nymphs that the Venerable Nanda, half-brother of the Exalted One, son of his mother's sister, is living the holy life; it appears that the Exalted One has guaranteed that he shall win five hundred pink-footed celestial nymphs."

As a result the Venerable Nanda's fellow-monks treated him as a hireling and as one bought with a price. And they addressed him accordingly, saying, "It appears that the Venerable Nanda is a hireling; it appears that the Venerable Nanda is one bought with a price. It appears that it is in the hope of winning celestial nymphs that he is living the religious life; it appears that the Exalted One has guaranteed that he shall win five hundred pink-footed celestial nymphs."

Now although his fellow-monks despised him, were ashamed of him, and tormented him by calling him "hireling" and "bought with a price," the Venerable Nanda, living in solitude, withdrawn from the world, heedful, ardent, and resolute, in no long time, even in this life, arrived at the knowledge, realization, and attainment of that supreme goal of the religious life for the sake of which good youths retire once and for all from the household life to the homeless life. This did he know: "Birth is at an end, lived is the holy life, done is what should be done; there is no more of this to come." And there was yet another venerable elder numbered among the arahants.

Now a certain deity came by night to the Teacher, illuminating the whole Jetavana; and bowing to the Teacher, he thus addressed him, "Reverend sir, the Venerable Nanda, son of the sister of the mother of the Exalted One, by extinction of the taints, even in this life himself abides in the knowledge, realization, and attainment of freedom from the taints, emancipation of the heart, emancipation by wisdom." And there arose within the Exalted One also knowledge of the following: "By extinction of the taints, Nanda, even in this life, himself abides in the knowledge, realization, and attainment of freedom from the taints, emancipation of the heart, emancipation by wisdom."

At the end of the same night the Venerable Nanda also approached the Exalted One, bowed to him, and spoke as follows, "Reverend sir, I release the Exalted One from the promise which he made when he guaranteed that I should win five hundred pink-footed celestial nymphs." The Exalted One replied, "Nanda, I myself grasped your mind with my own mind and saw, 'By extinction of the taints, Nanda, even in this life, himself abides in the knowledge, realization, and attainment of freedom from the taints, emancipation of the heart, emancipation by wisdom.' Likewise a deity informed me of the fact, saying, 'By extinction of the taints, Nanda, even in this life, himself abides in the knowledge, realization, and attainment of freedom from the taints, emancipation of the heart, emancipation by wisdom.' When, therefore, Nanda, you ceased to cling to the things of the world, and your heart was released from the taints, at that moment I was released from that promise." Then the Exalted One, knowing the meaning of this matter, three times spoke this solemn utterance:

"He that has crossed the mud and crushed lust's thorn,
Attained delusion's end, is unmoved in ease or pain."

Now one day the monks approached the Venerable Nanda and asked him, "Friend Nanda, earlier you said, 'I am dissatisfied.' Do you say the same thing now?" – "Brethren, I am in no way inclined to the life of a layman." When the monks heard his answer, they said "Venerable Nanda says that which is not true, utters falsehood. On former days he used to say, 'I am dissatisfied,' but now he says, 'I am in no way inclined to the life of a layman.'" And at once they went and reported the matter to the Exalted One. The Exalted One replied, "Monks, in former days Nanda's personality was like an ill-thatched house, but now it has come to be like a well-thatched house. From the day he saw the celestial nymphs, he has striven to reach the goal of a monk's practice, and now he has reached it." So saying, he pronounced the following stanzas:

13. Even as rain penetrates
    A house badly thatched,
    So likewise lust penetrates
    An uncultivated mind.

14. As rain does not penetrate
    A house well thatched,
    So lust does not penetrate
    A well-cultivated mind.

44. A Certain Monk

HAVING RENOUNCED ALL FORCE.... This instruction was given by the Teacher while he was in residence at Jetavana with reference to a certain monk.

It appears that this monk, upon receiving a subject of meditation from the Teacher, retired to the forest, applied himself diligently to the practice of meditation, and attained arahantship. Thereupon he said to himself, "I will inform the Teacher of the great blessing which I have received," and set out from the forest.

Now a woman living in a certain village through which he passed had just had a quarrel with her husband, and as soon as her husband was out of the house, said to herself, "I will return to the house of my family." So saying, she set out on the road. As she went along the road, she saw the elder. "I'll keep not far from this elder," she thought, and followed close behind him. The elder never looked at her at all.

When her husband returned home and saw his wife nowhere about the house, he concluded to himself, "She must have gone to the village where her family lives," and followed after her. When he saw her, he thought to himself, "It cannot be that this woman would enter this forest all by herself; in whose company is she going?" All of a sudden he saw the elder. He thought, "This monk must have taken her away with him," and went up to the monk and threatened him. Said the woman, "This good monk never so much as looked at me or spoke to me; do not say anything to him." Her husband replied, "Do you mean to tell me that you took yourself off in this fashion? I will treat him as you alone deserve to be treated." And in a burst of rage, out of hatred for the woman, he beat the elder soundly, and having done so, took the woman with him and returned home.

The elder's whole body was covered with weals. After his return to the monastery the monks who massaged his body noticed the weals and asked him, "What does this mean?" He told them the whole story. Then the monks asked him, "Friend, but when this fellow struck you thus, what did you say? Did you get angry?"

"No, friends, I did not get angry." Thereupon the monks went to the Teacher and reported the matter to him, saying, "Reverend sir, when we asked this monk, 'Did you get angry?' he replied, 'No, friends. I did not get angry.' He does not speak the truth, he utters falsehood." The Teacher listened to what they had to say and then replied, "Monks, those who have rid themselves of the defilements have laid aside force; even for those that strike them, they cherish no anger." So saying, he pronounced the following stanza:

> 405. Having renounced all force
> Against creatures weak and strong,
> Who causes not to kill nor kills—
> That one I call a brāhmaṇa.

45. The Elder Cūḷa Panthaka

BY ENERGY AND HEEDFULNESS.... This instruction was given by the Teacher while he was in residence at Veḷuvana with reference to Cūḷa Panthaka, Little Wayman the Elder.

The Birth of Cūḷa Panthaka

We are told that the daughter of a rich merchant of Rājagaha, upon reaching the age of maturity, was provided by her mother and father with quarters on the topmost floor of a seven-storied palace and guarded with excessive care. But in spite of this, maddened with the madness of youth and lusting for a man, she had intercourse with her own slave. Frightened to think that others also might find out about her misconduct, she said to him, "It is out of the question for us to live here any longer. If my mother and father discover my misconduct, they will tear me limb from limb. Let us go live elsewhere."

So taking a few necessary things they could carry in the hand, they left the house by the principal door. "It matters little," said they, "where we go, so long as we go and live where others will know nothing about us." So saying, the two set out together. They took up their residence in a certain place and lived together, with the result that the young wife conceived a child in her womb. When her unborn child reached maturity, she took counsel with her husband, saying, "If I give birth to my child in a place far removed from my family, it will bring suffering to both of us. There is but one place for us to go, and that is home to my parents." But her husband, fearing that if he himself went there he would be killed, kept postponing the day of their departure, saying, "We will go today; we will go tomorrow."

The wife thought to herself, "This simpleton realizes the enormity of his offense and therefore dares not go. After all, a mother and a father are one's best friends. Let this fellow go or not; at any rate I intend to go." So while her husband was out of the house, she put the household utensils away, and informing her next-door neighbours that she was going home to her parents, she started out

184

on the road. When her husband returned to the house and failed to see her, he inquired of the neighbours where she had gone. Hearing that she had gone to her parents, he set out after her as fast as he could and overtook her on the road. And right there she gave birth to her child. "What is it, wife?" asked the husband. "Husband, it is a son." – "What shall we do now?" – "That for which we intended to go home to my parents has happened by the way. Why, therefore, should we go there? Let us return to our own home."

Agreeing that this was the best plan, husband and wife returned to their own home. Since their son had been born by the way, they gave him the name Panthaka, Wayman. In no long time the young wife conceived a second child in her womb. (All is to be related in detail precisely as before.) Since this child also was born by the way, they gave him the name Cūla Panthaka, Little Wayman, calling the older son Mahā Panthaka, Big Wayman. Taking their two sons, they returned to their own place of residence.

While they were living there, Mahā Panthaka heard other boys speak of their uncles and grandparents. So one day he asked his mother, "Mother, other boys speak of their grandfather and grandmother. Haven't we any relatives?" – "Yes, my son. You have no relatives living here, but you have a grandfather, a rich merchant, living in Rājagaha, and we have many other relatives living there too." – "Why don't we go there, mother?" The mother evaded telling her son why she did not go there. But the children repeated the question time and again. Finally she said to her husband, "These children weary me excessively. Will my mother and father eat us alive when they see us? Come, why not let the children see the family of their grandparents?" – "I should not dare meet them face to face, but I will escort you there." – "Very well; some means must be found by which the children can see their grandparents."

So mother and father took the children, and arriving at Rājagaha in due course, took up their residence in the hall of a certain woman near the gate of the city. Then the mother of the children sent word to her mother and father that she and her children had arrived. When her parents received this message, they said to each other, "As we have passed through the round of existences, perhaps we have not previously had a son or a daughter; but these two have grievously offended against us, and it is out of the question for them to stand in our sight. Let these two take as much money

185

as they need and go and live in some pleasant place. However, let them send the children here." So the two took the money which was sent to them, and giving their children into the hands of the messengers who came, sent them to their grandparents. Thus it happened that the children were brought up in the home of their grandparents.

Of the two children, Cūla Panthaka was still very young. Mahā Panthaka, however, used to accompany his grandfather to hear the Buddha teach the Dhamma. And as the result of his frequent visits to the Teacher, his heart inclined to going forth. Accordingly he said to his grandfather, "If you would give me your permission, I should like to go forth as a monk."

"What did you say, dear grandson? There is no one in the whole world whose going forth would give me so much pleasure as your own. If you are able to do so, by all means go forth."

Cūla Panthaka as a Monk

Accordingly the grandfather took Mahā Panthaka to the Teacher, who said, "Householder, you have got a boy?"

"Yes, reverend sir, this is a grandson of mine who desires to become a monk under you." The Teacher asked a certain monk to ordain the boy as a novice. The elder assigned to him as a subject of meditation the first five of the constituent parts of the body, and then ordained him. The youth learnt by heart a considerable portion of the Word of the Buddha, kept residence during the season of the rains, obtained acceptance as a monk, and by diligently applying himself to meditation attained arahantship.

As Mahā Panthaka passed his time in the bliss of deep meditation, in the bliss of the fruit of the path, he thought to himself, "Assuredly it is in the power of Cūla Panthaka to experience this same bliss." Therefore he went to the treasurer his grandfather and said to him, "Great treasurer, if you will give your kind permission, I should like to let Cūla Panthaka go forth as a monk."

"By all means let him go forth, reverend sir." We are told that the treasurer was profoundly attached to the dispensation of the Buddha, and that when asked, "Of which daughter of yours are these two children the sons?" he felt ashamed to say, "Of my daughter who ran away," and that for these two reasons he was only too glad to give them permission to go forth as monks.

So the Elder Mahā Panthaka let his brother Cūḷa Panthaka go forth and established him in the precepts. But Cūḷa Panthaka, when he had gone forth, proved a dullard. Indeed in four months he was unable to learn by heart this single stanza:

> Even as the red lotus sweetly scented
> Appears in the morn full blown, replete with scent,
> Behold the Buddha, Angīrasa, resplendent
> Blazing like the sun in the sky.

It seems that in the dispensation of the Buddha Kassapa he had possessed great wisdom, but that, after entering the religious life, he ridiculed and made fun of a certain monk who was a dullard while the latter was trying to learn the Sacred Word; and that this monk, embarrassed by the ridicule to which he was subjected, was unable either to learn the passage by heart or even to repeat it. As the result of that act, Cūḷa Panthaka was reborn as a dullard, and every sentence he learned put the preceding sentence out of his mind; indeed four months passed while he was striving to learn this one stanza.

Thereupon Mahā Panthaka said to his brother, "Cūḷa Panthaka, it is not in your power to master this religion. In four months you have not been able to learn a single stanza. How can you ever hope to reach the goal of the religious life? Leave the monastery at once." So saying he expelled him. But Cūḷa Panthaka was sincerely attached to the dispensation of the Buddha, and the last thing in the world he wished to do was to leave the Order and return to the life of a householder.

Now at that time Jīvaka Komārabhacca, taking an abundant supply of garlands and of various kinds of perfumes, went to his own mango grove, rendered honour to the Teacher, listened to the Dhamma, and then rising from his seat and paying obeisance to the Teacher, approached Mahā Panthaka, who was steward of the Order, and asked him, "Reverend sir, how many monks are living with the Teacher?" – "Five hundred." – "Tomorrow, reverend sir, bring the five hundred monks presided over by the Buddha and take a meal in our house." – "Lay disciple, the bhikkhu Cūḷa Panthaka is a dullard and has made no progress in the Dhamma. I accept the invitation for all except him."

When Cūḷa Panthaka heard that, he thought to himself, "The elder accepts an invitation for all these monks, but in accepting it, deliberately leaves me out. Beyond a doubt my brother's affection for me is gone. Of what profit to me any longer is this religion? I will return to the life of a householder and spend my days giving alms and doing other works of merit." So on the following day, very early in the morning, he set out with the intention of returning to the life of a householder. Very early in the morning also the Teacher surveyed the world, and seeing this incident, preceded Cūḷa Panthaka to the gate and walked back and forth on the same road Cūḷa Panthaka would take.

As Cūḷa Panthaka came along, he saw the Teacher, and approaching him, paid obeisance to him. Said the Teacher, "But, Cūḷa Panthaka, where are you going at this hour of the day?" – "Reverend sir, my brother has expelled me, and therefore I intend to return to the householder's life." – "Cūḷa Panthaka, it was at my hands that you went forth. Therefore when your brother expelled you, why did you not come to me? Come now, what have you to do with the life of a householder? You shall remain with me." So saying, the Teacher stroked him on the head with his hand, the palm of which was marked with the wheel, and taking him with him, went and seated him over against the Perfumed Chamber. And creating by his supernormal power a perfectly clean cloth, he gave it to him, saying, "Cūḷa Panthaka, remain right here, face towards the east, rub this cloth, and say as you do so, 'Dirt-remover! Dirt-remover!'" Just then meal-time was announced, whereupon the Teacher, accompanied by the Order of Monks, went to the house of Jīvaka and sat down on the seat prepared for him.

Cūḷa Panthaka sat down, facing the sun, and rubbed the cloth, saying as he did so, "Dirt-remover! Dirt-remover!" As he rubbed the piece of cloth, it became soiled. Thereupon he thought, "This piece of cloth was perfectly clean before. But through this body of mine it has lost its original character and has become soiled. Impermanent, indeed, are all conditioned things!" And grasping the thought of decay and death, he developed insight. The Teacher, knowing that Cūḷa Panthaka's mind had attained insight, said, "Cūḷa Panthaka, think not that only a piece of cloth has become soiled and dyed with impurity. Indeed within you are lust, impurity, and other defilements; remove them." And sending forth a luminous image of himself, the Teacher, sitting before him, present in bodily form as it were, pronounced the following stanzas:

"Lust, not dust, is dirt truly called,
To lust is the term 'dirt' truly given;
Having abandoned this dirt, O monks,
Live in the Teaching of one free from dirt.

Hate, not dust, is dirt truly called,
To hate is the term 'dirt' truly given;
Having abandoned this dirt, O monks,
Live in the Teaching of one free from dirt.

Delusion, not dust, is dirt truly called,
To delusion is the term 'dirt' truly given;
Having abandoned this dirt, O monks,
Live in the Teaching of one free from dirt."

At the conclusion of the stanzas, Cūḷa Panthaka attained arahantship together with the supernormal powers, and with the analytical knowledges also a knowledge of the Tipiṭaka.[1]

It appears that in a previous state of existence he had been a king. Once, while making a ceremonial circuit of the city, with sweat pouring down his forehead, he wiped his forehead with a clean cloth, whereupon the cloth became soiled. Thought he: "By reason of this body of mine a cloth so clean as this has lost its former character and become soiled. Impermanent, indeed, are all conditioned things!" Thus did he acquire the concept of impermanence. In consequence of this, in a later existence, a "dirt-remover" became his salvation.

Jīvaka Komārabhacca offered water of donation to the Buddha. The Teacher, covering the bowl with his hand, said, "Jīvaka, are there no monks in the monastery?" Mahā Panthaka replied, "No, reverend sir, there are no monks in the monastery." Said the Teacher, "But, Jīvaka, there are!"

"Very well," said Jīvaka, and sent a man to find out. Said he, "Go to the monastery and find out whether or not there are any

---

1. The supernormal powers (*iddhi*) include such powers as the ability to become invisible, to walk on water, to fly through the sky, etc. The Tipiṭaka is the collection of Buddhist scriptures consisting of the three "baskets": Vinaya, Suttanta, and Abhidhamma.

monks there." At that moment Cūḷa Panthaka said to himself, "My brother says, 'There are no monks in the monastery.' I will show him that there are monks in the monastery." And forthwith he filled the whole mango grove with monks. Some of them were making robes, others were dyeing robes, others were repeating the sacred texts. Thus did Cūḷa Panthaka create by supernormal power a thousand monks, each different from every other. So when Jīvaka's messenger saw the numerous monks, he returned and told Jīvaka, "Noble sir, the entire mango grove is full of monks." And right there the Elder Cūḷa Panthaka did as follows:

> Panthaka, multiplying himself a thousandfold,
> Sat in the charming mango grove until he was sent for.

The Teacher said to the man, "Go to the monastery and say, 'The Teacher summons Cūḷa Panthaka.' " The man went and said what he was told to say. Thereupon the cry went up from a thousand throats, "I am Cūḷa Panthaka! I am Cūḷa Panthaka!" The man returned and said, "Reverend sir, they all say they are Cūḷa Panthaka." Said the Teacher, "Well then, go and take by the hand the first monk that says, 'I am Cūḷa Panthaka,' and the rest will disappear." The man did so. Immediately the thousand monks disappeared. The Elder Cūḷa Panthaka returned with the man who came for him.

At the end of the meal the Teacher addressed Jīvaka, "Jīvaka take Cūḷa Panthaka's bowl, and he will pronounce the words of thanksgiving for you." Jīvaka took his bowl. The Elder Cūḷa Panthaka, like a young lion roaring a lion's roar, pronounced the words of thanksgiving, ranging through the whole of the Tipiṭaka. The Teacher arose from his seat, and surrounded by the Order of Monks, went to the monastery. After the monks had shown the Teacher the customary attentions, the Teacher, in front of the Perfumed Chamber, admonished the Order of Monks with an admonition of the Happy One, assigned a subject of meditation, dismissed the Order of Monks, and entered the Perfumed Chamber.

One day in the Hall of Truth the monks began a discussion: "Friends, in four months Cūḷa Panthaka was unable to learn by heart a stanza of four verses; but because he never relaxed his effort he became established in arahantship and has just now become master of the family of Dhamma transcending all worlds."

The Teacher came in and asked, "Monks, what is it that you are sitting here now talking about?" When they told him, he said, "Monks, a monk of roused up effort in my Teaching cannot fail to make himself master of the Dhamma that transcends all worlds." So saying, he pronounced the following stanza:

25. By energy and heedfulness,
     By taming and by self-control,
     The wise man should make an isle
     That no flood can overwhelm.

46. Two Fellow-monks

THOUGH OFTEN HE RECITE THE SACRED TEXTS.... This instruction was given by the Teacher while he was in residence at Jetavana with reference to two fellow-monks.

For at Sāvatthī lived two men of good families who were inseparable friends. On a certain occasion they went to the monastery, heard the Teacher teach the Dhamma, renounced the pleasures of the world, gave their hearts to the dispensation of the Buddha, and went forth. When they had kept residence for five years with preceptors and teachers, they approached the Teacher and asked about the duties in his religion. After listening to a detailed description of the duty of meditation and the duty of study, one of them said, "Reverend sir, since I became a monk in old age, I shall not be able to fulfil the duty of study, but I can fulfil the duty of meditation." So he had the Teacher instruct him in the duty of meditation as far as arahantship, and after striving and struggling attained arahantship together with the analytical knowledges. But the other said, "I will fulfil the duty of study." He acquired by degrees the Tipiṭaka, the Word of the Buddha, and wherever he went, taught the Dhamma and chanted it. He went from place to place reciting the Dhamma to five hundred monks and was preceptor of eighteen large communities of monks.

Now a company of monks, having obtained a meditation subject from the Teacher, went to the place of residence of the older monk, and by faithful observance of his admonitions attained arahantship. Thereupon they paid obeisance to the elder and said, "We desire to see the Teacher." Said the elder, "Go, friends, greet the Teacher in my name, and likewise greet the eighty chief elders, and greet my fellow-elder, saying, 'Our teacher greets you.'" So those monks went to the monastery and greeted the Buddha and the elders, saying, "Reverend sir, our teacher greets you." When they greeted their teacher's fellow-elder, he replied, "Who is he?" Said the monks, "He is your fellow-monk, reverend sir."

Said the younger monk, "But what have you learned from him? Of the Dīgha Nikāya (Long Collection) and the other Nikāyas, have you learned a single Nikāya? Of the Three Piṭakas, have you learned a single Piṭaka?" And he thought to himself, "This monk does not know a single stanza containing four verses. Soon after he went forth, he took rags from a dust heap, entered the forest, and gathered a great many pupils about him. When he returns, it behooves me to ask him some questions." Now somewhat later the older monk came to see the Teacher, and leaving his bowl and robe with his fellow-elder, went and greeted the Teacher and the eighty chief elders, afterwards returning to the place of residence of his fellow-elder. The younger monk showed him the customary attentions, provided him with a seat of the same size as his own, and then sat down, thinking to himself, "I will ask him a question."

At that moment the Teacher thought to himself, "Should this monk annoy my son, he is likely to be reborn in hell." So out of compassion for him, pretending to be going the rounds of the monastery, he went to the place where the two monks were sitting and sat down on the seat of the Buddha already prepared. (For wherever the monks sit down, they first prepare the seat of the Buddha, and not until they have so done do they themselves sit down. Therefore the Teacher sat down on a seat already prepared for him.) And when he had sat down, he asked the monk who had taken upon himself the duty of study a question on the first concentration. When the younger monk had answered this question correctly, the Teacher, beginning with the second concentration, asked him questions about the eight attainments and about the form and formless worlds, all of which he answered correctly. Then the Teacher asked him a question about the path of stream-entry, and he was unable to answer it. Thereupon the Teacher asked the monk who was an arahant, and the latter immediately gave the correct answer.

"Well done, well done, monk!" said the Teacher, greatly pleased. The Teacher then asked questions about the remaining paths in order. The monk who had taken upon himself the duty of study was unable to answer a single question, while the monk who had attained to arahantship answered every question he asked. On each of four occasions the Teacher bestowed applause on him. Hearing this, all the deities, from the gods of earth to the gods of the world of Brahmā, including the nāgas and the garuḍas, shouted their applause.

193

Hearing this applause, the pupils and fellow-residents of the younger monk were offended at the Teacher and said, "Why did the Teacher do this? He bestowed applause on each of four occasions on the old monk who knows nothing at all. But to our own teacher, who has thoroughly learnt everything by heart and is at the head of five hundred monks, he gave no praise at all." The Teacher asked them, "Monks, what is it you are talking about?" When they told him, he said, "Monks, your own teacher is in my dispensation like a man who tends cows for hire. But my son is like a master who enjoys the five products of the cow at his own good pleasure." So saying, he pronounced the following stanzas:

19. Though often he recite the sacred texts,
     The heedless man who does not practise
     Is like a cowherd counting other's cattle:
     He has no share of the holy life.

20. Though little he recite the sacred texts,
     If he practises in accordance with Dhamma,
     Rid of delusion, lust, and hate,
     In wisdom perfect, a heart well-freed,
     One who clings not here or hereafter—
     He has a share of the holy life.

47. The Elder Sappadāsa

THOUGH ONE SHOULD LIVE A HUNDRED YEARS.... This instruction was given by the Teacher while he was in residence at Jetavana with reference to the Elder Sappadāsa.

At Sāvatthī we are told, the son of a good family, after hearing the Teacher teach the Dhamma, went forth and obtained acceptance as a monk. Becoming discontented after a time, he thought to himself, "The life of a layman is not suited to a youth of station like me; but even death would be preferable to remaining a monk." So he went about considering ways of killing himself.

Now one day, very early in the morning, the monks went to the monastery after breakfast, and seeing a snake in the hall where the fire was kept, put it into a jar, closed the jar, and carried it out of the monastery. The discontented monk, after eating his breakfast, drew near, and seeing the monks, asked them, "What's that you've got, friend?" – "A snake, friend." – "What are you going to do with it?" – "Throw it away." The monk thought to himself, "I will commit suicide by letting the snake bite me." So he said to the monks, "Let me take it; I'll throw it away."

He took the jar from their hands, sat down in a certain place, and tried to make the snake bite him. But the snake refused to bite him. Then he put his hand into the jar, waved it this way and that, opened the snake's mouth and stuck his finger in, but the snake still refused to bite him. So he said to himself, "It's not a poisonous snake, but a house-snake," threw it away, and returned to the monastery. The monks asked him, "Did you throw away the snake, friend?" – "Friends, that was not a poisonous snake; it was only a house-snake." – "Friend, that was a poisonous snake all the same; it spread its hood wide, hissed at us, and gave us much trouble to catch. Why do you talk thus?" – "Friends, I tried to make it bite me, and even stuck my finger into its mouth, but I couldn't make it bite." When the monks heard this, they were silent.

Now the discontented monk acted as barber of the monastery; and one day he went to the monastery with two or three razors, and laying one razor on the floor, cut the hair of the monks with the other. When he removed the razor from the floor, the thought occurred to him, "I will cut my throat with this razor and so put myself out of the way." So he went to a certain tree, leaned his neck against a branch, and applied the blade of the razor to his windpipe. Remaining in this position, he reflected upon his conduct from the time of his acceptance as a monk, and perceived that his conduct was flawless, even as the spotless disk of the moon or a cluster of transparent jewels. As he surveyed his conduct, a thrill of joy suffused his whole body. Subduing the feeling of joy and developing insight, he attained arahantship together with the analytical knowledges. Then he took his razor and entered the monastery enclosure.

The monks asked him, "Where did you go, friend?" – "Friends, I went out thinking to myself, 'I will cut my windpipe with this razor and so put myself out of the way.' " – "How did you escape death?" – "I can no longer commit suicide. For I said to myself, 'With this razor I will sever my windpipe.' But instead of so doing, I severed the taints with the razor of knowledge." The monks said to themselves, "This monk speaks falsely, says what is untrue," and reported the matter to the Exalted One. The Exalted One listened to their words and replied, "Monks, those that have rid themselves of the taints are incapable of taking their own life."

"Reverend Sir, you speak of this monk as one who has rid himself of the taints. But how did it come about that this monk, possessed of the faculties requisite for the attainment of arahantship, became discontented? How did he come to possess those faculties? Why didn't that snake bite him?"

"Monks, the simple fact is that snake was his slave in a past life, his third previous existence, and therefore did not dare to bite the body of his own master." Thus briefly did the Teacher explain this cause to them. Thereafter that monk was known as Sappadāsa ("having a snake as his slave").

The monks, after hearing the Exalted One explain the matter, asked him a further question: "Reverend sir, this monk says that he attained arahantship even as he stood with the blade of his razor pressed against his windpipe. Is it possible to gain the path of arahantship in so short a period of time?"

"Yes, monks, a monk who strives with all his might may gain the path of arahantship in raising his foot, in setting his foot on the ground, or even before his foot touches the ground. For it is better for a man who strives with all his might to live but a single instant than for an idle man to live a hundred years." So saying, he pronounced the following stanza:

112. Though one should live a hundred years
Lazy, of little effort,
Yet better is life for a single day
For one who makes a steady effort.

48. The Elder Pūtigatta Tissa

NOT LONG, ALAS, AND IT WILL LIE.... This instruction was given by the Teacher while he was in residence at Sāvatthī with reference to the Elder Pūtigatta Tissa, Tissa with the Putrid Body.

A certain youth of good family who lived at Sāvatthī heard the Teacher teach the Dhamma, gave his heart to the dispensation, and went forth as a monk. After his acceptance into the Order he became known as the Elder Tissa. As time went on, an eruption broke out on his body. At first appeared pustules no bigger than mustard seeds, but as the disease progressed they assumed successively the size of kidney beans, chickpeas, jujube seeds, emblic myrobalans, and vilva fruits. Finally they burst open, and his body became covered with open sores. In this way he came to be called the Elder Pūtigatta Tissa. After a time his bones began to disintegrate, and no one was willing to take care of him. His under and upper robes, which were stained with dried blood, looked like net cakes. His fellow-residents, unable to care for him, cast him out, and he lay down on the ground without a protector.

Now the Buddhas never fail to survey the world twice a day. At dawn they survey the world, looking through the extent of the galaxy towards the Perfumed Chamber, taking cognizance of all they see. In the evening they survey the world, looking from the Perfumed Chamber and taking cognizance of all that is without. Now at this time the Elder Pūtigatta Tissa appeared within the net of the Exalted One's knowledge. The Teacher, knowing that the monk Tissa was ripe for arahantship, thought to himself, "This monk has been abandoned by his associates; at the present time he has no other refuge than me." Accordingly the Teacher departed from the Perfumed Chamber, and pretending to be making the rounds of the monastery, went to the hall where the fire was kept. He washed the boiler, placed it on the brazier, waited in the fire-room for the water to boil, and when he knew it was hot, went and took hold of the end of the bed where that monk was lying.

At that time the monks said to the Teacher, "Please depart, reverend sir; we will carry him in for you." So saying, they took up the bed and carried Tissa into the fire-room. The Teacher caused a measure to be brought and sprinkled hot water. He caused the monks to take Tissa's upper garment, wash it thoroughly in hot water, and lay it in the sunshine to dry. Then he went, and taking his stand near Tissa, moistened his body with hot water and rubbed and bathed him. At the end of his bath his upper robe was dry. The Teacher caused him to be clothed in his upper robe and caused his under robe to be washed thoroughly in hot water and laid in the sun to dry. As soon as the water had evaporated from his body, his under robe was dry. Thereupon Tissa put on one of the yellow robes as an under garment and the other as an upper robe, and with his body refreshed and mind tranquil lay down on the bed. The Teacher took his stand at Tissa's pillow and said to him, "Monk, consciousness will depart from you, your body will become useless and, like a log, will lie on the ground." So saying, he pronounced the following stanza:

> 41. Not long, alas, and it will lie—
>   This body here upon the earth,
>   Rejected, void of consciousness,
>   And useless as a rotten log.

At the conclusion of the lesson the Elder Pūtigatta Tissa attained arahantship and reached final Nibbāna. The Teacher performed the funeral rites over his body, and taking the relics, caused a shrine to be erected.

The monks asked the Teacher, "Reverend sir, where was the Elder Pūtigatta Tissa reborn?" – "He has reached final Nibbāna, monks." – "Reverend sir, how did it happen that such a monk, having the supporting tendencies to attain arahantship, came to have a diseased body? Why did his bones disintegrate? Through what deed in a former birth did he obtain the dispositions requisite for the attainment of arahantship?" – "Monks, all these things happened solely because of deeds he committed in a previous existence." – "But, reverend sir, what did he do?" – "Well then, monks, listen.

Story of the Past: The Cruel Fowler

In the dispensation of the Buddha Kassapa, Tissa was a fowler. He used to catch birds in large number, and most of these he served to royalty. Most of those he did not give to royalty he used to sell.

199

Fearing that if he killed and kept the birds he did not sell, they would rot, and desiring to prevent his captive birds from taking flight, he used to break their leg-bones and wing-bones and lay them aside, piling them in a heap. On the following day he would sell them. When he had too many, he would have some cooked also for himself.

One day, when well-flavoured food had been cooked for him, a monk who was an arahant stopped at the door of his house on his round for alms. When Tissa saw the elder, he made his mind serene and thought, "I have killed and eaten many living creatures. A noble elder stands at my door, and an abundance of well-flavoured food is in my house. I will therefore give him alms." So he took the monk's bowl and filled it, and having given him well-flavoured food, saluted the monk respectfully and said: "Reverend sir, may I obtain the highest fruit of the Dhamma you have seen." Said the elder in his words of rejoicing, "So be it." (*End of Story of the Past.*)

"Monks, it was through the meritorious deed Tissa then did that this fruit accrued to him. It was because he broke the bones of birds that his body became diseased and his bones disintegrated. It was because he gave well-flavoured food to the arahant that he attained arahantship."

49. The Elder Vaṅgīsa

WHO, OF BEINGS, KNOWS THEIR DEATH.... This instruction was given by the Teacher while he was in residence at Jetavana with reference to the Elder Vaṅgīsa.[1]

It seems that there lived at Rājagaha a brahmin named Vaṅgīsa who could tell in which of the states of existence men were reborn after death. He would rap on their skulls and say, "This is the skull of a man who has been reborn in hell; this man has been reborn as an animal; this man has been reborn as a ghost; this is the skull of a man who has been reborn in the human world."

The brahmins thought to themselves, "We can use this man to prey upon the world." So clothing him in two red robes, they took him about the country with them, saying to everyone they met, "This brahmin Vaṅgīsa can tell by rapping on the skulls of dead men in which of the states of existence they have been reborn; ask him to tell you in which of the states of existence your own kinsmen have been reborn." People would give him ten pieces of money or twenty or a hundred according to their several means, and would ask him in which of the states of existence their kinsmen had been reborn.

After travelling from place to place, they finally reached Sāvatthī and took up their abode near the Jetavana. After breakfast they saw throngs of people going with perfumes, garlands, and the like in their hands to hear the Dhamma. "Where are you going?" they asked. "To the monastery to hear the Dhamma," was the reply. "What will you gain by going there?" asked the brahmins, "There is nobody like our fellow-brahmin Vaṅgīsa. He can tell by rapping on the skulls of dead men in which of the states of existence they have been reborn. Just ask him in which of the states of existence your own kinsmen have been reborn."

"What does Vaṅgīsa know!" replied the disciples, "There is no one like our teacher." But the brahmins retorted, "There is no one like Vaṅgīsa," and the dispute waxed hot. Finally the disciples said, "Come now, let us go find out which of the two knows the

---

1. He was the foremost poet in the Sangha. A collection of his verses is found in the Saṃyutta Nikāya, Chap. 8, and Theragāthā, 1209–79.

more, your Vaṅgīsa or our teacher." So taking the brahmins with them, they went to the monastery.

The Teacher, knowing that they were on their way, procured and placed in a row five skulls, one each of men who had been reborn in the four states of existence: hell, the animal world, the human world, and the worlds of the gods; and one skull belonging to a man who had attained arahantship. When they arrived, he asked Vaṅgīsa, "Are you the man of whom it is said that by rapping on the skulls of dead men you can tell in which of the states of existence they have been reborn?" – "Yes," said Vaṅgīsa. "Then whose is this skull?" Vaṅgīsa rapped on the skull and said, "This is the skull of a man who has been reborn in hell." – "Good, good!" exclaimed the Teacher, applauding him. Then the Teacher asked him about the next three skulls, and Vaṅgīsa answered without making a mistake. The Teacher applauded him for each answer he gave and finally showed him the fifth skull. "Whose skull is this?" he asked. Vaṅgīsa rapped on the fifth skull as he had on the others, but confessed that he did not know in which of the states of existence the man had been reborn.

Then said the Teacher, "Vaṅgīsa, don't you know?" – "No," replied Vaṅgīsa, "I don't know." – "I know," said the Teacher. Thereupon Vaṅgīsa asked him, "Teach me this charm." – "I cannot teach it to one who has not gone forth." Thought the brahmin to himself, "If I only knew this charm I should be the foremost man in all India." Accordingly he dismissed his fellow-brahmins, saying, "Remain right here for a few days; I intend to go forth." And he went forth in the presence of the Teacher, obtained acceptance as a monk, and was thereafter known as Elder Vaṅgīsa.

They gave him as his subject of meditation the thirty-two constituent parts of the body and said to him, "Repeat the preliminary words of the formula." He followed their instructions and repeated the preliminary words of the formula. From time to time the brahmins would ask him, "Have you learned the formula?" and the elder would answer, "Just wait a little! I am learning it." In but a few days he attained arahantship. When the brahmins asked him again, he replied, "Friends, I am now unable to learn it." When the monks heard his reply, they said to the Teacher, "Reverend sir, this monk utters what is not true and is guilty of falsehood." The Teacher replied, "Monks, do not say so. Monks,

202

my son now knows all about the passing away and rebirth of beings." So saying, he pronounced the following stanzas:

419. Who, of beings, knows their death,
      Their being born in every way,
      Detached, well-faring, enlightened too—
      That one I call a brāhmaṇa.

420. Him whose bourn men do not know,
      Neither devas nor minstrels divine,
      Pollutions destroyed, an arahant—
      That one I call a brāhmaṇa.

Part VIII

The Attainments of Nuns

50. Mahā Pajāpatī Gotamī

IN WHOM IS NO WRONG-DOING.... This instruction was given by the Teacher while he was in residence at Jetavana with reference to Mahā Pajāpatī Gotamī (the Buddha's aunt and foster-mother).

When the circumstances requiring the eight important conditions (for admitting nuns) had arisen, the Exalted One proclaimed them and Mahā Pajāpatī Gotamī accepted them by bowing her head, just as a person accustomed to the wearing of ornaments accepts a garland of fragrant flowers by bowing his head. So likewise did all the members of her retinue. She had no preceptor or teacher other than the Exalted One himself. Thus she received acceptance as a nun.

On a subsequent occasion the members of her retinue commented on the manner in which this nun was admitted to full membership in the Order, saying, "Mahā Pajāpatī Gotamī has no teacher or preceptor; by herself alone and with her own hand she received the yellow robes." On hearing this, other nuns were dissatisfied and from then on refused to keep Uposatha day or to celebrate the Pavāraṇā ceremony with her.[1] And going to the Tathāgata, they reported the matter to him. The Teacher listened to what they had to say and then replied, "I myself conferred the eight important conditions on Mahā Pajāpatī Gotamī. I alone am her teacher; I alone am her preceptor. Those who have renounced bad conduct by way of body, speech, and mind, those who have rid themselves of the evil passions, should never entertain feelings of dissatisfaction." And teaching the Dhamma, he pronounced the following stanza:

> 391. In whom is no wrongdoing
> By body, speech, or mind,
> In these three ways restrained—
> That one I call a brāhmaṇa.

---

1. The ceremony for inviting mutual admonition, held at the end of the rains residence.

51. The Elder Nun Uppalavaṇṇā

'AS SWEET AS HONEY' THINKS THE FOOL.... This instruction was given by the Teacher while he was in residence at Jetavana with reference to the nun Uppalavaṇṇā.

We are told that Uppalavaṇṇā made her earnest wish at the feet of the Buddha Padumuttara, and that after performing works of merit for a hundred thousand cycles of time, as she passed from birth to birth among gods and humans, she passed from the world of the gods in the dispensation of the present Buddha and was reborn in Sāvatthī as the daughter of a rich merchant. The hue of her skin was like the hue of the calyx of the blue lotus, and therefore they gave her the name Uppalavaṇṇā. When she reached marriageable age, all the princes and merchants in India, without a single exception, sent gifts to the merchant her father, asking him to give them his daughter in marriage.

Thereupon the merchant thought to himself, "I shall not be able to satisfy the wishes of all, but I shall find some way out of the difficulty." So he summoned his daughter and said to her, "You might become a nun." Now she was in her last existence before attaining Nibbāna, and therefore his words were to her, as it were, oil a hundred times refined, sprinkled on her head. Therefore she replied, "Dear father, I will become a nun." So he prepared rich gifts in her honour, and conducting her to the Order of Nuns, had her go forth.

Not long after she had gone forth, her turn came to unlock the Uposatha hall. After she had lighted the lamp and swept the hall, her attention was attracted to the flame of the lamp. And standing there, she looked repeatedly at the flame; and concentrating her attention on the element of fire, she entered into a state of deep concentration. Consummating the deep concentration, she attained arahantship together with the analytical knowledges.

Some time later she went on a pilgrimage for alms in the country, and on her return entered the Dark Forest. At that time it was not forbidden to nuns to reside in a forest. There they built her a hut, set up a bed, and hung curtains round. From the forest she went to Sāvatthī to receive alms, and then set out to return to her

208

hut. Now a cousin of hers, a young brahmin named Ānanda, had been in love with her ever since she lived the household life; and when he heard where she had gone, he went to the forest ahead of the nun, entered the hut, and hid under the bed.

On her return the nun entered the hut, closed the door, and sat down on the bed, unable to see in the dark, because she had just come in out of the sunlight. As soon as she sat down on the bed the youth crawled out from under and climbed on top. The nun cried out, "Fool, do not ruin me! Fool, do not ruin me!" But the youth overcame her resistance, worked his will on her, and went his way. As if unable to endure his wickedness, the great earth burst asunder, and he was swallowed up and reborn in the great hell of Avīci.

The nun told the other nuns what had happened, and the nuns told the monks, and the monks told the Exalted One. Having heard this the Teacher addressed the monks as follows, "Monks, the fool, whoever he may be, whether monk or nun, or lay disciple male or female, who commits an evil act, acts with as much joy and happiness, with as much pleasure and delight, as though he were eating honey or sugar or some other sweet-tasting substance." And joining the connection and instructing them in the Dhamma, he pronounced the following stanza:

69. "As sweet as honey" thinks the fool
So long as the evil is unripe,
But when the evil deed ripens,
Then to the fool comes suffering.

Some time later the throng assembled in the Dhamma hall and began to discuss the incident: "Even those that have rid themselves of taints like the pleasures of love and gratify their passions. Why should they not? They are not kolapa-trees or ant-hills, but are living creatures with bodies of moist flesh. Therefore they also like the pleasures of love and gratify their passions." The Teacher drew near and asked them, "Monks, what are you sitting here now talking about?" They told him. Then he said, "Monks, they that have rid themselves of the taints neither like the pleasures of love nor gratify their passions. For even as a drop of water which has fallen upon a lotus leaf does not cling to it or remain there, but rolls over and falls off; even as a grain of mustard seed does not cling to the point of an awl or remain there, but rolls over and falls off; precisely so sensual love does not cling to the heart of one who has rid himself of the taints nor remain there." And joining the connection, he instructed them in the Dhamma by pronouncing the following stanza, found in the Chapter on the Brāhmaṇa:

401. Who, like water drops on a lotus leaf,
Or mustard seed on a needle point,
Clings not to sensual pleasures—
That one I call a brāhmaṇa.

Now the Teacher summoned King Pasenadi Kosala and said to him, "Your majesty, in this religion young women of good family, as well as young men of good family, renounce many kinsfolk and much wealth, go forth and take up residence in the forest. In case women reside in the forest, it is possible that evil-minded men, inflamed by lust, may conduct themselves towards them with disrespect and arrogance, do them violence, and bring their religious life to naught. Therefore a place of residence for the Order of Nuns should be erected within the city." The king agreed to this and had a place of residence for the Order of Nuns erected on one side of the city. From that time on the nuns resided only within the city.

52. The Elder Nun Kisā Gotamī

THOUGH ONE SHOULD LIVE A HUNDRED YEARS.... This instruction was given by the Teacher at Jetavana, with reference to Kisā Gotamī.

Kisā Gotamī Marries a Rich Merchant's Son

Once upon a time, the story goes, a merchant worth four hundred millions lived at Sāvatthī. Suddenly all of his wealth turned into charcoal. The merchant, overwhelmed with grief, refused to eat and took to his bed. One day a certain friend of his came to see him and asked him, "Sir, why are you so sorrowful?" The merchant told him what had happened. Said his friend, "Sir, do not give yourself over to sorrow. I know a way out of the difficulty, if you will but make use of it."

"Well, sir, what am I to do?"

Said his friend, "Spread matting in your shop, and pile the charcoal on it, and sit down as if you were selling it. People will come along and say to you, 'Most merchants sell such things as clothing and oil and honey and molasses; but you are sitting here selling charcoal.' Then you must say to them, 'If I can't sell what belongs to me, what am I to do?' But again someone may say, 'Most merchants sell such things as clothing and oil and honey and molasses, but you are sitting here selling yellow gold.' Then you must say, 'Where's any yellow gold?' Your customer will say, 'There it is!' Then say, 'Let me have it.' Your customer will bring you a handful of charcoal. Take it, cover it with your hands, and presto! It will turn into yellow gold. Now if your customer should be a maiden, marry her to your son, turn over your four hundred millions to her, and live on what she gives you. But if your customer should be a youth, marry your daughter to him as soon as she reaches marriageable age, turn over your four hundred millions to him, and live on what he gives you."

"A fine plan indeed!" said the merchant. So he piled the charcoal up in his shop, and sat down as if he were selling it. People came along and said to him, "Most merchants sell things such as clothing and oil and honey and molasses; but you are sitting here selling charcoal." To such as asked this question, he replied as follows, "If I can't sell what belongs to me, what am I to do?" There came one day to the door of his shop a certain maiden, the daughter of a poverty-stricken house. Her name was Gotamī, but by reason of the leanness of her body she was generally known as Kisā Gotamī. She came to buy something for herself; but when she saw the merchant, she said to him, "My good sir, most merchants sell such things as clothing and oil and honey and molasses; but you are sitting here selling yellow gold." – "Maiden, where is there any yellow gold?" – "Right there where you are sitting." – "Let me have some of it, maiden." She took a handful of the charcoal and placed it in his hands. No sooner had it touched his hands than presto! It turned into yellow gold.

Then said the merchant to her, "Which is your house, maiden?" Said she, "Such and such, sir." The merchant, perceiving that she was unmarried, married her to his own son. He then gathered up his wealth (what was previously charcoal turning into yellow gold at his touch), and gave the four hundred millions into her charge. In time she became pregnant, and, after ten lunar months, gave birth to a son. But the child died as soon as he was able to walk.

Kisā Gotamī Seeks Mustard Seed for Her Child

Now Kisā Gotamī had never seen death before. Therefore, when they came to remove the body for burning, she forbade them to do so. She said to herself, "I will seek medicine for my son." Placing the dead child on her hip, she went from house to house inquiring, "Do you know anything that will cure my son?" Everyone said to her, "Woman, you are stark mad that you go from house to house seeking medicine for your dead child." But she went her way, thinking, "Surely I shall find someone who knows medicine for my child."

Now a certain wise man saw her and thought to himself, "This young woman has no doubt borne and lost her first and only child, nor has she seen death before; I must help her." So he said to her, "Woman, I myself do not know how to cure your child, but I know of one who has this knowledge." – "Sir, who is it that knows?" – "Woman, the Teacher knows; go and ask him." – "Good sir, I will go and ask him."

So she went to the Teacher, paid obeisance to him, stood at his

212

side, and asked him, "Venerable sir, is it true, as men say, that you know how to cure my child?" – "Yes, I know that." – "What shall I get?" – "A pinch of white mustard seed." – "I will get that, venerable sir. But in whose house shall I get it?" – "In whose house neither son nor daughter nor any other has yet died." – "Very well, venerable sir," said she, and paid obeisance to him.

Then she placed the dead child on her hip, entered the village, stopped at the door of the very first house, and asked, "Have you here any white mustard seed? They say it will cure my child." – "Yes." – "Well then, give it to me." They brought some grains of white mustard seed and gave them to her. She asked, "Friends, in the house where you dwell has son or daughter yet died?" – "What are you saying, woman? As for the living they are few; only the dead are many." – "Well then, take back your mustard seed; that is no medicine for my child." So saying, she gave back the mustard seed.

After this manner, going from house to house, she plied her quest. There was not a single house where she found the mustard seed she sought; and when the evening came, she thought, "Ah! It's a heavy task I took upon myself. I thought that I alone had lost a child, but in every village the dead are more in number than the living." While she reflected thus her heart, which until then was soft with mother's love, became firm. She took the child and discarded him in the forest. Then she went to the Teacher, paid homage to him, and stood to one side.

Said the Teacher, "Did you get the pinch of mustard seed?" – "No, I did not, venerable sir. In every village the dead are more in number than the living." Said the Teacher, "You imagined vainly that you alone had lost a child. But all living beings are subject to an unchanging law, and it is this: The Prince of Death, like a raging torrent, sweeps away into the sea of ruin all living beings, but still their longings are unfulfilled." And instructing her in the Dhamma, he pronounced the following stanza:

> 287. In flocks and children finding delight
> With a mind clinging – just such a man
> Death seizes and carries away,
> As a great flood a sleeping village.

213

As the Teacher uttered the last part of the stanza, Kisā Gotamī was established in the fruit of stream-entry. Likewise did many others also obtain the fruit of stream-entry, and the fruits of the second and third paths. Kisā Gotamī requested the Teacher to let her go forth; accordingly he sent her to the Order of Nuns and directed that they let her go forth. Afterwards she obtained acceptance as a nun and came to be known as the nun Kisā Gotamī.

One day it was her turn to light the lamp in the Uposatha hall. Having lighted the lamp, she sat down and watched the tongues of flame. Some flared up and others flickered out. She took this for her subject of meditation and meditated as follows: "Even as it is with these flames, so also is it with living beings here in the world: some flare up, while others flicker out; only those who have reached Nibbāna are no more seen."

The Teacher, seated in the Perfumed Chamber, sent forth a radiant image of himself, and standing as it were face to face with her, spoke and said: "Even as it is with these flames, so also is it with living beings here in the world: some flare up, while others flicker out; only those who have reached Nibbāna are no more seen. Therefore, better is the life of one who sees Nibbāna, though living but for an instant, than the lives of those who endure for a hundred years and yet do not see Nibbāna." And joining the connection, he instructed her in the Dhamma by pronouncing the following stanza:

114. Though one should live a hundred years,
    Not seeing the Deathless State,
    Yet better is life for a single day
    For one who sees the Deathless State.

At the conclusion of the discourse Kisā Gotamī, even as she sat there, attained arahantship together with the analytical knowledges.

53. The Elder Nun Paṭācārā

THOUGH ONE SHOULD LIVE A HUNDRED YEARS.... This instruction was given by the Teacher, while in residence at Jetavana, with reference to the nun Paṭācārā.

Paṭācārā, we are told, was the daughter of a wealthy merchant of Sāvatthī. Her father was worth four hundred million, and she was exceedingly beautiful. When she was about sixteen years old, her parents provided quarters for her in a palace seven stories high, and there they kept her, on the topmost floor, surrounded by guards. But in spite of these precautions, she misconducted herself, and it was with her own page.[1]

Now it so happened that her father and mother had promised her in marriage to a certain young man who was her social equal, and finally they set the wedding day. When the day was close at hand, she said to the page, "My parents tell me that they intend to give me in marriage to a young man who comes of such and such a family. Now you know very well that when I am once inside my husband's house, you may bring me presents and come to see me all you like, but you will never, never get in. Therefore, if you really love me, don't delay an instant, but find some way or other of getting me out of this place."

"Very well, my love, this is what I will do: tomorrow, early in the morning, I will go to the city gate and wait for you at such and such a spot; you manage, somehow or other, to get out of this place and meet me there."

On the following day he went to the appointed place and waited. Paṭācārā got up very early in the morning, put on soiled garments, disheveled her hair, and smeared her body with red powder. Then, in order to outwit her keepers, she took a waterpot in her hand, surrounded herself with slave-maidens, and set out as if she intended to fetch water. Escaping from the palace, she went to the appointed place and met her lover. Together they went a long way off, and took up their abode in a certain village. The husband tilled the soiled, and gathered firewood and leaves in the forest.

---

1. The opening portion of this story closes resembles the opening of story No. 45. See pp.186-87.

215

The wife fetched water in her waterpot, and with her own hand pounded the rice, did the cooking, and performed the other household duties. Thus did Paṭācārā reap the fruit of her own wrongdoing.

By and by, she became pregnant, and when the time for her delivery was near at hand, she made the following request to her husband, "Here I have no one to help me. But a mother and father always have a soft spot in their heart for their child. Therefore take me home to them, that I may give birth to my child in their house." But her husband refused her request, saying to her, "My dear wife, what are you saying? If your mother and father were to see me, they would subject me to all manner of tortures. It is out of the question for me to go." Over and over again she begged him, and each time he refused her.

One day when her husband was away in the forest, she went to the neighbours and said, "Should my husband ask you where I have gone when he returns, tell him that I have gone home to my parents." And having said this she closed the door of her house and went away. When her husband returned and observed that she was not there he inquired of the neighbours and they told him what had happened. "I must persuade her to return," thought he, and set out after her. Finally he caught sight of her, and overtaking her, begged her to return with him. But try as he might, he was unable to persuade her to do so.

When they reached a certain place, the birth pains came upon her. She said to her husband, "Husband, the birth pains have come upon me." So saying, she made her way into a clump of bushes, laid herself upon the ground, and there, with much tossing about and pain, she gave birth to a son. Then she said, "What I set out to go home for is over." So back again to their house she went with him, and once more they lived together.

After a time she became pregnant again. When the time for her delivery was at hand, she made the same request of her husband as before and received the same answer. So she took her child upon her hip and went away just as she had before. Her husband followed her, overtook her, and asked her to return with him. This she refused to do. Now as they went on their way, a fearful storm arose, out of due season. The sky was ablaze with flashes of lightning, and rent asunder, as it were, with thunder claps, and there was an incessant

216

downpour of rain. At that moment the birth pains came upon her. She said to her husband, "Husband, the birth pains are come upon me; I cannot stand it; find me a place out of the rain."

Her husband went here and there, axe in hand, seeking materials for a shelter. Seeing some brushwood growing on the top of an ant-hill, he set about to chop it down. Hardly had he begun his work when a poisonous snake slipped out of the ant-hill and bit him. Instantly his body was burned up, as it were, by flames of fire shooting up within him, his flesh turned purple, and right on the spot he fell down dead.

Paṭācārā, suffering intense pain, watched for her husband to return, but in vain. Finally she gave birth to a second son. The two children, unable to withstand the buffeting of the wind and the rain, screamed at the top of their lungs. The mother took them to her bosom, and crouching upon the ground with her hands and knees pressed together, remained in this posture all night long. Her whole body looked as though there were no blood left in it, and her flesh had the appearance of a sere and yellow leaf.

When the dawn rose, she took her newborn son, his flesh as red as a piece of meat, and placed him on her hip. Then she gave the older boy one of her fingers to hold, and with the words, "Come, dear child, your father has left us," set out along the same path her husband had taken. When she came to the ant-hill, there on top of it she saw her husband lying dead, his flesh purple, his body rigid. "All on account of me," said she, "my husband has died upon the road," and wailing and lamenting, she continued her journey.

When she came to the river Aciravatī, she observed that by reason of the rain, which had lasted all night long, the river was swollen knee-deep, and in places waist-deep. She was too weak to wade across the stream with the two children; therefore she left the older boy on the near bank and carried the younger across to the far side. Breaking off a branch of a tree and spreading it out, she laid the child on it. Then thinking to herself, "I must return to my other child," she took leave of the younger boy and turned to recross the stream. But she could hardly bring herself to leave the little one, and again and again she turned around to look at him.

She had barely reached midstream when a hawk caught sight of the child, and mistaking him for a piece of hawk, swooped down from the sky after him. The mother, seeing the eagle swoop

217

down after her child, raised both her hands and screamed with a loud voice, "Begone, begone!" Three times she screamed, but the hawk was so far away that he failed to hear her, and seizing the boy, flew up into the air with him.

When the older boy, who had been left on the near bank, saw his mother stop in the middle of the river and raise her hands, and heard her scream with a loud voice, he thought to himself, "She is calling me." And in his haste he fell into the water. In this way her younger son was carried off by a hawk, and her older son swept away by the river. And she wailed and lamented, saying, "One of my sons has been carried off by a hawk, the other swept away by the water; by the roadside my husband lies dead." And thus wailing and lamenting, she went on her way.

As she proceeded on her way, she met a certain man coming from Sāvatthī. She asked him, "Sir, where do you live?" – "In Sāvatthī, my good woman." – "In the city of Sāvatthī, in such and such a street, lives such and such a family. Do you know them, sir?" – "Yes, my good woman, I know them. But please don't ask me about that family. Ask me about any other family you know." – "Sir, I have no occasion to ask about any other. This is the only family I wish to ask about." – "Woman, you give me no opportunity to avoid telling you. Did you observe that it rained all last night?"

"Indeed I did, sir. In fact, I am the only person the rain fell on all night long. How it came to rain on me, I will tell you by and by. But just tell me what has happened to the family of this wealthy merchant, and I will ask you no further questions."

"My good woman, last night the storm overturned that house, and it fell on the merchant and his wife and his son, and they perished, all three, and their neighbours and kinsmen are even now burning their bodies on one funeral pyre. Look there, my good woman. You can see the smoke now."

Instantly she went mad. Her clothing fell off from her body, but she did not know that she was naked. And naked as at her birth she wandered round and round, weeping and wailing and lamenting, "Both my sons are dead; my husband on the road lies dead; my mother and father and brother burn on one funeral pyre."

Those who saw her yelled, "Crazy fool! Crazy fool!" Some flung rubbish at her, others showered dust on her head, others pelted her with clods of earth.

It so happened that at this time the Teacher was in residence at Jetavana monastery. As he sat there in the midst of his disciples teaching the Dhamma, he saw Paṭācārā approach from afar, and he recognized in her one who for a hundred thousand cycles of time had fulfilled the Perfections, one who had made her earnest wish and attained it.

We are told that in the dispensation of the Buddha Padumuttara she had seen the Teacher Padumuttara assign to an elder nun, an expert in the Vinaya, pre-eminence among those who are versed in the Vinaya. It seemed as if the Teacher were taking her by the arm and admitting the nun to the Garden of Delight. So she formed her resolve and made this aspiration, "May I also obtain from a Buddha like you pre-eminence among nuns versed in the Vinaya." The Buddha Padumuttara, extending his consciousness into the future and perceiving that her aspiration would be fulfilled, made the following prophecy: "In the dispensation of a Buddha to be known as Gotama, this woman will bear the name Paṭācārā, and will obtain pre-eminence among nuns versed in the Vinaya."

So when the Teacher beheld Paṭācārā approaching from afar, her aspiration fulfilled, her earnest wish attained, he said, "There is none other that can be a refuge to this woman, but only I." And he caused her to draw near to the monastery. The moment his disciples saw her, they cried out, "Do not let that crazy woman come here." But he said to them, "Do not hinder her." And when she had come near, he said to her, "Sister, regain your mindfulness!" Instantly, through the power of the Buddha, she regained her mindfulness. At the same moment she became aware that her clothing had fallen off from her body; and recovering at once her shame and fear of wrongdoing, she crouched upon the ground.

A certain man threw her his outer cloak. She put it on, and approaching the Teacher, prostrated herself before his golden feet. Having so done, she said, "Venerable sir, be my refuge, be my support. One of my sons has been carried off by a hawk, the other swept away by the water; by the roadside my husband lies dead; my father's house has been wrecked by the wind, and in it have perished my mother and father and brother, and even now their bodies are burning on one funeral pyre."

The Teacher listened to what she had to say and replied, "Paṭācārā, be troubled no more. You have come to one who is able to be your shelter, your refuge. What you have said is true. One of your sons has been carried off by a hawk, the other swept away by the water; by the roadside your husband lies dead; your father's house has been wrecked by the wind, and in it have perished your mother and father and brother. But just as today, so also all through this round of existences, you have wept over the loss of sons and others dear to you, shedding tears more abundant than the waters of the four oceans." And he uttered the following stanza:

> But little water do the four oceans contain,
> Compared with all the tears that man has shed,
> By sorrow smitten and by suffering distraught.
> Woman, why heedless do you still remain?

In this way the Teacher discoursed on the round of existences without conceivable beginning. As he spoke, the grief which pervaded her body became less intense. Perceiving that her grief had become less intense, he continued his discourse as follows: "Paṭācārā, to one who is on his way to the world beyond, neither sons nor other relatives can ever be a shelter or a refuge. How much less can you expect them to be such to you in this present life! One who is wise should clarify his conduct, and so make clear the path that leads to Nibbāna." So saying, he instructed her in the Dhamma by pronouncing the following stanzas:

> 288. No sons are there for shelter,
> Nor father, nor related folk;
> For one seized by the Ender
> Kinsmen provide no shelter.

> 289. Having well understood this fact,
> The wise man well restrained by virtues
> Quickly indeed should clear
> The path going to Nibbāna.

At the conclusion of the discourse, Paṭācāra obtained the fruit of stream-entry and the taints within her, as numerous as the particles of dust on the whole wide earth, were burnt away. Many others likewise obtained the fruit of stream-entry and the fruits of the second and third paths. Paṭācāra, having obtained the fruit of stream-entry, requested the Teacher to let her go forth. The Teacher sent her to the Order of Nuns and directed that she go forth. Afterwards she obtained acceptance as a nun and by reason of her happy demeanour (*paṭitācārattā*) came to be known as Paṭācāra.

One day she filled her waterpot with water, and pouring out water, bathed her feet. As she poured out the water, she spilled some on the ground. The water ran a little way and disappeared. The second time it went a little farther. The third time a little farther yet. So she took this very incident for her subject of meditation, and fixing accurately in her mind the three occurrences, she meditated thus: "Even as the water I spilled the first time ran a little way and disappeared, so also living beings here in the world are dying in youth. Even as the water I spilled the second time ran a little farther, so also living beings here in the world are dying in the prime of life. Even as the water I spilled the third time ran a little farther yet, so also living beings here in the world are dying in old age."

The Teacher, seated in his Perfumed Chamber, sent forth a radiant image of himself, and standing as it were face to face with her, spoke and said: "Paṭācāra, it would be far better to live but a single day, even but a single moment, and see the rise and fall of the five aggregates, than to live a hundred years and not see." And joining the connection, he instructed her in the Dhamma by pronouncing the following stanza:

113. Though one should live a hundred years
     Not seeing rise and fall,
     Yet better is life for a single day
     For one who sees rise and fall.

At the conclusion of the discourse Paṭācāra attained arahantship together with the analytical knowledges.

54. The Elder Nun Bahuputtikā

THOUGH ONE SHOULD LIVE A HUNDRED YEARS.... This instruction was given by the Teacher while he was in residence at Jetavana with reference to Bahuputtikā.

In a certain household at Sāvatthī, we are told, were seven sons and seven daughters. All of them married as soon as they were old enough, and were happy, as was indeed their nature. After a time their father died. But the mother, the eminent female lay disciple, even after the death of her husband, did not relinquish control of his property for some time. One day her sons said to her, "Mother, now that our father is dead, what is the use of your retaining his property? Can we not support you?" She listened to their words, but said nothing. After they had spoken to her several times about the matter, she thought to herself, "My sons will look after me; why do I need to I keep the property separate for myself?" So she divided the estate into two parts and distributed them among the children.

After a few days had passed, the wife of her eldest son said to her, "Apparently this is the only house our excellent mother visits; she acts as though she had given both parts of her estate to her eldest son." In like manner did the wives of her other sons address her. So likewise did her daughters address her whenever she entered their houses, from the eldest to the youngest. With such disrespect was she treated that finally she said to herself, "Why should I live with them any longer? I will go forth and live the life of a nun." So she went to the nuns' convent and asked to go forth. They let her go forth and when she had obtained acceptance she went by the name of Bahuputtikā the nun.[1]

"Since I have gone forth in old age," she thought, as she performed the major and minor duties assigned to nuns, "it behooves me to be heedful; I will therefore spend the whole night in meditation. On the lower terrace, putting her hand on a pillar, she guided her steps thereby and meditated. Even as she walked back and forth, fearful that in the dark places she might strike her head against a tree or against some other object, she put her hand

---

1. The name "Bahuputtikā" means "one with many children."

on a tree and guided her steps thereby and meditated. Resolved to observe only the Dhamma taught by the Teacher, she considered the Dhamma and pondered the Dhamma and meditated.

The Teacher, seated in the Perfumed Chamber, sent forth a radiant image of himself, and sitting as it were face to face with her, talked with her, saying: "Bahuputtikā, though one should live a hundred years, were one not to behold the Dhamma I have taught and meditate thereon, it would be better for one to live but a moment and behold the Dhamma I have taught." And joining the connection and teaching the Dhamma, he pronounced the following stanza:

115. Though one should live a hundred years
Not seeing the supreme Dhamma,
Yet better is life for a single day
For one who sees the supreme Dhamma.

At the conclusion of the stanza, Bahuputtikā became an arahant possessed of the analytical knowledges.

55. The Elder Nun Dhammadinnā

FOR WHOM THERE IS NO OWNERSHIP.... This instruction was given by the Teacher while he was in residence at Veḷuvana with reference to the nun Dhammadinnā.

For one day, while she was living the household life, her husband Visākha, a lay disciple, heard the Teacher preach the Dhamma and attained the fruit of the third path. Thereupon he thought to himself, "I must now turn over all of my property to Dhammadinnā."[1] Now it had previously been his custom on returning home, in case he saw Dhammadinnā looking out of the window, to smile pleasantly at her. But on this particular day, although she was standing at the window, he passed by without so much as looking at her. "What can this mean?" she thought. "Never mind, when it is meal-time, I shall find out." So when meal-time came, she offered him the usual portion of boiled rice. Now on previous days it had been his custom to say, "Come, let us eat together." But on this particular day he ate in silence, uttering not a word. "He must be angry about something," thought Dhammadinnā.

After the meal Visākha settled himself in a comfortable place, and summoning Dhammadinnā to his side, said to her, "Dhammadinnā, all the wealth that is in this house is yours. Take it!" Thought Dhammadinnā, "Persons who are angry do not offer their property and say, 'Take it!' What can this mean?" After a time, however, she said to her husband, "But, husband, what about you?" – "From this day forth, I shall engage no more in worldly affairs." – "Who will take the spittle you have rejected? In that case permit me also to become a nun." – "Very well, dear wife," replied Visākha, giving her the desired permission. And with rich offerings he escorted her to the nuns' convent and had her go forth. After she had obtained acceptance as a nun she was known as the nun Dhammadinnā.

Dhammadinnā yearned for the life of solitude and so accompanied the nuns to the country. Residing there, in no long time she attained arahantship together with the analytical knowledges.

---

1. A non-returner has abandoned all greed and possessiveness.

Thereupon she thought to herself, "Now, by reason of me, my kinsfolk will perform works of merit." Accordingly she returned once more to Rājagaha. When the lay disciple Visākha heard that she had returned, he thought to himself, "What can be her reason for returning?" And going to the nuns' convent and seeing the nun, his former wife, he saluted her and seated himself respectfully on one side.

Thought he, "It would be highly improper for me to say to her, 'Noble sister, are you discontented?'[2] I will therefore ask her this question." So he asked her a question about the path of stream-entry, and she immediately answered it correctly. Continuing this line of questioning, the lay disciple asked about the remaining paths also. He did not stop, however, at this point, but continuing his questions, asked her about arahantship. "Wonderful, brother Visākha!" exclaimed Dhammadinnā. "But if you desire to know about arahantship, you should approach the Teacher and ask him this question."[3]

Visākha saluted the nun, his former wife, and rising from his seat and going to the Teacher, repeated to the Exalted One their talk and conversation. Said the Teacher, "What my daughter Dhammadinnā said was well said. In answering these questions I also should answer it in the very same way." And expounding the Dhamma, he pronounced the following stanza:

421. For whom there is no ownership
Before or after or midway,
Owing nothing and unattached—
That one I call a brāhmaṇa.

---

2. Discontented with the holy life of celibacy, implying a desire to return to lay status.

3. Their conversation is recorded in Majjhima Nikāya No. 44.

56. The Elder Nun Rūpanandā

THIS IS A CITY MADE OF BONES.... This instruction was given by the Teacher while he was in residence at Jetavana with reference to the nun Janapada-Kalyāṇī Rūpanandā.

The story goes that one day Janapada-Kalyāṇī thought to herself, "My eldest brother has renounced the glory of dominion, has become a monk, and has now become the foremost being in the world, even the Buddha; his son, Rāhula Kumāra, has become a monk; my husband has become a monk; so also has my mother become a nun. Seeing that all these kinsfolk of mine have adopted the holy life, why should I continue any longer to live the household life? I, too, will become a nun." Accordingly she went to the Order of Nuns and became a nun, not at all because of faith, but solely because of love for her kinsfolk. Because of her wondrous beauty, she became known as Rūpanandā ("Beautiful Delight").

One day she heard that the Teacher had said, "Beauty of form is impermanent, involved in suffering, and non-self; so likewise are feeling, perception, the aggregate of mental states, and consciousness, impermanent, involved in suffering, and non-self." Thereupon she said to herself, "In that case he would find fault even with my own form, so beautiful to look upon and so fair to see." Therefore she avoided meeting the Teacher face to face.

Now the residents of Sāvatthī, having given alms early in the morning, took upon themselves the Uposatha precepts. In the evening, clad in spotless upper garments and bearing garlands and flowers in their hands, they assembled at Jetavana to hear the Dhamma. And the Order of Nuns also, desiring to hear the Dhamma, went to the monastery and heard the Dhamma. And having heard the Dhamma, they entered the city, praising the virtues of the Teacher as they entered.

(For there are four standards of judgement prevailing among persons who dwell together in the world. However, there are very few persons in whom the sight of the Tathāgata does not arouse a feeling of satisfaction. Those who judge by what they see, look upon the golden-hued body of the Tathāgata, adorned with the major marks and the minor marks, and are satisfied with what they see.

Those who judge by what they hear, listen to the report of the Teacher's virtues through many hundreds of births, and to his voice, endowed with the eight excellences, in the preaching of the Dhamma, and are satisfied with what they hear. *Those who judge by austerities* are satisfied with his austere robes and so forth. *Those whose standard of judgement is the Dhamma* reflect: "Such is the virtue of the Master, such is his meditation, such is his wisdom; in virtue and meditation and wisdom the Exalted One is without an equal, is without a peer." Thus they also are satisfied. Indeed those who praise the virtues of the Tathāgata lack words with which to tell their praises.)

Rūpanandā listened to the nuns and the female lay disciples as they recited the praises of the Tathāgata, and having listened, said to herself, "In extravagant terms do they tell the praises of my brother. Suppose he were to find fault with my beauty of form during one single day. How much could he say in that length of time? Suppose I were to go with the nuns, and without letting myself be seen, look upon the Tathāgata, hear him preach the Dhamma, and then return?" So she said to the nuns, "Today I too will go and hear the Dhamma." Said the nuns, "It has taken a long time to arouse in Rūpanandā a desire to wait upon the Teacher. Today, by reason of her, the Teacher will preach the Dhamma with many and various details." And with delighted hearts, taking her with them, they set out.

From the moment Rūpanandā started out, she kept thinking to herself, "I will not let him see who I am." The Teacher thought to himself, "Today Rūpanandā will come to pay her respects to me; what manner of lesson will do her the most good?" As he considered the matter further, he came to the following conclusion: "This woman thinks a great deal of her beauty of form and is deeply attached to her own person. It will therefore be of advantage to her if I crush out the pride she feels in her beauty of form by means of beauty of form itself, even as one draws out one thorn with another thorn." Accordingly, when it was time for her to enter the monastery, the Teacher put forth his power and created a young woman about sixteen years of age. Surpassing beauty did she possess; she wore crimson garments; she was adorned with all her ornaments, and stood before the Teacher with fan in hand, swinging the fan back and forth.

Now both the Teacher and Rūpanandā beheld this woman. As Rūpanandā entered the monastery with the nuns, she took her place behind the nuns, saluted the Teacher respectfully, and sat down among the nuns. Having done so, she surveyed from head to foot the person of the Teacher, richly brilliant with the major marks, resplendent with the minor marks, surrounded by a halo a fathom in extent. Then she saw the phantom of a woman standing near the Teacher and surveyed her face, glorious as the full moon. Having surveyed this woman, she surveyed her own person and compared herself to a crow standing before a royal goose of golden hue. For from the moment she looked upon this phantom, created by supernatural power, her eyes rolled back and forth. "Oh, how beautiful is her hair! Oh, how beautiful is her forehead!" she exclaimed. She was fascinated by the glorious beauty of every part of her body, and she became possessed with intense desire for equal beauty herself. The Teacher, observing that she was fascinated by the beauty of the woman, proceeded to teach her the Dhamma.

First he transformed the woman from a maiden about sixteen years of age to a woman about twenty years of age. Rūpanandā surveyed her form again, was quickly filled with a feeling of disappointment, and said to herself, "This form is by no means the same as it was before." Gradually the Teacher transformed her, first into a woman who had given birth to one child, then into a woman of middle life, finally into a decrepit old woman. Rūpanandā watched every stage of the transformation saying to herself, "Now this has disappeared, now that has disappeared." When, however, she saw her transformed into a decrepit old woman, and surveyed her standing there, teeth broken, hair gray, body bent, crooked as a curved beam, forced to lean on a cane, trembling in every limb, she was filled with great dispassion.

Then the Teacher caused disease to overmaster the woman. Casting away her cane and her palm-leaf fan, she screamed aloud, fell upon the ground, and rolled over and over, wallowing in her own urine and excrement. Rūpanandā looked upon her and was filled with great dispassion. Then the Teacher showed the death of that woman. Straightaway her body began to bloat. From its nine wound-like openings oozed pus and worms like lamp-wicks. Crows and dogs fell on her and tore her. Rūpanandā looked and thought, "In this very place this woman has come to old age, has come to

228

disease, has come to death. Even so, this body of mine will come to old age, disease, and death." Thus she came to behold her own body in its impermanence; and as a result of doing so, she also saw her body as suffering and as devoid of self.

Straightaway the three modes of existence[1] appeared to her like houses set on fire, or like carrion tied to her neck, and her mind sprang forth to the meditation subject. The Teacher, perceiving that she had beheld her own body in its impermanence, considered within himself, "Will she, or will she not, by herself be able to get a firm footing?" Straightaway he became aware of the following: "She will not be able; she must have support from without." Accordingly, out of consideration for her welfare, he taught her the Dhamma by pronouncing the following stanzas:

Behold, Nandā, this assemblage of elements called the body;
It is diseased, impure, putrid; it oozes and leaks; yet it is
    desired of simpletons.
As is this body, so also was that; as is that body, so also will
    this body be.
Behold the elements in their emptiness; go not back to the
    world;
Cast away desire for existence and you shall go to perfect
    peace.

Thus, with reference to the nun Nandā, did the Exalted One pronounce these stanzas.

Directing her thought in a way conformable to his teaching, Nandā attained the fruit of stream-entry. Thereupon the Teacher, desiring that she should dwell with insight upon the three paths and the three fruits, and desiring to teach her to meditate upon the void, said to her, "Nandā, think not that there is an essence in this body; for there is not the least essence in this body. This body is but a city of bones, made by building up three hundred bones." So saying, he pronounced the following stanza:

---

1. The planes of sensuality, subtle form, and formlessness.

150. This is a city made of bones
Plastered with flesh and blood,
In it are stored decay and death
As well as pride and detraction.

At the conclusion of the lesson the nun Nandā attained arahantship; the multitude also profited by the lesson.

Of related interest from BPS

The Dhammapada: The Buddha's Path of Wisdom
Translated by Acharya Buddharakkhita.
The most beloved Buddhist classic of all time, an anthology of 423 verses on the ethics, meditation, and wisdom of Buddhism. This edition includes the original Pali text and a clear English translation which ably conveys the spirit and content of the original. Introduction by Bhikkhu Bodhi.
BP 203S, 2007   158 pp.

The Buddha and his Disciples
S. Dhammika
In this book the life the Buddha is explored through the perspective of his interactions with his disciples and contemporaries, using society of the time as background. An accessible work especially suited for young people and newcomers to Buddhism.
BP 423S   114 pp.

Tales from Kosambi
By Paul Pothecary
This book bringstogether the most important events that occurred in and around Kosambi to create a lively, imaginative and accessible narrative that interweaves historical figures, events and important aspects of the Buddha's teachings with fascinating accounts of life in northeast India more than 2500 years ago.
BPS 429S, 2010   132 pp.

See the current BPS catalogue for price information.

THE BUDDHIST PUBLICATION SOCIETY

The BPS is an approved charity dedicated to making known the Teaching of the Buddha, which has a vital message for all people.

Founded in 1958, the BPS has published a wide variety of books and booklets covering a great range of topics. Its publications include accurate annotated translations of the Buddha's discourses, standard reference works, as well as original contemporary expositions of Buddhist thought and practice. These works present Buddhism as it truly is—a dynamic force which has influenced receptive minds for the past 2500 years and is still as relevant today as it was when it first arose.

You can support the BPS by becoming a member. All members receive the biannual membership book and are entitled to discounts on BPS books.

For more information about the BPS and our publica-tions, please visit our website, or write an e-mail, or a letter to the:

Administrative Secretary
Buddhist Publication Society
P.O. Box 61
54 Sangharaja Mawatha
Kandy • Sri Lanka
E-mail: bps@bps.lk
web site: http://www.bps.lk
Tel: 0094 81 223 7283 • Fax: 0094 81 222 3679